WILLIE'S
Chocolate
BIBLE

FOR MY MOTHER AND HENRY

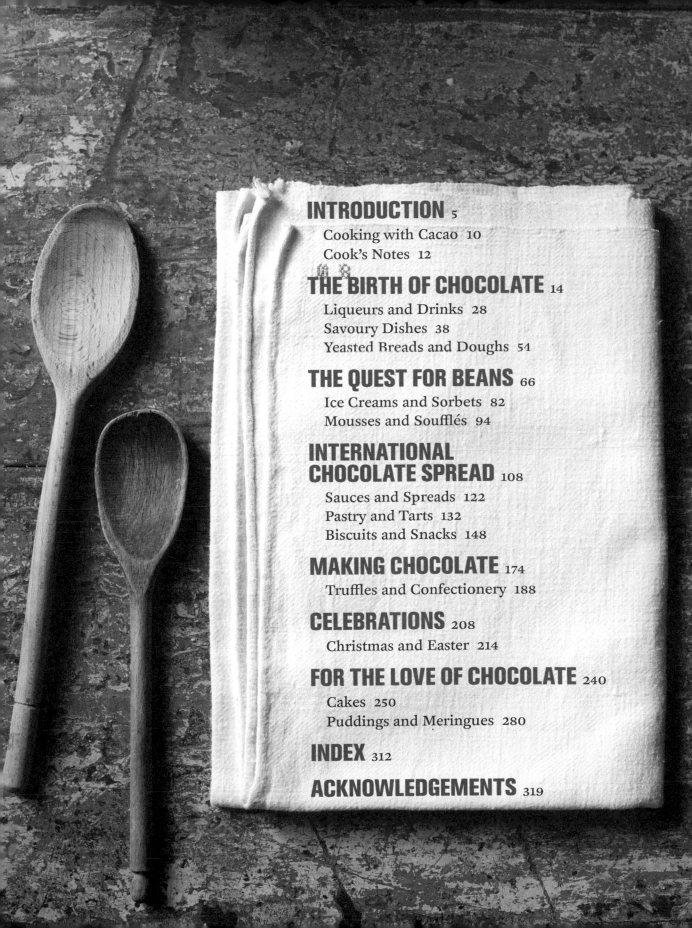

INTRODUCTION

High above my farm in Venezuela, next to the old abandoned sugar refinery in the cloud forests of San Pablo, stands a lone cacao tree. The beans it produces are pure, unadulterated Creole, whiter than white, untouched for hundreds of years, beans that the Aztecs would have recognized. When I first came across this tree, while walking up the mountain above the farm, I sat down beneath it with a feeling that there was something almost sacred about it. And, as I looked out at a sea of virgin rainforest, I suddenly experienced a sense of time rewinding, back to when cacao originated in the Amazon Basin, thousands of years ago.

Cacao and chocolate had become a passion for me soon after I bought the Hacienda El Tesoro in 1995. Founded in 1640 as a cacao plantation, three and a half centuries later the farm was still producing a modest crop of cacao twice a year. I'll never forget my first harvest, the November after we moved in. Scooping the seeds from the pod was no easy job: my fingers were bruised and my nails stung from the acidity of the juice and the fragments of shell that slipped beneath them, yet the soreness was far outweighed by the satisfying feeling of producing something from the earth.

My farm manager Bertillio Araujo and his nephew Ricardo Soto took me through the long, labour-intensive process of harvesting, fermenting and drying the beans. Later they taught me the rudiments of chocolate-making in my kitchen, where I learned to pan-roast the beans, shell them and feed them through my old Corona coffee grinder to produce cacao liquor.

Tasting the cacao liquor made from my El Tesoro beans was a revelation. Rich, chocolaty and fruity, this wasn't like any other chocolate I'd tried. Mixing it with water and honey, I heated it up and drank a miraculous, mind-blowing cup of hot chocolate. It was so delicious and distinct that I actually felt a little uncomfortable about how unfamiliar I was with this new flavour. Why hadn't I ever tasted anything like it? How could it be so different from chocolate as I'd known it up to this point? What's more, I was almost immediately struck by an extraordinary physical feeling of energy and well-being. It was unbelievable, fantastic, a surge of dynamism. From that moment, I was determined to discover more about cacao, its origins and history.

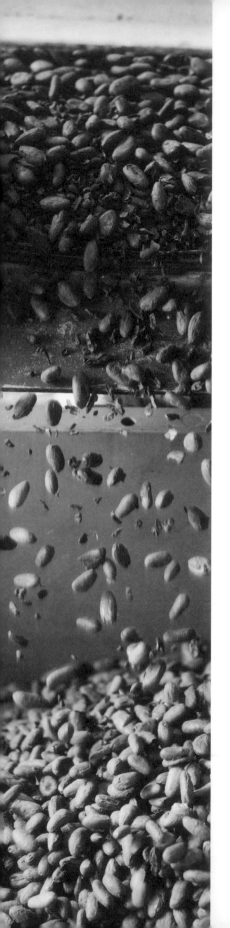

What I went on to find out amazed me – the more I read and heard from chocolate lovers, growers and makers, the more interested I became. Chocolate is steeped in history. It's been a revered luxury for thousands of years, driving people to lie, cheat, seduce, wage war, trade, create, build and destroy. But how and where did the story start? I was desperate to know.

My cacao plantation had been neglected for years, so I decided to improve and replant large areas, at the same time expanding cacao production. I travelled the length and breadth of Venezuela searching for the purest strains of cacao. At every plantation I visited, I whipped out a cast-iron pan, a fan and a small grinder with which to process the beans on offer there. By then I'd worked out that the most effective way to gauge the individual flavour, subtle taste notes and quality of the beans was to make a truffle mix by combining the cacao liquor with sugar and a local type of cream. I ate a lot of this delicious mixture during my quest, but I was never completely satisfied. The perfect bean I was looking for proved to be elusive.

Finally, I found myself hurtling down a network of dirt tracks in my quest for the remote, legendary Costa Maya hacienda, where the cacao trees were reputed to be of an ancient, pure strain. Costa Maya was, and always had been, a coffee plantation, like all the other haciendas in the region, which meant that the cacao trees on the farm hadn't cross-pollinated with other cacao trees when they were planted a century before. After a couple of false starts, I found Costa Maya; at last I had located the perfect beans! I bought 350 pods, germinated the seeds inside them back at El Tesoro, painstakingly planted them on the farm and began to focus on growing high-quality cacao.

Meanwhile, experimenting in the farmhouse kitchen, I played around with all kinds of chocolate recipes, adjusting and adapting them according to the jungle ingredients I had to hand. I made delicious ganaches, sauces, puddings, cakes, coulis and ice creams, using mangoes and guyabanos. I also started producing 100% cacao bars and selling them at the market downtown and through guesthouses and *posadas* in the local area. Chocolate had become an all-consuming passion.

I realized that every stage of the chocolate-making process can affect the flavour of the finished product, from the soil and climate right up to the roasting, grinding and beyond. A whole new world had opened up to me and I revelled in the discoveries I was making. Now that I knew how to make good cacao, my

experiments in the kitchen began to run wild. I found that
I could do almost anything with cacao: I could go savoury or
sweet, I could go rich, or I could use it as a condiment, a flavour-
enhancer, like salt. I found that adding just a small amount can
augment and bring out the flavours of food, or simply add depth
and richness and body. The possibilities seemed endless. I used
it to enrich stews and sauces, risottos, soups, curries and *moles*.

Eventually, after moving back to England, I built a chocolate
factory from scratch in Devon and filled it with beautiful antique
cacao-processing machines, some of which date back to the late
nineteenth century. That's when I began to learn about further
stages of making chocolate, including conching and tempering.
It still amazes me how much care and attention goes into
cultivating cacao and all the stages it takes just to produce the
dried bean – and then the processes necessary to make a bar of
chocolate on top of that! It's astounding. I can't think of another
foodstuff that requires so many processes to reach the finished
product. And then, like a fine wine, you leave the bar to settle
for three weeks to improve its flavour.

Since the El Tesoro cacao harvest still wasn't large enough
to produce the volume of chocolate that I wanted to make,
I carefully sourced two other high-quality and distinct types of
Venezuelan cacao beans, Rio Caribe and Carenero, each from a
different region of the country, with gorgeous flavour notes that
reflect their individual habitats. From the start, my approach to
making chocolate was all about flavour.

First, I made a 100% cacao bar for use in cooking and for hot
chocolate drinks. People loved it, so inevitably I decided to start
making a sweet chocolate bar, using a high percentage of
excellent cacao from Venezuela and Peru and a relatively small
amount of Cuban organic raw-cane sugar. It wasn't easy; I had
to find new machines and teach myself a whole new way of
processing. Making sweet chocolate introduces even more
variables into the mix; for instance, adding the sugar to the early
milling process of the nibs is crucial because it absorbs the
flavour of the beans as they are being ground.

Instead of focusing on the many different types of cacao,
chocolatiers have traditionally created a variety of chocolate
flavours by adding ingredients, blending it with anything from
orange to pepper and chilli. And there's no doubt that extra
elements can have a wonderfully enhancing effect on ordinary
chocolate, just as the right blend of spices can turn an average

supermarket red into a good mulled wine. But when you think that a high-quality cacao has a potential range of around 400 different flavour notes, that soil, climate, harvesting, drying, fermenting and roasting can make a profound difference to its taste and that different chocolatiers can produce totally different flavours from the same crop of cacao beans, you wonder why the origin and provenance of cacao has been overlooked for so long.

Ever since I built my factory, my mission has been to seek out cacao's many flavours and reintroduce them to a world that has grown used to bland, mass-produced blends of chocolate. Fortunately, an increasing number of people have been taking notice of high-quality chocolate and how its flavour notes and subtleties make it comparable to fine wine. There's been a revolution in the way many people approach chocolate, which has definitely helped me along the way.

When I don't know something, I'm never afraid to ask. So I've built what I have on the knowledge of others in the chocolate-growing and -processing industry. I call them the chocolate romantics and I've learned so much from them, as well as from books, about the origins and history of cacao. In the meantime, I've been collecting recipes as I go, endlessly exploring the possibilities of cooking and creating with chocolate.

In my last book, *Willie's Chocolate Factory Cookbook,* many of the recipes were based on my farmhouse kitchen experiments and had a rustic, home-cooking feel to them. This time I bring you something more sophisticated and every bit as delectable. I've met date farmers from Syria and tried out sugar-free desserts, using date and fig syrup; I've played with green walnuts from my mother and stepfather's farm in Wales to make Nocino; I've explored Spanish patisserie on my trips to Spain; and I've added recipes that I couldn't bear to part with before, like Willie's Cacao Bean Ice Cream. I've also included my secret weapon for children: Chocolate and Blackberry Lava Cakes – gooey puddings, where the fruit coulis breaks its way to the surface like volcanic lava and flows down the chocolate 'slopes'!

Here's the story of how I searched for knowledge, recipes and new beans, and of how I discovered the secret of making sweet chocolate that retained the beautiful flavours of the cacao I've sourced from all over the world. I've travelled far and wide in my quest to make fantastic chocolate, but often it feels like the journey has only just started. From Venezuela to Madagascar, Mexico to Bali, there's still so much more to discover!

COOKING WITH CACAO

Cacao adds richness and depth to many dishes, savoury and sweet. It's excitingly versatile, offering different flavour profiles in different dishes. The robust flavour notes, which survive at higher cooking temperatures, are great for casseroles and other savoury dishes, while the subtle, fruity notes shine through in a simple sauce or mousse. The trick in savoury dishes is to use it as a condiment, and how much you use depends to a degree on personal taste, as with salt and pepper. It's incredibly easy too: just stir the grated cacao into the dish (or as described in the recipes).

For sweet dishes, such as truffles or a mousse, where you are looking for the fine, fruity flavour notes, you need a more delicate approach, which is one reason why the cacao for a sweet dish is usually melted in a bain-marie (a bowl set over a saucepan of gently simmering water). Another reason is that cacao on its own can catch and burn if put in a pan over direct heat.

Ways to grate or crumble a bar of cacao

1. Grate by hand on the coarse side of a kitchen grater.
2. Grate in a food processor, using the carrot-grating disc.
3. Place the cacao on a chopping board and chop coarsely with a chef's knife. The cacao will start to flake off the bar in chunks that will melt easily.

Note:
- Cacao will melt the moment it touches anything above body temperature, so there is no need to grate it too finely.
- There's no need to store cacao in the fridge; it just makes grating or chopping it harder.

Tempering chocolate

When chocolate is to be used for dipping and coating, such as when making truffles and confectionery or for decorating a cake, tempering makes it more malleable and glossy. The easiest way to temper small amounts of chocolate by hand at home is called 'seeding', which involves stirring unmelted chocolate into melting chocolate that has been heated to 45°C. You will need a sugar thermometer, plus a heatproof bowl, a spatula and a pan of gently simmering water to do this.

To temper 300g chocolate, first roughly break up or chop 200g of it and finely grate the remaining 100g. Place the roughly chopped chocolate in a heatproof bowl set over a pan of gently simmering water until melted, making sure that the bottom of the bowl is not in contact with the hot water. Use the sugar thermometer to check the temperature of the chocolate. When it has reached 45°C, remove from the heat and stir in the 100g finely grated chocolate. Keep stirring until the temperature of the mixture drops to 28°C for dark chocolate, or 26°C for milk or white chocolate. Set the bowl over the pan of gently simmering water again and heat to 31–33°C for dark chocolate, or 28–29°C for milk or white chocolate. The chocolate is now tempered and ready for use.

I have generally found the smallest amount of chocolate that you can successfully temper in this way is about 300g. If you don't need that much for a recipe, you can store the remainder in a cool place until needed.

Cacao nibs

Sometimes a recipe calls for cacao nibs. This is the cacao after it has been fermented, roasted and winnowed, but before it has been ground, refined and conched. You can buy cacao nibs from specialist retailers or online; they are often sold under their French name, *grue de cacao*.

Substituting other chocolates

When you use 100% cacao, you get the full flavour of the bean, with nothing added and nothing taken away. If you can't get 100% cacao, experiment with other high-percentage chocolates. Try 85% for savoury dishes. In sweet dishes, experiment with the 70% chocolates: use more 70% chocolate than you would 100% cacao and reduce other ingredients, especially sugar and cream or butter, accordingly.

Stockists of Willie's Cacao are listed on the website: www.williescacao.com

COOK'S NOTES

In my recipes:
- All eggs are medium and free-range.
- 1 tsp is the equivalent of 5ml
- 1 tbsp is the equivalent of 15ml
- All cocoa powder should be non-alkalised

Oven temperatures

My oven is fan-assisted and so all temperatures in this book refer to a fan-assisted oven. For those of you with conventional ovens, I have given a guide below. You can simply add 20 degrees to the temperature I give in the recipes. However, all ovens vary and it will not take long for you to get to know your own oven.

WILLIE'S FAN OVEN	CONVENTIONAL OVEN	GAS MARK
120°C	140°C/275°F	1
130°C	150°C/300°F	2
150°C	170°C/325°F	3
160°C	180°C/350°F	4
170°C	190°C/375°F	5
180°C	200°C/400°F	6
200°C	220°C/425°F	7
210°C	230°C/450°F	8

Sterilizing bottles and jars

A number of the drinks on pages 28–37, and several of the sauces, spreads and pastes on pages 122–32, are more likely to keep well if the bottles or jars they are stored in are sterilized first. Use only heatproof containers and start by washing them thoroughly with hot water and washing-up liquid. Rinse well, then place in a large pan of boiling water for about 10 minutes. Drain, then dry upside-down in a warm oven, set at about 110°C. Fill the bottles or jars while they are still warm and seal with tightly fitting metal screw-tops or corks, that have also been sterilized in boiling water then dried in a warm oven.

Equipment

Certain equipment is specified at the end of some ingredients lists as it makes a successful result easier to achieve. Feel free, however, to adapt whatever equipment you have to hand.

THE BIRTH OF CHOCOLATE

I'm never happier than when I'm making chocolate and I've got my finger in a bowl of it, tasting it every step of the way, from bean to bar. The rivers of chocolate that flow in my factory and the rhythm of the conching machine are the music of my life. I have to be one of the luckiest people alive, because my quest to make great chocolate also takes me on the cacao trail across the world, around the Equator, in search of the finest beans. Every trip turns up something new.

While I was visiting a plantation in Colombia on one of my bean-tasting expeditions, I came across a young girl eating the white pulp that surrounds the beans inside a cacao pod. Her father had opened the pod for her with a machete, skilfully removing the upper casing to reveal a small mountain of pulpy seeds inside.

As her dad and I walked through the trees, discussing the growing conditions of the plantation, she happily followed behind us, sucking on the delectable pulp and spitting out the bitter-tasting beans.

'Es bueno?' I asked her.

'Deliciosa!' she admitted shyly, her cheeks bulging.

Cacao pulp must have been what first attracted the native peoples of South America to the cacao pod, not to mention all the other forest animals. Sweet and tangy, often with citrus, even sherbety notes, it's a mouthwatering treat that my kids can't get enough of when we're on my farm in Venezuela. Eating it, you would never guess that it bore any relation to chocolate – and perhaps the ancient peoples of Amazonia were none the wiser either. There is evidence that they sucked the pulp and used it to make a beverage, probably an alcoholic one, but like the plantation owner's daughter, they threw away the beans. It wasn't until much later, and much further away, that the seeds were cultivated into cacao.

I was keen to explore the origins of chocolate as soon as I bought the Hacienda El Tesoro, which has a history of growing and processing cacao that dates back to 1640. In England, I searched out books and documents that would inform me, and I avidly read one particular book, *The Chocolate Tree* by Allen M. Young (Smithsonian Nature Books), which is full of edifying facts and stories. My neighbour, Kai Rosenberg, who owns four haciendas below my farm, was always quoting it at me. 'I've read it!' I kept telling him. But he kept on quoting it to me nonetheless.

That's how I learned that the cacao tree evolved in the lowland rainforests of the Upper Amazon Basin. Not much is known about it in its wild, early form. Some experts believe it's possible that the tree we know today is the result of selective cross-breeding by prehistoric South American peoples, or perhaps it evolved naturally. Either way, two distinct strains – criollo and forastero – made the long journey north from the lower, eastern flanks of the Andes to Central America, where the Mokaya people of the Pacific coast and the pre-Olmecs living around the coast of the Gulf of Mexico cultivated cacao and came to understand its true benefits.

How did the cacao tree make its way north? Again, no one knows for sure. Perhaps it happened through natural distribution, with the pods being carried by the sea along the coast, or maybe the ancient Amazonians had begun to realize that the seeds had a stimulating effect and took them along as they migrated up through the continent. Since cacao pods remain attached to the trees, unless they are picked by animals or humans, they must have been helped on their way.

What seems certain from sample analysis is that chocolate-making was born in Mexico. Traces of theobromine, a bitter alkaloid found in cacao that resembles caffeine, have recently been found on fragments of drinking vessels that date back as far as 1900 BC, in the Mexican state of Chiapas.

It makes sense that the Mokaya and pre-Olmecs were the first people to experiment with processing cacao, because they were the first people in the region to settle down in organized villages, where they had more time and space than their nomadic predecessors to experiment with food. First, they invented a process called nixtamalization, a way of soaking maize and cooking it using lime, which unlocked nutritious amino acids, reduced any toxins, improved the flavour and made it easier to grind.

Unlike the boiled, pounded or ground maize that people were eating before, nixtamalized maize could be kneaded into a smooth dough and made into tortillas and tamales. The sixteenth-century Spanish invaders were appalled when they first came across this process; they thought that the natives were poisoning their food with lime, whereas in fact they were bumping up the nutrients.

Once the pre-Olmecs had sorted out their staple diet, they could relax and play around with other foods, including cacao, which grew on trees in the shade of the jungle canopy all around them. They would only have needed to leave a basket of cacao beans idle for a few days to have recognized the changes wrought by fermentation, which is essential to the development of a chocolaty flavour. As with so many breakthroughs in history, it was probably some happy accident, combined with the natural inquisitiveness of the human mind, that led to one of the greatest discoveries in the history of food.

From there it would have been a short step to discovering that processed cacao is delicious, nutritious and energizing. They roasted it in earthenware pots, crushed it between stones and added water, making it into a drink that was so healthy and stimulating that it wasn't long before they began to prize cacao beans above all their other resources. They grew to revere it so much that they used it as currency – yes, cash actually grew on trees back then! One sixteenth-century chronicler noted that a rabbit was worth ten beans and a slave could be bought for a hundred beans.

But cacao wasn't by any means easy money because the tree that produces cacao isn't at all easy to grow. It is fussy, requiring the hot, damp conditions that can only be found 20 degrees north and 20 degrees south of the Equator; it must be planted next to taller trees that protect it from direct sun; and it won't bear fruit until it's three to five years old. Even then, each tree produces just 1000 beans a year, which is only enough to make about a kilo of chocolate.

The cacao tree won't thrive at high altitudes where temperatures drop to below 16°C; it demands year-round moisture; and it is vulnerable to all kinds of diseases, from moulds and rots to a catastrophic growth known as 'witch's brooms'. What's more, cacao farming is incredibly labour-intensive and time-consuming. Even today, every stage of the process, from planting, irrigating and harvesting to fermenting and drying is done mainly by hand. That's why nearly all the world's cacao trees are grown on small family farms. A lot of work, care and attention is needed to produce really fine cacao.

The early colonials noted that cacao was used as a medicine among the native peoples of Mexico and Guatemala. It was reputed to build strength, aid digestion and combat tiredness, anaemia, fever and low sex drive, among other complaints. Modern research has also shown it to have many health benefits. In a pilot study at Brunel University in the UK, Dr Emma Ross,

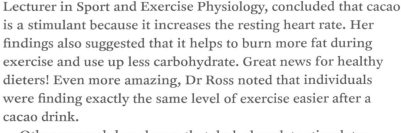

Lecturer in Sport and Exercise Physiology, concluded that cacao is a stimulant because it increases the resting heart rate. Her findings also suggested that it helps to burn more fat during exercise and use up less carbohydrate. Great news for healthy dieters! Even more amazing, Dr Ross noted that individuals were finding exactly the same level of exercise easier after a cacao drink.

Other research has shown that dark chocolate stimulates feel-good endorphins, contains flavonoids, which are a powerful antioxidant, and serotonin, which acts as an anti-depressant. New studies have suggested that eating dark chocolate can be beneficial to blood circulation and may even lower blood pressure (www.livescience.com/health).

It's therefore maddening to think that most of the chocolate we now drink and eat is not in the slightest bit nutritious, but just plain fattening. Your average chocolate confectionery bar contains no more than 5–10% cacao liquor; the rest is mainly fat and sugar. In the last 150 years, as manufacturing methods have advanced, the mass market has transformed chocolate from the all-time healthy drink into the all-time unhealthy luxury.

Yet even in its most diluted and polluted form, the world is still as crazy about chocolate as the Maya people were 3000 years ago, when they descended from the highlands of Guatemala and began saying the pre-Olmec word *kakawa* or *kakaw* with wonder in their eyes, having mixed enough with the Olmec descendants to realize that there was a magic bean in their midst.

By AD 250, the Maya were enjoying a cultural explosion that saw fantastic cities, palaces and temples spring up throughout northern Guatemala and the southern Yucatán in Mexico. They painted, carved, sculpted, made pottery and wrote books and, in their writings, arts and crafts, they celebrated the rituals that had sprung up around cacao. There are gods depicted doing all kinds of things with cacao pods and beans, from offering up plates piled high with beans to piercing their ears and splattering blood all over them. Children were anointed with perfumed cacao in naming ceremonies; sacrificial victims were plied with it before they went to their death; and the elite class were buried with bowls, jars and cylindrical vases filled with frothy cacao drinks to give them the strength and energy they needed to make their way into the next life.

The Maya probably drank all kinds of cacao mixtures, some hot, some cold, some warm, spicy or sweet, adding herbs, honey or chilli peppers for flavour, or maize starch as a thickener. The cacao and maize drinks were highly nutritious, combining the amino acids that were released by soaking the maize kernel in lime, plus all the life-giving elements that cacao offers.

After the roasted beans had been pounded and water added, a foam rose up on the surface and this froth was considered the most desirable part of the drink. The Maya, and the Aztecs after them, went to extraordinary lengths to increase the foam, endlessly pouring the cacao and water from a great height from one vessel into another. This is a very natural way of agitating the cacao to remove the bitterness and bring out its intense flavour notes, which in its modern, mechanized form is known as conching. Later, the Spanish managed to sidestep this exhausting process by inventing a wooden swizzle stick – called a *molinillo* – to beat the liquid with and raise the foam. Funnily enough, although the chocolate drink we consume today barely resembles the drink of old, we still love the idea of frothy hot chocolate, with added cream or machine-aerated milk.

The Aztecs seem to have preferred their chocolate drink cold; they flavoured it with chilli, honey flowers, peanut butter and vanilla. Chocolate was an elitist drink for them, as it had been for the Maya; like the Maya they offered it up to their gods and it was restricted mainly to the priest, warrior and merchant classes. It was drunk on special occasions, at ceremonies, festivals and sacrificial offerings, and often combined with a common red food colouring called achiote. It must have been frightening to see priests offering up sacrifices to the gods, with blood-like fluid dripping from their mouths!

It is interesting that the Maya and Aztecs consumed so many varieties of drinking chocolate, whereas today we favour a standard mix of chocolate, sugar and milk. Why aren't we keener on flavouring our hot chocolate, perhaps with chilli or vanilla? Once I had discovered the wonders of cacao in my farmhouse kitchen, it didn't take me long to start adding ingredients to my chocolate drinks. There was nutmeg growing on the lawn outside the farmhouse, so naturally it was one of my first additions, and I went wild about the combination of chocolate and chilli, which we also grew on the farm. I could see why the Aztecs used more chilli than sweeteners in their *cacahuatl* (literally 'cacao water'.) I'm convinced that the chilli opens up the flavour receptors in the mouth, enhancing and complementing the full complex flavours of the cacao.

I was constantly experimenting with cacao in cooking when I lived at El Tesoro. My great friend Linny Gentle-Cadeau, a chocolatier who came to stay on the farm in 2001, taught me about raw infusion and the delicious flavours that you can create by immersing an ingredient in cream overnight. We had a go at infusing virtually every edible thing we could find, from coriander and nutmeg to peeled ginger and lemongrass. There was a jungle of stuff going on in the fridge, all jammed into various pots and piles. It was a roller-coaster of flavours in those days and I had a lot of fun making truffles out of the flavoured cream and cacao. The El Tesoro cacao was always fantastically fruity, so it was mind-blowing to combine it with the many kinds of fruit that grew on the farm, as well as with herbs, ginger and chillies. We only ever used what was at hand – and the results were mixed – but I made some really interesting discoveries.

My farm manager Bertillio and his assistant Ricardo were constantly introducing me to new fruits and plants because they knew I was fascinated by all the different exotic varieties that were growing around us. Whenever we were walking in the jungle, we always seemed to come across something new. One day, while we were high in the cloud forest collecting bananas, Bertillio tripped and nearly fell over.

'OK, Bertillio?' I asked.

The next minute, he had pulled up a root and he kept on pulling it, following it and coiling it up under his arm. It was like watching something out of a cartoon, as he went on pulling up and rolling this root into a seemingly endless coil. Eventually, he peeled off the bark and said, 'We are going to make a drink from this!' He looked very pleased with himself. Apparently the root was a stimulant – it was the go-go root – and he was eager to combine it with cacao. We tried it later; it wasn't hugely tasty, but the combination of the stimulating effects of the cacao and the go-go root was dynamic.

The cabalonga nut came up in conversation while Bertillio was watching Linny and me playing with infusions. According to local fable in Choroni, the cabalonga helps to cure cancer. 'Why don't you make a truffle that cures cancer?' Bertillio suggested. It was definitely worth a try. After all, what could be better than an anti-cancer truffle? Of course, it was impossible to test its efficacy, but it was delicious.

Because the cabalonga was such a hard nut, much more resistant than nutmeg, we had to grate it into the cream rather than steeping it whole, and then we strained the gratings out later. There is no other flavour like the cabalonga: it's slightly bitter, like a less aromatic nutmeg, and slightly reminiscent of a green walnut. Years later, my cabalonga infusion trials came to mind as I was walking around my mother and stepfather's garden in Wales, where they grow green walnuts. Ding! I was inspired to make chocolate Nocino.

Another medicinal plant that grew on the farm was *caña dos indios*, a purplish cane that is smashed up and put in water. It was reputed to clean out the kidneys and urinal tract; the locals swore by it. But possibly the most legendary plant was *la baca*, a tree up the mountain. When you cut it with a machete, the tree bled 'milk'. Local lore had it that the Indians used *la baca* milk as a supplement to breast milk and we always wondered what it would be like to make truffles out of it, substituting the milk for the cream. That's something I definitely plan to try the next time I go back to the farm.

My neighbour Enrique, the ex-Prefect of Maracay, became a great friend and he was also interested in making infusions – only his were alcohol-based! He had flasks full of *aguardiente* (literally 'firewater') stuffed with berries, nuts, leaves and fruits. He would sit on his verandah for hours, slowly sipping his delicious infused grog. I was always asking, 'What does this leaf do?' or 'What's the effect of that root?'

'That leaf is really mellow,' he would say. 'In case it is too mellow, you counteract it with this root, which really picks you up, followed by this one, which has a dreamy effect.' He was doing with *aguardiente* what I was doing it with cream. Soon he was adding cacao to his hooch!

While Enrique attracted visitors to his lovely home with his assortment of flavoured liqueurs, I found that people were often popping into El Tesoro, hovering around the kitchen, drawn by the aroma of my latest cacao experiment. It wasn't long before I realized that cacao nibs are great for cooking. Nibs are roasted, shelled beans and they have a wonderfully nutty flavour and a crunchy texture. While chocolate is all about the melt – the sensuousness of seeping flavours – nibs offer deep chocolaty crunchiness. Since they go rancid within a couple of weeks if you don't make them into chocolate, they always guarantee a fresh, honest flavour. You can use nibs like nuts in cooking: they add all the zing of the raw roasted bean, plus texture, and they can also be used decoratively.

I was constantly challenging myself to come up with something new. My inventions included chocolate wasabi, alcoholic drinks, various ice creams and cacao nib tea; I also made fish burgers mixed with wild coriander and dusted in grated cacao instead of flour, and I seasoned whole rump steaks with cacao. Sorbets were an all-time favourite because it wasn't always possible to get good double cream. And, of course, everyone loved our range of El Tesoro truffles.

At the very least, I'd whip up one of my special hot chocolate drinks for anyone who came to visit. It always seemed to make people smile, and the next time I saw them, they'd regale me with tales of how energized it had made them feel. A hot chocolate drink never fails to put people in a good mood, I find. It's not only a comfort drink when you use fine chocolate – although it retains that appeal – it also feels very nourishing and sustaining.

On one occasion chocolate even helped my wife Tania and me to escape from a potentially sticky situation on one of our road trips around Venezuela. We were travelling in the dead of night from Mérida, high in the Andes, to the flatlands. We had been driving for ages along winding mountain roads before we eventually hit a long straight road, at which point I looked at the petrol gauge and realized that we were low on fuel and miles and miles from the nearest petrol station. We freewheeled all the way down to the bottom of the slopes, somehow managing to stay awake despite the monotony of the straight road, which felt endless. The hours ticked by: now it was three, now four in the morning. Suddenly we hit something and the car span out of control; the steering wheel didn't respond for a few seconds. Then a blast of brightness lit up the night and, before we knew it, we were surrounded by soldiers with their guns out, expressions of sheer panic on their faces.

We were in shock because of our near-accident, and so were they because we had appeared out of nowhere. It turned out that we had hit a 'sleeping policeman' at a military block. Fortunately, no tyres had been punctured. The soldiers demanded to see our papers. At this point we had a dilemma. Do we play the dumb tourists? Do we speak Spanish or do we conveniently not speak Spanish? We waited anxiously as they searched our vehicle.

The discovery of cacao in the boot of the car immediately changed the mood. The next minute we were making hot chocolate inside the guardhouse and the terrifying soldiers had transformed. There is something about sweetened chocolate that makes everybody happy. Before you knew it, there was laughter, smiling and chatting. As we left, they waved us off like old friends. What's more, we'd been refreshed by a powerful pick-me-up and could continue to drive for the rest of the night.

Christopher Columbus was the first European to set eyes on cacao, on his fourth voyage to the 'New World' that he had 'discovered' 12 years previously. According to an account written by his son Ferdinand, he was heading for Jamaica when he landed on the island of Guanaja, around 50 kilometres north of Honduras, on 15 August 1502. That same day, a huge canoe came into view across the turquoise waters around the island; it was a Maya trading canoe, the size of a galley ship, stocked up with maize, manioc, maize wine and what appeared to be almonds, but were in fact cacao beans.

Columbus immediately realized that cacao was important to the natives because when he captured the canoe and brought its goods on board his ship, the Maya merchants couldn't take their eyes off the cacao, scurrying to pick up every bean that fell on deck. But the great explorer never tasted it or understood *why* it was so precious. He was too focused on finding gold to understand what he was missing. He is said to have presented it to Ferdinand and Isabella at the Spanish court on his return, but they dismissed it out of hand as being too bitter. So it wasn't until 1517, when the Spaniards invaded the Yucatán, that anyone outside Mexico began to catch on. In 1519, Hernán Cortés and his crew watched the great Aztec ruler Moctezuma knocking back cacao in huge quantities and were fascinated to see how assiduously his attendants whipped up a foam before serving it up.

Cacahuatl wasn't an instant hit with the settlers. One of the first Europeans to describe the experience of quaffing the bitter, frothy beverage, the Milanese explorer Girolamo Benzoni, wrote that it was 'more a drink for pigs than a drink for humanity'. He struggled to understand why it was so expensive and why he was laughed at whenever he turned down a cup of it. The Jesuit José de Acosta also hated it, writing in his *Natural and Moral History*,

published in 1590, 'It disgusts those who are not used to it, for it has foam on top, or a scum-like bubbling.' Yet he acknowledges that Spanish men and women had become addicted to it by then.

Many Spanish invaders took native women as wives and they and their Creole descendants inevitably adopted the custom of drinking cacao. Crucially, though, they began to adapt it to their European tastes by adding cane sugar and substituting cinnamon, black pepper and aniseed for chilli and achiote. They also found a way of making instant hot chocolate, by manufacturing a tablet of ground cacao that could be dissolved with sugar in hot water.

I like to think that the Aztecs used cacao in cooking, although we don't know for sure. Today, Mexico is famous for its savoury *moles*, or sauces, containing chocolate. The innovation of *mole poblano* is often attributed to Spanish nuns in Mexico during the mid-seventeenth century, but there's no real proof of this. However, there is firm evidence that it was used in pies, pastas and meat dishes in northern Italy from 1680 onwards, so maybe the Italians were the first European innovators and perhaps the Creole population of Mexico was also experimenting with cacao in its cooking.

I think cacao is a fantastic ingredient in savoury cooking, and I remember the first time I discovered that chocolate wasn't just for sweet dishes. I was in the mountains in Santo Domingo with Tania, her sister Sophie and a Venezuelan friend called Hamish, who had dropped out of medical school and opened a restaurant in Santo Domingo. Hamish took us fishing at Laguna Negra, 1500 metres up in the mountains, where mushrooms grew so thickly that we couldn't avoid leaving our footprints in them.

One night, Hamish and I went fishing. We were so high up and it was so clear and bright that the stars were practically in our faces. The climate there is very localized and the weather can change in second. Suddenly, the sky blackened and it started to rain. When the rain stopped, the clouds swirled around us so quickly that soon we were enveloped in a dense mist. You could hardly see further than the end of your nose. And then, the next instant, the moonlight cut through the mist.

We were unlucky with the fish and disastrously I fell in the river. Hamish and I made our way back to the tent, where Sophie and Tania were asleep. I had to sleep in my wet clothes. What made it worse was that the four of us were squashed into a two-man tent: when one person wanted to turn over, everyone had to turn over, which woke everyone up.

In the morning, Hamish made his special Andean soup to revive us. He fried onions and garlic and added diced potatoes, then some fresh milk and wild coriander and finally dropped in a couple of eggs to poach. After breakfast, we trekked back down to Santo Domingo and made puff pastry filled with mushrooms gathered from the mountainside and seasoned with cacao. I remember being blown away by the way the cacao complemented the mushrooms, adding depth and richness and thickening the juices.

Later on, when I'd bought El Tesoro, it didn't surprise me to learn that the seventeenth-century Italians were keen on using cacao in their savoury dishes. So many Italians have settled in Venezuela over the years that their cuisine has a very strong presence, and you often come across a fusion of Venezuelan and Italian cooking. Since I love Italian food, in one of my experiments on the farm, I combined cacao with juicy homegrown basil, pine and cashew nuts and a fantastic pecorino cheese that we bought from Maracay, plus a gorgeous imported Italian olive oil. The result? Chocolate pesto! Back in England, while doing a massive cook-off at my sister's house, we made chocolate pasta by adding cacao to the pasta dough. I cooked it up for the kids with a bolognese sauce and it blew them away. They would live on pasta if they could, but this was just phenomenal. They absolutely loved it.

I followed a similar tangent on one of my most recent quests for beans, when I travelled from Venezuela to Colombia and then on to Mexico, tracing the journey that cacao originally made thousands of years ago as it migrated up from the Amazon Basin. I was very keen to find a Mexican bean that I could make into fine chocolate, partly because Mexican cacao is important. It represents the birth of chocolate, way back in pre-Olmec times; I was looking for a bean that would reflect those origins and flavours.

I went to Villahermosa, in the state of Tabasco, where cacao plantations flourished among the Olmecs, Maya and Aztecs for many centuries before Spanish colonization. Tabasco state, especially the eastern side, is alive with chocolate – just bursting with it! The land is productive because it's well irrigated by various rivers; this area had the reputation for growing the highest-quality cacao right up until the nineteenth century. The ancient peoples of Mesoamerica fought vicious wars for control of the territory.

Across from my hotel was the Parque La Venta Olmec museum, where an incredible array of colossal stone heads and Olmec carvings are on display. Although my days in Villahermosa were jam-packed with visiting cacao plantations, I had a couple of hours to visit the park. As I wandered around, looking at these stunning artefacts, I couldn't help feeling an incredible admiration for these people. What an incredible civilization! It was awesome to think about their use of cacao thousands of years ago.

On my way between two plantations, my guide Mariano said, 'Is there anything else you'd like to see?'

Naturally I said, 'Can we visit the market?'

I always think that visiting countries is a bit like visiting friends; I can't help opening my friends' fridges to see what's inside – and for me, markets are the larders of a country. Mariano took me to the bustling market of Comalcalco, where I bounced along the aisles looking at stalls packed with chillies and cacao, thinking I'm going to make a *mole*! Searching out ingredients that would make it more authentically Mexican, I asked to have a quick sample of some local honey. Wow! It was unbelievably tasty and distinct.

I spotted women rushing around in the market canteen and headed over to try their *mole*. First they served up a glass of cold hibiscus tea and then along came the mole: two pieces of chicken in a dark sauce, spicy, chocolaty and rich. It wasn't quite hot enough for me so I reached for the *salsa picante*. A little fire in the mouth always helps to awaken the taste buds! In my usual fashion, although I'm not supposed to, I wolfed my food down and set off to explore again.

Within seconds, I had fallen in love with a giant pestle and mortar made of volcanic rocks, even before Mariano explained the health benefits of grinding your spices in it – apparently the minerals in the lava mix with whatever is ground. Immediately I began imagining myself grinding vast amounts of spices and garlic, making a *mole* for everyone, perhaps having a *mole* party. I had to buy it, even though it weighed 30 kilos. Unbelievably, I managed to get away without paying excess baggage on the plane home! Mariano and I nearly did our backs in getting it to the car, but it was worth it.

Back in Villahermosa, I made a beeline for the central market, desperate to try a cup of *pozol*, a popular drink also known as *chorote*, which is made from roasted cacao beans, ground maize

and sugar. It's a traditional drink in Tabasco, and surprisingly refreshing, with a watery oatmeal chocolaty flavour. As well as filling you up and providing slow-burn energy, it counters the tropical heat. For this reason it's often drunk by cacao plantation workers, especially during harvest time.

The central market was gigantic and it felt like we were going round in circles before I found the *pozol* stalls. I parked myself at the nearest counter and began chatting to the owner, a typically friendly Mexican woman. Soon she was ladling chocolate *pozol* out of a large urn into a cup for me. On the counter in front of me were several balls of maize dough used for making tortillas; beside them was a ball of *pozol* dough, which looked exactly like the maize dough except for its chocolaty colour. Suddenly I had a brainwave. 'Hey, you could make chocolate tortillas from the *pozol* dough, couldn't you?'

The stall owner frowned comically. 'No,' she said, 'you make tortillas from the maize dough. The *pozol* dough is for drinks.'

'But if you *wanted* to, surely you could make chocolate tortillas from the *pozol* dough,' I pressed, aware that I was coming across as a particularly stupid gringo.

'Not really,' she said with a laugh.

'But it would be possible, wouldn't it?' I continued.

'Well, it would be possible,' she said uncertainly.

Yee-ha! Who would help me try making chocolate tortillas? Anyone? I bought a ball of *pozol* dough and rushed from one tortilla stall to the next. 'No!' people kept saying. 'You've bought the wrong dough!'

Since no one would help me on the busy ground floor, I ran upstairs to where there was less traffic. Finally, I found someone who would help me. Paulo and Juanita, comrades in food, said that of course they would let me try using *pozol* dough to make tortillas. I borrowed their tortilla maker, which flattened the dough into a pancake; we filled it with the *pozol* dough and into the hot oil it went.

By the time I was on my third black bean chocolate tortilla, I had attracted a lunch companion. She agreed that my *pozol* tortilla was the best tortilla she had ever eaten. As I left, joking and laughing, I told Paulo and Juanita to put up a sign saying, 'Chocolate tortillas today!' And who knows what tomorrow...

LIQUEURS
AND
DRINKS

EUROPEAN HOT CHOCOLATE

The Europeans modified Aztec cacao drinks to create something they considered more palatable. One significant change was the addition of sugar. They also liked to add various eastern spices, such as cinnamon, nutmeg and cloves, and crushed rose petals or jasmine flowers were sometimes stirred in as flavourings. Milk was a later addition, and I've chosen not to use it here.

Serves 6

90g 100% cacao, finely grated

450ml water

¼ tsp ground cinnamon

3 tbsp sugar

⅓ vanilla pod, or ¼ tsp vanilla essence

Place the cacao, water, cinnamon and sugar in a saucepan. Scrape out the seeds from the vanilla pod, if using, but add both the pod and seeds to the pan. Bring to the boil, stirring frequently, then lower the heat and simmer gently for about 5 minutes, or until the mixture thickens a little. Remove and discard the vanilla pod. Whisk well to create a light foam. Remove from the heat and stir in the vanilla essence, if using instead of the pod. Serve hot.

AZTEC HOT CHOCOLATE

Cacao has been consumed as a drink for thousands of years in Central America. This recipe is based on a typical Aztec beverage. The light heat from the chilli helps open up the subtle chocolate flavours. I have used ancho chilli, which is mild, but the Aztecs would have used many other types with varying heats. Experiment to suit your taste and mood.

Serves 6

90g 100% cacao, finely grated

450ml water

1 tsp ancho chilli powder

¾ tsp achiote powder (optional)

⅓ vanilla pod, or ¼ tsp vanilla essence

½ tbsp honey

Tip the cacao, water, chilli and achiote powder, if using, into a saucepan. If you are using a vanilla pod, scrape out the seeds and add them, with the pod, to the pan. Bring to the boil, stirring frequently, then lower the heat and simmer gently for about 5 minutes, or until the mixture thickens slightly. Take out and discard the vanilla pod, then whisk well to create a light foam. Remove from the heat and, if using vanilla essence, stir it in now. Serve piping hot in small cups, or leave to cool a little and serve, as the Aztecs would have done, at room temperature.

CHOCOLATE ADVOCAT

This is a truly sumptuous, sweet liqueur (*opposite*). Because of the high alcohol and sugar content, it will keep well for at least a year. A small glass of it, served with a biscuit, makes an instant – if rather alcoholic – pudding. It is also a wonderful topping for homemade ice cream.

Makes 1 litre

160g Indonesian Javan Light Breaking 69% chocolate, roughly chopped

1 vanilla pod

4 large egg yolks

300g caster sugar

400g unsweetened evaporated milk

300ml cognac

75ml 80% pure alcohol (ask a wine merchant or pharmacist to get it for you)

Melt the chocolate by placing it in a heatproof bowl set over a pan of gently simmering water, making sure the bottom of the bowl is not in contact with the water. Leave to cool slightly.

Meanwhile, split the vanilla pod, scrape out the seeds and place them in a blender or food processor with the egg yolks and sugar. Blitz to combine, then, while the blender or processor is running, add the evaporated milk in a slow steady stream.

Next, with the blender or processor still running, first add the melted chocolate, then the cognac and alcohol. When everything is well combined, pour the mixture through a sterilized funnel into a sterilized 1-litre jar or bottle and cork or seal. Leave to stand for at least 2 hours, ideally longer, before drinking. To serve, pour the quantity required into a saucepan and heat gently until warm.

CACAO NIB AND CHILLI TEA

The first cacao tea I ever tried was made from the waste of roasted cacao shells from Hacienda El Rosario in Venezuela; the second was made from cacao nibs. Variations on this drink are endless. Instead of chilli, you can use your favourite herbs or spices, such as lemongrass, ginger or nutmeg. Or, if drinking after a heavy meal, try adding a sprinkling of fennel seeds or a sprig of mint, as both are excellent digestives.

1 tbsp cacao nibs per person

¼ large dried mild chilli, or a small pinch of mild chilli powder

1 large teacup boiling water, per person

Place the cacao nibs and chilli in a teapot or heatproof jug. Add the boiling water, stir and leave to brew for about 5 minutes. Strain before drinking.

CACAO NIB AND VANILLA COGNAC

This makes a superb after-dinner drink, or it can be used wherever cognac is called for in a recipe involving chocolate (*opposite, left*). I enjoy straight cognac, but this is something really special. The only problem is keeping your hands off it while it matures!

Makes 350ml

150g cacao nibs

300ml cognac

1 vanilla pod

Place the cacao nibs, cognac and vanilla pod in a sterilized bottle. Seal well and leave to infuse for a 2–3 months. Strain before drinking.

CHOCOLATE NOCINO

This is a variation on the Italian liqueur Nocino (*opposite, right*). In Italy, the under-ripe green walnuts used are traditionally picked on midsummer's day. But in the cooler British climate, you're unlikely to find any available until at least the middle of July. As well as being a superb drink, this liqueur can be used as an ice-cream topping or for flavouring desserts. You can also make it with grappa or brandy instead of vodka.

Makes 2 litres

25–30 green walnuts

125g cacao nibs

175g granulated sugar

Zest of 1 lemon

1 cinnamon stick

½ vanilla pod

4 whole cloves

1 litre vodka

Quarter the walnuts and place with all the other ingredients, except the vodka, in a sterilized 2-litre glass jar. Pour in the vodka, seal the jar and leave to stand in a cool place for at least 2 months, shaking from time to time, until the liqueur has turned from yellow to a rich dark brown. It is now ready to drink. Strain, preferably through muslin to remove all trace of the spices and other flavourings. Pour into sterilized bottles and seal. It will keep well for 2–3 years – in fact, the flavours become richer and deeper with age.

CHOCOLATE MILKSHAKE

I grew up on homemade milkshakes. We made them using milk from our two Saanen goats, Nina and Sophie. However, if you don't have a ready supply of goats' milk, you can use full-fat organic cow's milk instead. Why not experiment by adding a slice or two of banana, or a handful of raspberries or blackberries, or a few chunks of fresh pineapple? You can vary the amount of cacao and sugar according to your taste (*opposite*).

Serves 2

50g 100% cacao

2 tbsp sugar

400ml full-fat organic milk

6 ice cubes

Put the cacao, sugar and half the milk in a saucepan and warm over a moderate heat until just starting to boil, stirring constantly to dissolve the sugar and cacao. Remove from the heat, stir in the remaining milk and leave to stand until cold. Chill in the refrigerator.

Pour the chilled chocolate milk into a blender, add the ice cubes and blitz for about 1 minute, until thoroughly mixed. Pour into tall chilled glasses and serve with a straw.

SLOE CHOCOLATE VODKA

This makes an unusual and stunning after-dinner liqueur, or you could offer it with a biscuit or slice of cake as dessert. You can serve it cold, but I prefer it gently warmed through. Just stand the bottle in a bowl of hot water for about 5 minutes before pouring into small glasses.

Makes about 750ml

500ml vodka

250g freshly picked sloes

100g granulated sugar (more if you prefer a sweeter drink)

200g Venezuelan Rio Caribe Superior 72% chocolate, roughly chopped

Place all the ingredients in a stainless steel saucepan. Heat very gently over a really low heat until the chocolate has melted and the mixture is hot, taking care not to let it boil. Carefully pour or spoon into a sterilized, wide-necked glass jar, seal and leave in a cool place for 2 months.

Strain, then pour through a sterilized funnel into a sterilized bottle and seal. Always shake the bottle before pouring, as the chocolate tends to settle on the bottom over time.

SAVOURY DISHES

MOLE NEGRO

This is one of my favourite Mexican dishes. Usually prepared for festivals and special occasions, it varies from region to region. The *mole*, or sauce, contains many different ingredients, but none of them dominates the others. Instead they combine to make a rich and distinctive blend. Don't be put off by how time-consuming the *mole* is to make. It can be prepared in advance and kept in the fridge for up to a week before using. Although there are a lot of chillies in this dish, they are all fairly mild, so it isn't particularly hot.

Serves 6–8

30g dried mulato chillies

30g dried ancho chillies

30g dried pasilla chillies

40g whole unblanched almonds

20g raw peanuts

25g sesame seeds

5g dried oregano

8 tbsp olive oil or goose fat

2 large onions, sliced

10 garlic cloves, finely sliced

2 large red peppers

4 large ripe tomatoes

100g pitted prunes

1 tortilla or 1 slice stale white bread, toasted

5cm cinnamon stick

1 litre chicken, turkey or beef stock

70g Madagascan Sambirano Superior 100% cacao, roughly chopped

Preheat the oven to 140°C.

Wipe the chillies to remove any dirt. Split them lengthways, removing and discarding the stems, seeds and any membranes. Arrange on a baking tray and roast in the preheated oven for 10 minutes, or until lightly browned. Remove from the oven, pour over enough boiling water to cover (keep the chillies submerged by placing a spoon on top of them) and leave to soak for 30 minutes. Tip into a blender or food processor with the soaking water and purée. Pass through a sieve or food mill and set aside.

Turn the oven up to 170°C. Spread the almonds and peanuts over a baking sheet and toast in the hot oven for 20–25 minutes, or until golden brown. Allow to cool, then blitz in a blender or food processor until finely ground. Set aside. Tip the sesame seeds into a frying pan and dry-roast over a medium heat until they start popping and are golden brown. Grind until fine, using a spice mill or a pestle and mortar, and set aside. Dry-roast and grind the oregano in the same way as the sesame seeds and set aside. Reset the oven to 200°C.

Heat 3 tablespoons of the oil in a frying pan. Add the onions and cook for 3–4 minutes, or until golden brown. Add the garlic to the pan and fry until dark brown, taking care not to burn, or the *mole* will be bitter. Remove from the heat and set aside.

Place the red peppers and tomatoes on a baking tray and roast in the hot oven for 40 minutes, adding the prunes to roast with them for the last 10 minutes. Skin and deseed the roasted peppers and tomatoes, then place in a blender or food processor along with the roasted prunes, ground almonds, peanuts, sesame seeds and oregano and the fried onions and garlic. Add the tortilla or bread. Blitz until smooth, then push through a fine sieve and set aside. Set the oven to 140°C.

2 tbsp Caco Nib Balsamic Vinegar (see page 127), or good-quality balsamic vinegar

1 tsp salt, plus more to taste

1 tbsp honey (optional)

2.5kg free-range chicken or turkey joints, a mixture of breasts, thighs and legs

Small bunch of finely chopped fresh coriander, to garnish

Pour 4 tablespoons of the remaining oil or fat into a large flameproof casserole. Add the cinnamon stick and fry over a moderate heat for 1–2 minutes. Tip in the tomato, pepper and nut mixture and fry over a moderate heat, stirring constantly, for another 2–3 minutes. Stir in the chilli purée and fry for a further 5 minutes, stirring constantly. Pour in 750ml stock and bring to the boil. Turn the heat down to low, then stir in the cacao, vinegar, salt and honey, if using. Cover and place in the hot oven for 2 hours.

Heat the remaining tablespoon of oil in a large frying pan. Add some of the chicken or turkey joints and fry on all sides until golden brown. Set aside and keep warm while browning the remaining chicken or turkey. This may have to be done in 2–3 batches, depending on the size of your frying pan. When all the chicken or turkey is browned, pour a spoonful or two of the remaining stock into the empty pan and bring to the boil over a high heat, scraping up any browned residue from the bottom of the pan. Pour over the browned chicken or turkey and set aside.

When the sauce is ready, remove the casserole from the oven and tip in the browned chicken or turkey legs, adding a little remaining stock if the *mole* is very thick. Re-cover, place over a medium-low heat on top of the stove and leave to simmer for 30 minutes. Add the remaining chicken or turkey joints and cook, covered, for a further 20–25 minutes over a gentle heat, or until the meat is cooked.

Garnish with chopped coriander and serve with corn tortillas or basmati rice and a green salad.

CRISPY CHINESE FIVE-SPICE BELLY OF PORK WITH A BITTER CHOCOLATE GRAVY

This is a great recipe, especially when it is made with meat from pigs fattened on potatoes and chocolate waste from my factory! As well as salting, the other key factor in achieving a crispy skin is for it to be slightly dried out and almost leathery before cooking. To help achieve this, place the pork in a dish, skin side up and uncovered, and leave in the fridge for 24 hours.

Serves 4–6

1kg piece belly pork

1 tbsp oil

1 tbsp fine sea salt

1 tbsp Chinese five-spice powder

1 large onion, thickly sliced

400ml chicken stock

7g Venezuelan Rio Caribe Superior 100% cacao

1 tbsp soy sauce

4 spring onions, shredded lengthways

Preheat the oven to 190°C.

Score the skin of the belly pork with a sharp knife, then lightly oil on all sides. Rub the sea salt well into the skin and rub the five-spice powder all over the underside.

Arrange the onions slices in the base of a roasting tin and lay the pork on top, skin side up. Roast in the hot oven for about 30 minutes. Lower the oven to 170°C and continue cooking for another hour. Check if the skin is really crispy and, if not, turn the oven up to 200°C and cook for a further 15–20 minutes. Don't worry about overcooking belly pork, as its high fat content will keep it from drying out.

When the pork is ready, remove from the oven, transfer to heatproof dish, cover loosely with foil and set aside to rest in a warm place.

While the meat is resting, make the gravy. Tip out and discard any liquid fat still in the roasting tin. Heat the stock in a saucepan over a medium heat, then pour into the roasting tin and stir, scraping up any caramelized bits in the tin. Pour this mixture back into the saucepan and bring to the boil. Lower the heat and cook gently for 5 minutes, then strain into fresh saucepan. Add the cacao and soy sauce and return to a gentle boil, stirring all the time until the cacao melts. Reduce to thicken slightly (although the gravy shouldn't be too thick). Taste and adjust the seasoning, if needed.

Remove the crackling from the pork, then slice the meat by dividing it between the ribs. Pour a little hot gravy onto each serving plate and top with slices of meat, placing a helping of crackling alongside. Scatter over the shredded spring onions and serve with steamed rice and spinach.

ROAST WILD DUCK WITH A CHOCOLATE AND ORANGE SAUCE

I used to keep ducks on my farm in Venezuela and always got on better with them than my chickens. I'm still not sure if that's why they were always tastier! Here's one of my favourite ways of preparing duck. The cacao balances the flavour of the orange and the richness of the sauce so well.

Serves 2

3 tsp fine sea salt

1 oven-ready wild duck

Small bunch of fresh thyme

1 tbsp butter

8 shallots, peeled

250ml duck or chicken stock

1 orange

1 tbsp Cacao Nib Balsamic Vinegar (see page 127), or good-quality balsamic vinegar

10g Venezuelan Rio Caribe Superior 100% cacao

1 heaped tsp quince or redcurrant jelly

Preheat the oven to 190°C.

Rub the salt all over the skin of the duck and place the thyme in the body cavity. Melt the butter in a roasting tin over a medium heat. Add the duck with the shallots and cook, turning regularly, until browned all over. Place in the hot oven and cook for 30 minutes if you like the meat rare, or 40 minutes for a medium-cooked bird. Don't overcook. Wild duck that is well done can be a little dry and tough.

While the duck is cooking, pour the stock into a saucepan and add a few strips of orange peel and the vinegar. Bring to a gentle simmer and leave to cook for about 5 minutes. Remove from the heat and set aside.

Take the cooked duck out of the oven and transfer to a warm dish along with the shallots. Cover loosely with foil, and leave in a warm place to rest while you make the gravy. Tip out any excess fat from the roasting tin. Place the tin over a medium heat and pour in the prepared stock, stirring to scrape up any caramelized bits in the bottom of the tin. Strain back into a fresh saucepan and stir in the cacao and jelly. Place over a low heat and cook, stirring, until the cacao and jelly melt. If necessary, cook a little longer to thicken slightly, then taste and adjust the seasoning. Add a squeeze or two of fresh orange juice, according to taste.

Divide the duck in half by cutting through the breastbone and place each piece on a warm serving plate. Pour a little hot gravy around the duck and serve the rest of the gravy separately in a warmed jug. Garnish with a few strips of orange zest and serve with mashed potato and a selection of steamed vegetables.

SADDLE OF ROE DEER WITH CHOCOLATE GRAVY AND SPICED RED CABBAGE

This is a great dinner-party dish and there's the bonus that most of the preparation can be done a day or two in advance. It is particularly good served with mixture of roasted root vegetables, such as potatoes, parsnips, carrots and Jerusalem artichokes, and homemade quince jelly.

Serves 6

4–5 tbsp olive oil

Small bunch of fresh thyme, roughly chopped

2 garlic cloves, sliced

Pinch of coarsely ground black pepper

2kg saddle of roe deer (ask your butcher to bone out the two fillets of meat from the saddle, giving you all the bones and sinews)

20g butter

FOR THE GRAVY:

2 onions, roughly chopped

2 carrots, roughly chopped

1 ripe tomato, roughly chopped

2 sticks celery, roughly chopped

3 bay leaves

8–10 sprigs fresh thyme

4 juniper berries

6 black peppercorns

350ml red wine

10g Venezuelan Hacienda Las Trincheras 100% cacao

Preheat the oven to 190°C.

Place the olive oil, thyme, garlic and black pepper in a large dish, add the two fillets of roe deer meat and turn until well coated in the olive oil and herb mixture. Cover and leave to marinate for at least 2 hours or preferably overnight in the fridge.

To make the gravy, put the onions, carrots, tomato and celery on a baking tray with the reserved bones and sinews from the meat and roast in the hot oven for about 1 hour, turning occasionally, until everything is well browned. Tip into a large pan, along with the bay leaves, thyme sprigs, juniper berries, peppercorns and red wine. Add enough water to cover and bring to the boil over a medium heat. Lower the heat and leave to simmer very gently for 3–4 hours. Strain through a sieve into a clean pan, return to the heat and continue to simmer until reduced to about 450ml liquid. Stir in the cacao and jelly until melted and well mixed in. Season to taste and, if the gravy is too thin, cook a little longer until it thickens slightly. Set aside until ready to serve.

Heat the olive oil for the red cabbage in a large pan over a medium heat. Add the onion and the thyme and fry for 3–4 minutes, or until soft. Stir in the cabbage and apples, then add the vinegar, cinnamon and orange zest and juice. Cover the pan, lower the heat and cook very slowly for about 30 minutes, or until the cabbage is tender, stirring occasionally. Set aside until ready to serve.

About an hour before serving, preheat the oven to 190°C.

To cook the meat, melt the butter in a roasting tin over a medium-high heat. When it is hot, add the meat, turning several times to brown lightly on all sides. Place in the hot oven and cook for about 6 minutes for very rare meat or 8 minutes for medium-rare meat. Don't overcook or the meat will be dry and

1–2 tbsp quince or redcurrant jelly

Salt and freshly ground black pepper

FOR THE RED CABBAGE:

1 tbsp olive oil

1 large red onion, finely sliced

1 tsp finely chopped fresh thyme

1 small red cabbage, sliced

2 Cox's apples, peeled, cored and sliced

1 tbsp Cacao Nib Balsamic Vinegar (see page 127), or good-quality balsamic vinegar

Pinch of ground cinnamon

Zest of ½ orange

Juice of 1 orange

leathery. Transfer the meat to a warm dish, cover loosely with foil and leave to rest in a warm place for 10 minutes while you reheat the red cabbage and gravy.

To serve, cut the meat into thick slices and divide between six warm serving plates. Place a couple of spoonfuls of red cabbage on each plate and pour some hot gravy around the meat.

ROAST PUMPKIN AND CACAO NIB SALAD

This dish is delicious served with grilled chicken or lamb. If you'd like a little extra heat, simply roast some mild fresh chillies with the pumpkin. When topped with a few slices of goats' cheese and served with some crusty bread on the side, it makes a lovely light lunch. You can use butternut squash instead of the pumpkin if you wish.

Serves 4

1kg pumpkin

5 tbsp olive oil

Juice of 1 lime

1 tbsp cider vinegar

1 tbsp honey

½ tsp salt

Large pinch of freshly ground black pepper

40g cacao nibs

200g mixed salad leaves

Preheat the oven to 200°C.

Peel the pumpkin, cut in half and discard the pith and seeds. Chop the flesh into approximately 3-cm cubes.

In a large bowl, whisk together the olive oil, lime juice, vinegar, honey, salt and pepper until well combined. Pour a third of this mixture into a small dish and set aside as a dressing for the salad at the end. Add the cubed pumpkin to the remaining mixture, along with the cacao nibs, and toss until it is all well coated.

Line a large roasting tin with baking paper. Tip the prepared pumpkin into it, spacing it out evenly. Roast in the hot oven for about 40 minutes, or until lightly browned, turning the pumpkin once or twice during cooking. Allow the pumpkin to cool down until it is only just warm.

Toss the salad leaves in a large serving bowl with the remaining dressing and top with the roasted pumpkin and cacao nibs. Serve immediately with crusty bread.

PORCINI AND CHOCOLATE RISOTTO

All my vegetarian friends say, 'Yes, Willie, but what do *we* do with cacao?' This risotto is the obvious option. The porcini mushrooms and cacao, both with distinct and powerful flavours and deep, rich colouring, make the perfect union.

Serves 4

100g dried porcini mushrooms

4–5 tbsp olive oil

1 onion, finely chopped

3 garlic cloves, finely chopped

25g butter

250g Arborio rice

1 litre hot chicken or vegetable stock

2 tbsp finely grated 100% cacao

Salt and freshly ground black pepper

Freshly grated Parmesan cheese, to serve

Place the porcini mushrooms in a small heatproof bowl. Cover with boiling water and leave to soak for at least 20 minutes.

Meanwhile, heat the oil in a large pan. Add the onion and garlic and fry over a gentle heat for 3–4 minutes, or until soft and translucent. Stir in the butter until melted, then stir in the rice.

Tip in the porcini, along with their soaking liquid. Bring to a gentle simmer, stirring continuously, until all the soaking liquid has been absorbed. Add a ladleful of hot stock and continue to simmer, stirring frequently, until the liquid has again been absorbed. Continue cooking, adding the stock and stirring in this way, until all the stock has been used up and the rice is plump and tender.

Finally, stir in the cacao, season with salt and black pepper to taste and serve with grated Parmesan sprinkled over the top.

WILD MUSHROOM STEW

Vegetarians and carnivores alike find this dish satisfying. The addition of cacao at the end thickens and enriches the gravy. To vary it, you could add a few freshly roasted chestnuts. Although making the stock takes a little extra time, it is worth it for the flavour. You can prepare the whole dish, up to adding the cacao, in advance, and then reheat and finish off on the day of serving.

Serves 4–6

30g dried porcini mushrooms, roughly chopped

1kg mix of wild and cultivated mushrooms (use at least 4 of porcini, trompettes, chicken of the wood, chanterelles, shiitake, chestnut, field and tiny button mushrooms)

40g butter

5 large garlic cloves, finely chopped

Salt and freshly ground black pepper

100ml glass vermouth, or dry white wine

2 tbsp olive oil

2 large onions, cut into 2cm cubes

2 fresh bay leaves

10g Venezuelan Hacienda Las Trincheras 100% cacao, grated

½–1 tbsp soy sauce

Small bunch of flat-leaf parsley, finely chopped

FOR THE STOCK:

2 large onions

3 tbsp olive oil

First make the stock. Cut the onions into 1cm slices. Heat the olive oil in a large pan, add the onions and salt and fry over a moderate heat until they are very brown and caramelized. Take care not to burn them as this will make the stock bitter.

Add all the remaining stock ingredients plus 1 litre cold water and bring to the boil. Lower the heat and leave to simmer for about 1 hour. Strain into a clean pan, return to a gentle boil and continue cooking until reduced to about 300ml liquid. Set aside.

Now prepare the stew. Stir the dried porcini mushrooms into the hot stock and set aside. Pick over and clean the wild mushrooms. Only resort to washing those that you cannot clean with a brush or cloth, such as the trompettes, which often grow in sandy soil. Leave the smaller mushrooms whole, and cut the larger ones either in half or into fat chunks, depending on shape and size.

Divide the prepared mushrooms into three batches. Melt about a third of the butter in a large frying pan and cook one batch of mushrooms over a medium heat until starting to soften. Add a little of the garlic with some salt and pepper to taste and a splash of the vermouth or wine and continue to cook, stirring, for another minute. Tip into a bowl and set aside while you cook the remaining batches of mushrooms in the same way.

Heat the olive oil in a large pan or flameproof casserole, add the onion cubes and fry until they are a nutty brown. Pour in the prepared stock, then add the cooked wild mushrooms, the bay leaves and the cacao. Bring to the boil and cook gently over a low heat for 5–7 minutes (don't overcook or you will lose the individual flavours of the mushrooms). Adjust the seasoning to taste with the salt, pepper and a little soy sauce. Serve garnished with a sprinkling of chopped parsley, accompanied by mashed potatoes, rice or with chocolate tagliatelle pasta (see page 56).

Pinch of salt

1 celery heart,
roughly chopped

2 carrots,
roughly chopped

2 bay leaves

Pinch of dried tarragon

2 sprigs fresh thyme

2 sprigs of parsley

Trimmings from the
fresh mushrooms
(see opposite)

1 tbsp soy sauce

This stew also makes a great pie filling. To use it in this way,
allow the stew to cool completely, then place in a large pie dish
or ovenproof casserole. Preheat the oven to 200°C and roll out
500g puff pastry to a thickness of about 3mm. Cut a long strip
off the pastry, just wider than the rim of the pie dish. Wet the
rim with a little water, then press the pastry strip down onto it.
Brush the strip with a little more water, then lay the sheet of
rolled-out pastry on top. Press down firmly along the edges to
seal, then trim off any excess. Cut a few slits in the pastry
topping and glaze by brushing with beaten egg. Bake in the
preheated oven for 40 minutes, until the pastry is golden
brown and puffed up. Serve immediately.

VINCISGRASSI

This is one of my all-time favourite recipes. Its origins lie in eighteenth-century Italy. The ingredients that lift it out of the ordinary are the chocolate pasta and the fresh white truffles that are shaved on at the end. If your budget can't stretch to fresh truffles, then white truffle oil is a good substitute. Instead of making six individual servings as described here, you can also make one large dish. It can be assembled and then frozen, ready to defrost and cook at a later date.

Serves 6

10g dried porcini mushrooms

750g fresh porcini mushrooms

75g butter

60g plain flour

2 fresh bay leaves

750ml full-fat milk

300ml double cream

1 recipe quantity Basic Chocolate Pasta Dough (see page 56)

200g Parmesan cheese, freshly grated

3 tbsp finely chopped flat-leaf parsley

1 fresh white truffle, or 5–6 tbsp white truffle oil

Place the dried porcini in a heatproof bowl. Cover with boiling water and leave to soak for at least 20 minutes.

Slice the fresh mushrooms, reserving 6 of the best central slices for garnish. Heat about 25g of the butter in a frying pan. Add the sliced mushrooms and cook for 2–3 minutes, or until very lightly browned. Remove from the heat and set aside.

Melt the remaining 50g butter in a saucepan over a medium-low heat. Add the flour and bay leaves and cook, stirring, for 1 minute. Take off the heat and gradually stir in the milk. Return to a low heat and bring slowly to the boil, stirring constantly, until you have a thick, creamy sauce. Stir in the cream and dried mushrooms with their soaking liquid and return to the boil. Remove and discard the bay leaves, then leave the sauce on one side while you roll out the pasta.

Cut the pasta dough into 8 equal pieces. First roll each piece out on a floured surface, then pass through a pasta machine, following the manufacturer's instructions, to produce 8 paper-thin pasta sheets. If you don't have a pasta machine, you can continue to roll out the dough on the floured surface using a rolling pin, but it is not as easy to get really thin sheets with this method. Lay the prepared pasta sheets on a flour-dusted surface and cut out 24 rounds, each about 20cm in diameter. Allow these pasta rounds to dry on a wire rack or on sheets of kitchen paper for at least 30 minutes before cooking.

Preheat the oven to 220°C. Bring a large pan of water to the boil. Plunge a couple of pasta rounds into the boiling water and cook for 1–2 minutes. Remove with a slotted spoon, plunge immediately into cold water and leave to drain on kitchen paper. Cook and drain the remaining pasta rounds in the same way.

Lightly grease 6 round 20-cm baking dishes. Place a freshly cooked pasta round in each dish, then top with a little of the creamy mushroom sauce, followed by a sprinkling of Parmesan and a few of the fried mushroom slices. Continue layering in this way, finishing with a layer of the creamy sauce, topped with a sprinkling of Parmesan and one reserved slice of fresh mushroom. Place the assembled vincisgrassi in the hot oven and cook for 12–15 minutes, or until golden brown on top.

Just before serving, sprinkle over a little chopped parsley and a shaving or two of white truffle, or a scant tablespoon of white truffle oil. Serve immediately with a green salad.

CHOCOLATE PESTO

Here cacao adds richness and warmth to a traditional pesto. The nutty spiciness of Venezuelan Carenero marries particularly well with the flavours of basil, pine nuts and Parmesan. For a quick, easy and sensational supper, stir this pesto into a bowl of your favourite freshly cooked pasta, or use it as a topping to a warm chicken salad.

Makes 150ml

75g fresh basil leaves

30g Parmesan cheese, crumbled

30g pine nuts

12g Venezuelan Carenero Superior 100% cacao, finely grated

12ml olive oil

Pinch of salt

Place all the ingredients in a blender or food processor and whizz to a coarse paste. If not using immediately, transfer to a sterilized jar or plastic container and seal with an airtight lid. The pesto will keep in the fridge for up to 2 weeks.

YEASTED BREADS AND DOUGHS

BASIC CHOCOLATE PASTA DOUGH

I remember the first time I made this. I used it for chocolate tagliatelle, which I served with Bolognese sauce. It blew away my little Evie. She loved it. Chocolate tagliatelle is also brilliant with a simple tomato and basil sauce, or Chocolate Pesto (see page 53) or Wild Mushroom Stew (see page 50). However, you can use this dough for any kind of pasta, including lasagne and stuffed pastas, such as ravioli and tortellini.

Makes 300g

30g Venezuelan Hacienda Las Trincheras 100% cacao, roughly chopped

200g '00' pasta flour

25g cocoa powder

2 large egg yolks

2 large whole eggs

Melt the cacao in a heatproof bowl set over a pan of gently simmering water, making sure that the bottom of the bowl is not in contact with the water. Set aside.

Sift the flour and cocoa powder together onto a wooden board or clean work surface. Make a well in the centre and put in the egg yolks, whole eggs and melted chocolate. Using the fingers of one hand, mix the eggs and chocolate together, gradually drawing in the flour and cocoa mixture to form a soft, but not sticky, dough. Add more flour or egg, if needed, to get the right consistency. Knead for 10–15 minutes, or until smooth and elastic. Wrap in cling film or a clean tea towel and leave in the fridge to chill for at least 1 hour before using.

The dough can also be made in a food processor or an electric mixer with a dough-hook attachment. Just place the flour and cocoa powder in the mixer or processor bowl, then add the eggs and melted chocolate and process for about 5 minutes, before wrapping and chilling.

To use, divide the dough into six or eight pieces and roll out each piece on a floured work surface until as close to paper-thin as possible. (Ideally, this should be done using a pasta machine.) Cut up the pasta sheets into whatever shape you wish to make.

BASIC PIZZA AND FOCACCIA DOUGH

The key factors in successful dough-making are getting the dough to the right consistency and leaving it to rise for at least 4–6 hours for the flavour to develop fully.

Makes 4 x 24-cm pizza bases or 2 large focaccie

500g strong white flour

1 heaped tsp salt

1 tbsp easy-blend yeast

300ml warm water

3 tbsp extra virgin olive oil

Sift the flour and salt into a large mixing bowl and stir in the yeast. Add the warm water and 2 tablespoons of the olive oil and mix thoroughly to form a soft, but not sticky, dough. Add more flour or water if necessary to achieve the right consistency. Turn out onto a lightly floured surface and knead for 10 minutes, until smooth and elastic. You can also make the dough in a food processor or an electric mixer with a dough-hook attachment. Simply place the flour, salt and yeast in the mixer or processor bowl, then add the warm water and olive oil and process for about 5 minutes.

Tip the dough into a large bowl that you have previously greased with the remaining tablespoon of olive oil. Cover with a clean tea towel, or place another large bowl upturned on top. Leave in a warm place for at least 4 hours to allow the dough to rise, doubling in size.

To use, tip the dough onto a floured surface and punch firmly to knock it back to its original size. Shape as you wish.

WILD MUSHROOM AND TALEGGIO PIZZA

If you cannot get hold of Taleggio cheese, you can use mozzarella here instead. However, I am a big fan of cooking with Taleggio. It has a wonderful flavour, which marries perfectly with the fruitiness of the cacao and the earthiness of the mushrooms.

Serves 2–4

300g wild mushrooms (you can use a mixture of cultivated mushrooms if wild ones are not available; just add a few slices of soaked and chopped dried porcini mushrooms to enhance the flavour)

30g butter

Salt and freshly ground black pepper

2 garlic cloves, finely chopped

½ recipe quantity Basic Pizza and Focaccia Dough (see page 57)

250g Taleggio cheese, cut into 2cm chunks

4 tbsp freshly grated Parmesan cheese

5g Madagascan Sambirano Superior 100% cacao

Small bunch of flat-leaf parsley, finely chopped

Wipe the mushrooms if they appear dirty. I only wash them if they are very gritty, otherwise you should never wash mushrooms. Cut in half or into thick slices if they are very large.

Melt the butter in a large frying pan, add the mushrooms, season to taste with salt and pepper and cook over a low to moderate heat for 5–8 mintues, or until they start to soften. Add the garlic just at the end of the cooking time. Leave to cool.

Tip the risen dough onto a floured work surface and knock it back to its original size. Divide into two pieces and shape each into a ball. Flatten slightly, then roll out to form two rounds, approximately 22cm in diameter. Lift each one up with both hands and stretch out the middle part, so the edges are thicker than in the centre. Lay each stretched round of dough on a lightly floured baking tray.

Sprinkle the cooled mushrooms evenly on the rounds of dough. Scatter the Taleggio evenly over the top, then sprinkle with the Parmesan. Leave in a warm place to rise for at least 1 hour.

Preheat the oven to 250°C. When the pizzas are ready, place in the hot oven and cook for 12–15 minutes, or until the dough is cooked through and crisp.

Remove from the oven and, with a potato peeler, shave the cacao over each pizza. Sprinkle with the parsley and serve immediately.

CACAO NIB FOCACCIA STUFFED WITH BASIL AND TALEGGIO

The cacao nibs on the outside of this bread lightly toast as it cooks. This adds a fragrant, nutty chewiness that contrasts with the softly melting fruitiness of the Taleggio cheese and the fragrant basil inside the bread. It is best served warm.

Makes 1

½ recipe quantity Basic Pizza and Focaccia Dough (see page 57)

25g cacao nibs

200g Taleggio cheese, cut into 1cm thick slices

12g fresh basil leaves

2 tbsp extra virgin olive oil

Tip the risen dough onto a floured work surface and knock it back to its original size. Divide into two pieces, one slightly smaller than the other, and shape each into a ball.

Sprinkle half the cacao nibs over a lightly floured surface. If the nibs are large, crush them a little with a pestle and mortar or a rolling pin. Roll out the smaller piece of dough evenly over the scattered nibs to form a circle approximately 24cm in diameter. Lift onto a lightly floured baking tray. Arrange the Taleggio slices on top, leaving a 2-cm border of dough around the edge. Scatter over the basil leaves, reserving a few as a garnish.

Again, lightly flour the work surface and sprinkle with the remaining cacao nibs, as before. Roll out the larger ball of dough evenly over the nibs to form a circle about 26cm in diameter. Wet the edges around the circle of dough on the baking tray and place the larger dough circle over it. Tuck the overhanging edge of the large circle under the small circle to neaten, then press down firmly all along the edges to seal in the filling.

Sprinkle the olive oil over the top. With a pair of scissors, snip about six holes in the central area of the bread, then scatter over the remaining basil leaves. Set aside in a warm place for about 2 hours, or until puffy and slightly risen.

Preheat the oven to 220°C and bake the bread for 12–15 minutes, or until lightly golden brown. Don't overcook – this bread should be slightly soft. Transfer to a wire rack and leave to cool for about 15 minutes before serving.

CACAO AND OLIVE BREAD

As I have always baked my own bread, it seemed only natural to mix cacao into a loaf. Here the cacao's nuttiness is a perfect foil for the meatiness of the olives. Try toasting this bread too, as it brings out the roasted flavours of the cacao even more.

Makes 1 large loaf or 10 rolls

300g plain white flour

100g strong wholemeal flour

1 tsp salt

1½ tsp easy-blend yeast

150ml full-fat milk

150ml water

75g Venezuelan Carenero Superior 100% cacao, chopped or grated

75ml extra virgin olive oil

200g green olives, pitted and chopped

1 egg yolk, beaten, or 1 tbsp milk

1 tbsp fennel seeds

Sift the flours and salt into a large mixing bowl and stir in the yeast. Warm the milk and water in a saucepan. Add the cacao and stir until it has melted. Pour in the olive oil and mix well. Tip this warm liquid into the bowl of dry ingredients and mix thoroughly to form a soft, but not sticky, dough. Add more flour or warm water if necessary to achieve the right consistency. Turn out onto a lightly floured surface and knead for 10 minutes, until smooth and elastic. You can also make the dough in a food processor or an electric mixer with a dough-hook attachment. Simply place the flour, salt and yeast in the mixer or processor bowl, then add the warm liquid and process for about 5 minutes.

Sprinkle the chopped olives over the dough and knead a little more to mix in. Place in a lightly greased bowl. Cover with a clean tea towel, or place another large bowl upturned on top. Leave in a warm place for at least 2 hours to allow the dough to rise, doubling in size.

Tip the risen dough onto a floured surface and knock it back to its original size. Press into a large, oiled bread tin or divide into ten pieces and shape each into a small roll. Place the rolls on an oiled baking tray. Lightly brush the top of the loaf or the rolls with either a little egg yolk or milk, then sprinkle over the fennel seeds. Leave in a warm place for about 1 hour, or until well risen (almost doubled in size)

Preheat the oven to 190°C and bake the bread: 45 minutes for the loaf, or 15 minutes for the rolls. To test if the bread is done, tap it sharply on the underside – it should sound hollow. If not, return to the oven for a further 3–5 minutes and test again. When fully cooked, turn the loaf out of the tin, or remove the rolls from the tray, and leave to cool on a wire rack.

CHOCOLATE, BLUEBERRY AND BUCKWHEAT BLINIS

Blinis are part of traditional Russian cuisine and are normally savoury. Here the chocolate adds a dash of sweetness and richness to the tangy blueberries and takes these blinis to new heights. They make great canapés for a summer party.

Makes about 25

25g strong white flour

50g buckwheat flour

Pinch of salt

1 tsp easy-blend yeast

45g caster sugar

75g Venezuelan Hacienda Las Trincheras 72% chocolate, roughly chopped

150ml warm full-fat milk

2 small eggs, separated

½ tsp vanilla essence

15g melted butter, plus extra butter for frying

125g blueberries

Crème fraîche, to serve

Sift the flours and salt into a large mixing bowl, then stir in the yeast and caster sugar to mix well.

Melt the chocolate in a heatproof bowl over a pan of gently simmering water, making sure the bottom of the bowl is not in contact with the water. Mix the warm chocolate and milk together in another large bowl. Add the eggs yolks, vanilla essence and melted butter and whisk to combine. Tip in the flour mixture and continue whisking to form a thick batter. Cover and leave in a warm place for about 2 hours.

Fold the blueberries into the batter. Whisk the egg whites until they form stiff peaks, then gently fold into the batter.

Heat a knob of butter in a large frying pan over a medium heat and, when hot, spoon three or four tablespoons of the batter into the pan, each spoonful forming a small round blini. Cook for 2 minutes, then turn the blinis over and cook for a further minute. The blinis should be golden and cooked through. Take care not to overcook as the addition of chocolate makes them easier to burn. Remove from the pan and keep warm while cooking the remaining batter.

Serve immediately, topped with a little crème fraîche. The blinis also go well with chocolate sauce (see pages 124–5).

PAIN AU CHOCOLAT

These take quite a bit of time to make, but are well worth the wait. If you want them for breakfast, you could always leave them in a cool kitchen, or in the fridge, to rise overnight, ready to bake in the morning. They can also be assembled and frozen for up to a month. To serve, just thaw and then leave to rise and bake in the usual way.

Makes 30

400g strong white flour

2 tsp salt

2 tsp easy-blend yeast

85g granulated sugar

220ml full-fat milk

220ml water

30g unsalted butter, melted

300g unsalted butter, softened to room temperature

300g Madagascan Sambirano Superior 71% chocolate

1 egg yolk, beaten, or 1 tbsp milk

Sift the flour and salt into a large mixing bowl and stir in the yeast and sugar. Add the milk, water and melted butter and mix well to form a soft, but not sticky, dough. Add more flour or water if necessary to achieve the right consistency. The dough could also be made in an electric mixer if you wish.

Transfer the dough to a large bowl, sprinkle over a little flour and leave for about 40 minutes to rise slightly.

On a lightly floured surface, roll the dough into a 20 x 40-cm rectangle. Cover with cling film and place in the fridge for 2–4 hours. Again, the dough will rise a little during this time.

Place the chilled dough on a floured work surface. Spread the softened butter over two-thirds of it, then fold the unbuttered area onto the buttered section, then the remaining buttered area on the top of this. Roll out to form a 30 x 80-cm rectangle and position it with a longer side facing you. Fold the left-hand third of the rectangle over to the right and then the right-hand third over that. Wrap in cling film and chill in the fridge for 1 hour.

Remove from the fridge, place on a floured work surface and roll out into a 30 x 80-cm rectangle about 5mm thick. Cut into 30 rectangles, each 8 x 10cm.

Cut the chocolate into 30 strips 2cm wide and place a strip along the length of each rectangle of dough. Fold one side of the dough over the chocolate. Brush a little beaten egg or milk along the edge of the opposite side and fold over to enclose the chocolate, pressing firmly to seal. Turn so that the seam is underneath. Line a large baking tray with baking paper and arrange the uncooked pains au chocolat on the tray. Leave in a warm place until about double in size. This can take 2–3 hours.

Preheat the oven to 220°C. When the pains au chocolat are ready to bake, brush lightly with beaten egg yolk or milk, then bake in the hot oven for 10–12 minutes, or until golden brown and slightly crisp on top.

THE QUEST FOR BEANS

When I first opened my factory in Devon, a great friend of mine told me, 'You'll get bored.' He thought that once I had achieved my goal of making chocolate, the repetition would get to me. 'After that, what's your next milestone?' he asked.

He was wrong, because it's not just about making chocolate. The thrill of discovering a fine new flavour and bringing it to the market will always drive me. I'm constantly on a quest for the Holy Grail of chocolate: the best beans, the richest flavours. Other chocolate companies are perhaps less romantic about doing business, because making chocolate with distinct flavours in small quantities doesn't make a lot of economic sense. But I just can't resist. For me, making chocolate is all about rediscovering the real tastes, textures and life-giving properties of a food that has been revered for thousands of years, but has somehow lost its way in the modern, commercial market.

Of course, Venezuelan chocolate was my first love and I still revel in its flavours. But when someone rings me and says, 'I've sourced some wild Nicaraguan beans for you,' a shiver of anticipation goes through me. The more I've learned about different cacao types, strains and flavours, the more interested I've become in sourcing the most delectable beans from other places. In fact, I sometimes feel as if I'm cataloguing the different cacao flavours of the world. I want to process them my way, preserving the fabric of the bean and the distinct flavour, and introduce as many of them as possible to chocolate lovers.

That's why I process up to 20 different bean samples from around the globe every month. At the time of writing, for instance, my factory has nine Colombian samples that have just been roasted and ground, three from Mexico, and 20 kilos of 70% chocolate made using a sack of beans from Sierra Leone. I've been sent some Cuban beans and two sets of Brazilian beans; another 13 samples are on their way from Colombia. And not long ago, some beans from Uganda turned up in the post, sent by a farmer who had looked me up on the Internet. They weren't fermented enough, but I could tell that they were very interesting trinitario beans. This is what fuels me - gorgeous flavours from different regions and climates! I don't think about making tons of money; I think about how I can bring those flavours to people who love great chocolate and want to try something new.

There's also a practical reason for sourcing beans from different places. When one of my first shipments was held up,

after I'd waited too long to order it, I became acutely aware that if my supply was ever interrupted, I'd have nothing to work with in the factory. Anything from a bad harvest to global climate change or political instability could lead to the loss of a supplier and leave me beanless, I realized. That's when I decided to branch out into other countries and flavours. I needed to be flexible about my supply and be able to make the best, most interesting chocolate on a consistent basis.

First, I thought of Peru. I have very fond memories of my two years of travelling in Peru during my twenties and feel a real affinity with the country. My great friend John Kehoe introduced me to Willem Bolk at Daarnhouwer & Co, a company of high-quality cacao brokers in Holland, who also came recommended by the Franceschi brothers, my bean brokers in Venezuela. I asked Willem whether there were any Peruvian samples I could try and he sent me a couple to experiment with. The San Martin beans were simply amazing in every way: the moment I tasted them, I knew I had to use them to make my 100% cacao bar. I then began to dream about making a range of sweet chocolate, using beans from around the world.

There are three varieties of Theobroma cacao, as it was officially named in 1753 by the Swedish scientist Carl von Linné. They are criollo, forastero and trinitario, and multiple hybrids exist of each strain. Criollo and forastero came first, but although they both evolved in the Amazon Basin, they are quite distinct from one another. Forastero is typically the hardier strain and has a higher yield of cacao pods. As a result, it's easier and cheaper to grow, which is why it accounts for more than three-quarters of the world's cacao crop. Forastero beans give a classic chocolate taste, but tend to lack the subtle flavour notes of the less robust, less productive criollo, which produces a much more interesting range of flavours and aromas.

Criollo beans are what the Maya and Aztecs went wild about, the strain that later seduced and enchanted Europeans in the

seventeenth and eighteenth centuries. Forastero is generally used to make mass-produced chocolate. It's consistent and reliable, but can be rather bland. Just as in Maya and Aztec times, when lower-grade cacao was mixed with maize and other seeds, while high-quality chocolate was drunk in a purer form, present-day manufacturers use cheaper, less interesting cacao to make average confectionery and save the fine, rare beans for making rich, flavoursome dark chocolate.

Since cacao is so variable, as well as so valuable, the chocolate industry has always attracted counterfeiters and swindlers. Aztec market traders, when selling cacao beans, often used to make their wares go further by mixing them up with avocado stones, bits of dough, wax, clay and anything else that could pass for the real thing. In Europe in the eighteenth and nineteenth centuries, chocolate was frequently diluted with brick dust or red lead, and lard was added to cacao butter to bulk it out. These days, the mainstream confectionery companies print their ingredients on the labels so that everyone can see how much fat, sugar and lecithin goes into your average bar, yet amazingly people still call it chocolate!

The trinitario bean has an interesting history. When virtually the entire crop of Trinidad's criollo cacao was wiped out in the eighteenth century – either by a hurricane or by a plant disease of some kind – forastero trees were introduced to the island, where they cross-pollinated with the few remaining criollo trees to produce a new strain of cacao. Trinitario is hardier than criollo, but tastier than forastero, so it's very versatile. Some of my favourite chocolates are made from trinitario beans.

Today, criollo tends to be the preferred bean of chocolate connoisseurs. There are many varieties of criollo cacao and almost all of them grow in Venezuela. Once upon a time, Venezuelan cacao was called 'Caracas' wherever it was imported, but now it is known by the region in which it grows, just like wine. Chuao, which is considered by some people to be among the world's finest cacao, comes from a village in Venezuela very near to my hacienda, where the soil and climate produce beans with a full, rich flavour. Porcelana Blanca, another highly prized variety, was originally called Maracaibo because it came from the area around Lake Maracaibo. Rio Caribe, one of my favourite trinitarios, grows in the beautiful northeast coastal region of Venezuela of the same name, not far from Puerto Carenero, where another beautiful trinitario is grown.

I learned to differentiate between all the different types of cacao on my journeys around Venezuela, when I was sourcing varieties of cacao to replant my hacienda and beans to process at my factory in England. As someone who had grown up thinking that chocolate had a fairly uniform flavour, I was taken aback by the different tastes and aromas that I came across. Each bean was distinct from the next! I soon realized that although criollo, forastero and trinitario each have general characteristics, it wasn't as simple as criollo having one flavour profile and trinitario having another. It was much more complex than that. Soil, climate, fermentation and roasting all have a huge impact.

As time went on, I was able to take an unroasted bean and shell it, eat it, taste the initial acidity and then focus on the distinguishing back notes, which are the cacao flavours in their infancy. The back notes are difficult to trace, but they are always there. I would immediatcly know if I was tasting a bean with merit, even before I roasted it my cast-iron pan, ground it and combined it with local cream to make a basic truffle and get a better idea of the flavour. Some of the more prolific hybrids of cacao can be quite acidic, but it doesn't mean the flavours aren't there. Anyway, acidic chocolate has its uses; it mixes particularly well with fillings in confectionery-making.

Back at the farm, I started experimenting with ice cream. It's a decadent way to taste the rich flavour notes of cacao; the double cream and egg yolks create a delicious wave of flavour, with the super rich taste of the cacao rolling in behind. Willie's Cacao Bean Ice Cream (see page 85) became one of my signature dishes. It's one of the most exciting ice creams ever, because people always love a surprise in ice cream – and what better surprise could you have than caramelized cacao nibs?

We would climb the shade trees and collect the vanilla pods from the vines that were creeping up them, dry them and infuse them into milk or cream. Before your lips even touched the milk, you could taste the vanilla. There was nothing like it. To caramelize the nibs, I used the beautiful sugar from the cloud forest in San Pablo. Everyone went wild about this ice cream and the way the sublime softness of the vanilla was followed by the sweetness of the caramelized sugar, with the slightly bitter chocolate flavour seeping in afterwards.

Double cream was very hard to find, though. Sometimes we'd be staying at people's haciendas in the middle of nowhere and they wouldn't even have milk, so when everyone looked at me to

produce a treat for dessert, I'd often make a sorbet, which only needed water. Sorbet is a lot more intense than ice cream and I found that it was a better way to reflect the intensity of the cacao. Mousse was another route to enjoying the flavour profiles, but in a lighter way: the flavour notes float.

When I first made sweet chocolate, I took it to my great friend Marco Pierre White for his approval, or disapproval, whichever it was going to be. Who better to ask than a Michelin-star chef? Marco has been hugely supportive of my chocolate, but I couldn't help being nervous. He loved my 100% cacao bar, but sweet chocolate is something else entirely. Marco suggested making a soufflé. 'It's the best way of tasting the flavour notes,' he said. His Chocolate Soufflé (see page 105) is sensational: the egg whites lighten up the rich, creamy chocolate custard to produce a beautiful airy, floating flavour. I've since made it using my entire sweet chocolate range.

Tasting chocolate is an art that I'm still learning. Like wine tasting, it's a complex business because there are at least 400 chocolate flavour notes. A number of different factors affect the tasting process. For instance, how the chocolate moves around your mouth has an impact on the flavour. The viscosity and how it melts are crucial. So there's a huge difference between a bar that's been kept in the fridge and a bar stored at room temperature. If the chocolate is cold, it will melt in your mouth more slowly than a room-temperature chocolate and taste different as a result. Ideally, you should eat chocolate at room temperature.

Dark chocolate takes longer to melt in the mouth than milk chocolate because more fat is melted during the process of making milk chocolate than dark chocolate, increasing its viscosity. Also, there is more cacao butter in milk chocolate, and cacao butter melts at room temperature.

Before you even start thinking about the adjectives you should be using to describe the flavour notes of the chocolate, you have to bear in mind that your taste buds vary during the day, so a tasting panel at 10 o'clock in the morning will produce different results at 2 o'clock in the afternoon. You should also wait for about two hours after eating, and avoid alcohol and smoking, which muddy the palate.

I've often been told that you should taste no more than four distinct chocolates at one session, although I've often broken that rule! Formal chocolate-tasting etiquette also requires that you agree your vocabulary before you sit down. The flavour terminology is very similar to that of wine. Common descriptive words include 'green', 'fruity', 'smoky', 'sacky', 'raisiny', 'flowery', 'citrusy', 'malty', 'piquant', 'vanilla', 'liquorice', 'caramel' and 'toffee'. 'Smoky' and 'mouldy' are flavours you can't get rid of. If a chocolate tastes smoky, the beans probably weren't dried with enough care; if it's mouldy, the beans may have been stored in the wrong conditions. There's nothing you can do to eradicate either of these mistakes in the factory, so it's important to get the post-harvesting process right in the first place.

I've detected a few strange flavour notes in some of the chocolate I've tasted. 'Spicy sausage' is one that springs to mind! And I remember trying a chocolate with Chloé Doutre-Roussel, who was the chocolate buyer at Fortnum & Mason at the time, and we both agreed that it had a strong aroma of Parma ham. Does anyone really want chocolate that tastes of Parma ham, I wondered? I have since sampled chocolate that came from India, which had a similar aftertaste, and I realized that its unusual flavour was probably to do with the way the beans were fermented.

Fermentation is crucial to the taste of cacao: without it, cacao beans won't develop a chocolate flavour, but if you mess it up, you can ruin a great cacao harvest. After the beans and pulp have been removed from the pod, they are placed in hardwood boxes, covered in banana leaves and turned twice a day to aerate them. Inside the boxes, the beans soon become a big mulchy mass and juice leaks from the pulp. The oxygen in the air activates the enzymes in the pulp sugar, causing it to acidify, which changes the chemical composition of the beans. Yeast cells, that grow and divide as a result of this change, produce alcohol and carbon dioxide, causing the beans to heat up; they give off a strong aroma as they reach temperatures of around 52°C. It's a natural chemical process and the most important stage is the rise in temperature: the porous shell of the cacao bean expands; there is traffic between inside and out; and the aroma of chocolate starts to develop.

Fermentation has been around for thousands of years, but it wasn't until the scientist Louis Pasteur identified what was happening during the process in 1856 that it was understood and formalized. The British later developed and systemized cacao fermentation on their plantations in Trinidad and Jamaica. So how did the Maya and Aztecs get it right? One theory is that

Ezequiel Cerreno, me, Juan de Dios and Alberto Franceschi. Talking cacao at Hacienda San Jose.

they put their cacao in boxes to let it drain before they put it out to dry, perhaps unaware that this process of natural fermentation was crucial to developing the chocolate flavour. For them, draining the pulp may simply have made the drying process easier; anyway, criollo beans need to be fermented for only a few days. Other varieties may take up to six days.

Fermentation has to be done properly, and no one understands this better than my bean brokers in Venezuela, the three Franceschi brothers. Whenever I go to my hacienda to oversee the cacao harvest, I never think twice about driving 12 hours across Venezuela to visit the Franceschis at their San José hacienda. Alberto, José Vicente and Juan de Dios are true chocolate romantics, fifth-generation cacao plantation owners who are passionate about growing the finest cacao.

I met the brothers during the long drawn-out process of trying to source beans to supply my fledgling factory in Devon. Since the El Tesoro crop didn't yield the amount of beans or variety of flavours that I needed for the volume of cacao bars I was planning to produce, in the autumn of 2006 I cast around for other suppliers, only to be let down by people almost everywhere I turned. I was an unknown buyer and, although as a cacao farmer I was permitted to buy and export cacao, I kept hitting a brick wall. After months of false leads and pulling my hair out, during which it began to look like all my dreams would crumble into the dust, my great friend John Kehoe saved the day when he introduced me to the Franceschis, who are the finest grower-brokers in Venezuela and have now become good friends.

The history of the Franceschis' San José plantation encapsulates the story of cacao growing in Venezuela over the last two centuries. Their great-great grandfather, José Vicente Franceschi José Vicentelli, arrived in Venezuela from Corsica in 1827, a French citizen and a consul. He set up as a cacao exporter and importer of European goods in Carúpano in 1830 and began advancing money to plantation owners. Gradually, he acquired plantations of his own, eventually managing about 5000 hectares of cacao in this region.

By 1890, the family were so important in the cacao business that they moved their headquarters from Carúpano to Paris, leaving behind some trusted Corsican families to continue the business in Venezuela. But after investing in French government bonds and railways, they lost everything during the First World

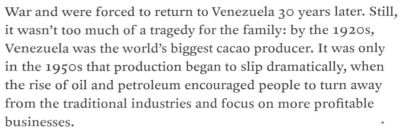

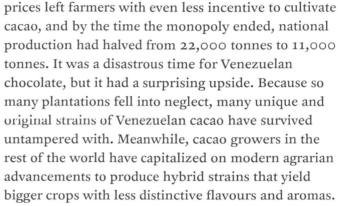

War and were forced to return to Venezuela 30 years later. Still, it wasn't too much of a tragedy for the family: by the 1920s, Venezuela was the world's biggest cacao producer. It was only in the 1950s that production began to slip dramatically, when the rise of oil and petroleum encouraged people to turn away from the traditional industries and focus on more profitable businesses.

Things became really bad when the government slapped a state monopoly on cacao exports between 1974 and 1991; fixed prices left farmers with even less incentive to cultivate cacao, and by the time the monopoly ended, national production had halved from 22,000 tonnes to 11,000 tonnes. It was a disastrous time for Venezuelan chocolate, but it had a surprising upside. Because so many plantations fell into neglect, many unique and original strains of Venezuelan cacao have survived untampered with. Meanwhile, cacao growers in the rest of the world have capitalized on modern agrarian advancements to produce hybrid strains that yield bigger crops with less distinctive flavours and aromas.

During the monopoly, the Franceschis sold all their cacao plantations except San José, the first one that their Corsican ancestor had acquired way back in 1840. They held on to it for romantic reasons, because it was integral to their family tradition and roots, but it soon became a money pit. They subsidized the property with their other businesses, but were unable to invest in the cacao. Over the 17 years that the monopoly lasted, the San José hacienda cacao rapidly deteriorated.

In 1989, the brothers held a family meeting. Everyone agreed that it was costing too much to keep the hacienda. But they still couldn't bear to let it go. Fortunately, the government opened up the market in 1991 and cacao became a potentially profitable business again. Driven by love of their land and strong feelings for family tradition, the brothers decided to replant the entire hacienda with the finest criollo plants and turn it into a model of cacao-growing excellence.

'In Venezuela, we had lost our criollo inheritance, because nobody was planting criollo anymore,' José Vicente told me. 'People were just growing trinitario, the hybrid of criollo and

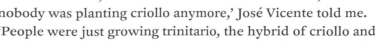

forastero. We decided to rescue criollo and replant the hacienda purely with criollo. Why? Because criollo fetched a higher price than other types of cacao, and when you have a plantation as big as this one, 180 hectares, it's very time- and money-consuming to restore it. So we needed to be different so that we could be more profitable.'

According to José Vicente, everybody had forgotten how to develop criollo, which is a little more delicate than trinitario and requires more work to grow successfully. At San José, they chose to replant by grafting from existing criollo trees to ensure the purity of their criollo varieties. 'If you produce it by seed, you risk cross-fertilization; the only way to guarantee that the cacao stays pure is by grafting or cloning,' he said. They selected healthy criollo trees with large white beans and set about taking cuttings and grafting them onto the roots of existing trees.

It was a huge effort to replant 180 hectares with grafted plants. 'We had a team of seven grafters and they grafted 150 trees a day,' José Vicente said. 'We divided the hacienda into lots of 10, 20 or 30 hectares and planted each lot with one of seven varieties of criollo cacao, mostly from the central part of Venezuela. They include Ocumare, Chuao, Guasare and Porcelana.'

I asked whether he had a favourite variety. 'For me, the Chuao is the best we have and it's better than the cacao from the Chuao plantation, because at the Chuao plantation they have introduced a lot of trinitario,' he said. 'It's a good hybrid with a high content of criollo plant, but the one we have is 100% pure. I'm sure it's going to be different.'

It's remarkable to think that José Vicente is a mechanical engineer with a master's degree in business administration. Like me, he's had no formal training in cacao growing or processing. But the dream of rebuilding the San José hacienda was incredibly powerful for him, just as replanting the El Tesoro hacienda was for me – only my plantation, at 15 hectares, was considerably smaller. I know exactly what he means when he says, 'Cacao is like a drug; once you become interested, you find a new world and become totally engrossed.' That's also the way it was for me.

San José now produces 30 tonnes of cacao and is aiming to produce 100 tonnes within four years. It's a beautifully managed plantation with just the right balance of light, shade, heat and moisture, and trees that are free from disease. Whenever I go there, it feels like I'm visiting the Garden of Eden; I buy as many beans from San José as the Franceschis will sell me.

The Franceschis' passion for cacao has taken the hacienda into the future. They are researching every aspect of growing and processing cacao, using science to improve their techniques, and are currently exploring new fermentation methods. One of their experiments involves injecting oxygen through tubes into the fermentation boxes to aerate the cacao without having to move it.

A few years ago, they hooked up with Domori, an Italian chocolate manufacturer, that helped with the financing of the replanting at San José. Now the Franceschis have built what they call 'a small laboratory' in Caracas, where two of their daughters and a son are making 70% criollo chocolate. 'Everybody loves cacao and chocolate in our family and everyone is involved in working with cacao in some way or another. It makes me very proud,' said José Vicente. And Venezuelan cacao production is now back up to 17,000 tonnes a year, and rising.

We went on to chat about cacao in Mexico and whether they could help me with sourcing some great Mexican beans. 'Funnily enough, we heard about some amazing criollo beans in Mexico,' Juan said. 'We flew up there to investigate and discovered that actually the cuttings had been brought from Aragua in Venezuela.' Aragua is the state next to mine!

'That's so fascinating,' I said, 'because a year ago, I was given some chocolate from a well-known chocolate manufacturer who said it was Porcelana. But what struck me about it was that it had a fantastic fruity flavour, very similar to my own El Tesoro chocolate.'

We both laughed when we realized that the Mexican plantation they had visited had supplied its beans to the company whose Porcelana chocolate I had sampled. That's the way the chocolate world loops! Five days later, while in Mexico, I paid a visit to the plantation and saw the big juicy Porcelana pods growing on its well-tended trees for myself.

However, the flavour profile was just too similar to my Venezuelan cacao. When I hit the cacao trail, I'm looking for home-grown Mexican or Colombian cacao. I want to source the authentic flavour of each country's cacao! I'm also keen on the idea of direct trade with cacao growers. Fairtrade is one thing, but putting money directly into the hands of the farmers who supply me with beans is a much more appealing idea.

So I was very interested to meet Marisol Hernandez Salazar, who approached me at the Real Food Festival at Earl's Court in London in May 2009, just after I had finished presenting my new Rio Caribe and Peruvian sweet chocolate. Marisol is the daughter of a Colombian potato farmer and she has plans to work with indigenous collectives around the world. She was taken by my relationship with my farm workers and the fact that I was buying beans directly. So how would I feel about meeting up with a collective of Colombian cacao growers? Marisol knew of a group who had turned their lives around by forming a cacao collective, after being forced by guerrillas to grow coca for decades.

Obviously, I was intrigued. Six months later, after a flying trip to my farm and a visit to San José and the Franceschis, I met up with Marisol at Bogotá airport, caught up on chocolate news and flew on to Bucamaranga. It was many years since I had last been in Colombia, but I was instantly reminded of the culture of good feeling and friendliness that characterizes this beautiful country.

The next morning we got up at 3.30 a.m. and took a taxi for five hours, north to Aguachica, winding through the mountains as dawn rose, catching glimpses of the occasional cacao tree through the breaking light. We travelled at high speed up the Rio Magdalena for an hour and a half through what appeared to be no man's land, and were greeted in Santa Rosa del Sur in the state of Bolivar by Marisol's contact, Don Miguel Angel Vargas Caro, and his chocolate gang.

I listened with fascination to the most amazing, heart-wrenching story of how the people of the area had lived under guerrilla rule for the last 30 years and been forced to grow coca, which is the basis for cocaine. The town and surrounding farms were a place of terror; murder and kidnapping were rife; children were forced to stop going to school and harvest coca leaves instead; many local girls and young women were forced into prostitution.

Then, six years ago, the area was transformed. The guerrillas were ejected and the local farmers came together and formed a collective. They ripped up the coca and planted cacao in its place. Behind these changes was Miguel Daza, a charismatic community leader who helped to found the workers' foundation Aprocasur (Association of Cocoa Producers in South Bolivar) in 2004. Tragically, Miguel was killed on the road between Santa Rosa and San Pablo in February 2008, in a suspected guerrilla

Miguel Daza
Cacao – Apuruxox
Colombia

ambush, but his legacy and the work of the collective continues to thrive.

The story was so powerful. We ended up in the central bodega in Santa Rosa, a depository for all the cacao beans from the surrounding farms. Some of the farmers had gathered to meet me and talk about their cacao, and I spent a couple of hours tasting beans and discussing their post-harvest methods. Some of the beans were well dried and fermented; some weren't quite dry enough or fermented enough, but it was an honest representation of what was going on within the collective.

I felt that they needed some guidance with their fermentation and drying, but the well-fermented and dried beans showed great promise and there was a definite eagerness among them to get it right. I recounted what Alberto Franceschi had told me a couple of days earlier: 'There are three main considerations when it comes to making a good chocolate: first is the genetics of the cacao; second is the post-harvesting – good fermentation and drying; third is the chef or chocolatier, who has the most responsibility for making the chocolate taste good.'

It's true that the chocolate-maker's role is very important, but the farmers needed to focus on what happens to the beans post-harvest. I explained that the pods need to be collected, sorted and then brought together to be fermented so that they can be processed as a whole, without inconsistencies in flavour. If there are different levels of fermentation within one shipment of cacao beans, making a consistent batch of chocolate will be impossible for the chocolate-maker in his factory.

I told them about the Madagascan cooperative I've been working with since 2009, after I was sent two sets of beans from Madagascar. The first sample came from a single hacienda and the second from a cooperative, a collection of growers. I was expecting the single estate bean to be the better option and provide a more consistent flavour, but I went for the cooperative's bean because the flavour jumped out at me. It went bling! I had to make chocolate from it!

When it came to naming the flavour notes, I decided on 'summer fruits' because there is something magical about the explosion of flavour in really fresh summer fruit. Both the 100% cacao bar and the sweet chocolate have subsequently been huge successes. People contact me all the time, going wild about the flavour, which is possibly more complex because the beans come from a combination of different plants. Watching me leap around gesticulating, as I described the outstanding qualities of my Madagascan chocolate, I think Don Miguel and his colleagues could tell that I was enthusiastic about working with cooperatives.

We continued to discuss post-harvesting methods. Drying the beans is less complex than fermenting, but it requires care and attention. After around 120 hours of fermentation, the beans are placed in the sun, first for a gentle dry, an hour in the morning and afternoon, when they need to be turned constantly. Exposure to the sun is then increased by the day, until the beans have been dried for up to 20 hours, usually over the course of a week. At El Tesoro, the way we make sure our beans are completely dry is to weigh them, put them out in the sun and weigh them again afterwards. When they weigh the same before and after, they're done. The optimum humidity of a dried bean is 7.5%. A bean that's too moist won't keep, and a bean that's too dry will break up and be difficult to roast because the broken pieces could easily burn in the roaster.

When we left the bodega, Don Miguel, Marisol and I went to visit Marlene Asevedo Romero's hacienda. Doña Marlene proudly walked me around her plantation and showed me the results of six years' hard work. I was impressed: her trees were a trinitario hybrid, well formed and well kept, growing in the shade of healthy avocado and passionfruit trees. As we walked down the neat avenues of cacao trees, Marlene told me how she and her family had lived in constant fear of guerrillas for 26 years. 'It was a terrible time, but I never lost hope, even when my husband was kidnapped,' she told me.

Now 38, strong, energetic and optimistic, Marlene appears to do everything on the farm, with some help from her four sons and her husband, when he isn't travelling. As well as keeping house, feeding her boys and cultivating cacao, she is studying for the eleventh grade in order to complete her education. After she had fed us all with a delicious vegetable soup and a main course of carne, frijoles y plátanos, I left her hacienda with a strong sense that her cacao was being grown with love. And to think that just seven years ago, the land was a coca plantation! I was full of admiration for the way she had turned the farm around. I suspect that she doesn't get a lot of sleep.

The hard work that goes into Marlene's plantation reminded me of a strange encounter I had with a chocolate company a couple of years ago, after the producer of my television

Visiting Marlene Asevedo Romero and her family at Santa Rosa, Colombia.

programme gave me a couple of bars of chocolate that came from Borough Market in London. One of them tasted off, so I sent it back. When I didn't hear from the company, I rang them up. The gentleman I spoke to said, 'We checked it and we all agreed it wasn't off.' I had to disagree!

He went into this long story about how the beans were Porcelana, from a very special plantation, where the crop is only allowed to fruit every seven years. I let him finish the story, then I said, 'That's remarkable, but I have to tell you something. I'm a cacao farmer and I'm amazed, because surely the cacao farmer who produced those beans would have had to charge you seven times the normal price, plus compound interest for all the years he had forfeited?'

Cacao-growing and -processing is a difficult enough industry as it is, without having to wait seven years before allowing the trees to fruit and produce a harvest. It sounded like a very tall story to me, and one that even the most imaginative of Aztec market traders would never have dared to tell.

ICE CREAMS AND SORBETS

WILLIE'S CACAO BEAN ICE CREAM

In my early days at the hacienda, when I first started roasting cacao beans and I wanted to turn those nibs into instant gratification, I caramelized them with sugar from the cloud forest. In itself, this is a great snack. But in this recipe, you savour the smooth ice cream, followed by the caramelized sugar, then the slightly bitter cacao nibs.

Serves 4

3 egg yolks

80g caster sugar

200ml full-fat milk

300ml double cream

½ vanilla pod, split lengthways

50g Cacao Nib Praline (see page 192), broken into large pea-sized pieces

Whisk the egg yolks and caster sugar together until pale and creamy. Heat the milk and cream over a low heat until just about to boil, then pour over the egg and sugar mixture, stirring constantly, until well combined. Strain through a sieve into a clean pan, add the vanilla pod and cook over a gentle heat, stirring constantly, until the mixture is thick enough to coat the back of a spoon.

Chill, then churn and freeze in an ice-cream maker, following the manufacturer's instructions. After churning for about 10 minutes or so and the ice cream is just starting to thicken and freeze, add the broken cacao nib praline. Firm up in the freezer before serving.

If you don't have an ice-cream maker, tip the chilled mixture into a bowl and place in the freezer for 2–3 hours, or until it starts to freeze around the edges. Stir well, then return to the freezer for another 2 hours. Remove, stir and freeze for another 2 hours. Repeat this process once more, this time stirring in the pieces of praline. Finally, return to the freezer and leave until firm. Transfer to a sealable container for longer-term storage.

MEXICAN CHOCOLATE ICE CREAM

Chocolate and chilli are great friends from the old days. For the Mayans and then the Aztecs, they were a favourite combination, and they make for a truly more-ish ice cream.

Serves 6

130g light muscovado sugar

15g slightly salted butter

75g lightly toasted whole almonds, roughly chopped

3 small dried medium-hot chillies, deseeded and finely chopped

90g Nicaraguan Wasala Superior 100% cacao, roughly chopped

80g Venezuelan Hacienda Las Trincheras 72% chocolate, roughly chopped

300ml double cream

300ml full-fat milk

4 large egg yolks, beaten

Put 40g of the muscovado sugar and all the butter in a saucepan and melt together over a gentle heat. Add the almonds and continue to cook for a 1–2 minutes, stirring constantly, until the nuts are well coated. Tip into a bowl and leave to cool completely. If the nuts have set together, hit them with a rolling pin, but not too much as you want biggish lumps. Mix with the chopped chillies and set aside.

Melt the cacao and chocolate together in a bowl set over a pan of gently simmering water, making sure the bottom of the bowl is not touching the water.

Place the cream, milk and remaining sugar in a saucepan and heat gently, stirring until the sugar dissolves. Bring almost to boiling point, then slowly pour onto the beaten egg yolks, stirring constantly. Pour the mixture through a sieve into a clean pan and place over a low heat. Cook, stirring constantly, until thick enough to coat the back of a spoon. Remove from the heat, pour into a bowl and leave to cool for about 5 minutes. While still warm, stir in the melted chocolates, then leave to cool completely, but don't refrigerate.

Churn and freeze in an ice-cream maker, following the manufacturer's instructions. After churning for about 10 minutes or so and the ice cream is just starting to thicken and freeze, add the almond and chilli mixture. Firm up in the freezer before serving.

If you don't have an ice-cream maker, tip the cooled mixture into a bowl and place in the freezer for 1–2 hours, or until it starts to freeze around the edges. Stir well, then return to the freezer for another 2 hours. Remove, stir again and freeze for another 2 hours. Repeat this process once more, this time stirring in the almond and chilli mixture. Finally, return to the freezer and leave until firm. Transfer to a sealable container for longer-term storage.

DEEP, DARK AND DELICIOUS ICE CREAM

Venezuela is a paradise for eating ice cream – and when it's hot and humid, there's nothing else like a really rich chocolate ice cream. This tastes so good that it's almost beyond belief!

Serves 6–8

900ml double cream

225ml full-fat milk

8 egg yolks

360g caster sugar

360g 100% cacao, finely grated

2 tsp vanilla essence

Pour the cream and milk into a large pan and bring to just below boiling point over a gentle heat. Remove from the heat and set aside.

Whisk the egg yolks and sugar until pale and creamy. Whisk a cupful of the warm cream mixture into the eggs and sugar, then pour this back into the pan containing the remaining cream mixture and cook over a low heat for 8–10 minutes, stirring constantly, until thick.

Remove from the heat, stir in the cacao until melted, then stir in the vanilla essence. Chill, then churn and freeze in an ice-cream maker, following the manufacturer's instructions. Firm up in the freezer before serving.

If you don't have an ice-cream maker, tip the chilled mixture into a bowl and place in the freezer for 2–3 hours, or until it starts to freeze around the edges. Stir well, then return to the freezer for another 2 hours. Remove, stir again and freeze for another 2 hours. Repeat this process once more. Finally, return to the freezer and leave until firm. Transfer to a sealable container for longer-term storage.

CHOCOLATE TRUFFLE, RUM AND RAISIN ICE CREAM

Try to use only the very best rum in this recipe, as it makes all the difference to the taste (*opposite*). You won't need an ice-cream maker.

Serves 4–6

100g large black raisins

4 tbsp dark rum

3 eggs, separated

100g icing sugar, sifted

250ml double cream

2 tbsp strong black coffee

24 small Rum and Raisin Truffles (see page 201)

Soak the raisins in the rum for 48 hours.

Whisk the egg whites until stiff, then whisk in the icing sugar a tablespoon at a time, until a stiff meringue mixture is formed. Whisk in the egg yolks

In a separate bowl, whisk the cream until it forms soft peaks, then whisk in the coffee. Fold gently into the egg mixture, followed by the soaked raisins and the truffles.

Transfer to a suitable, sealable container and freeze overnight.

CHOCOLATE CHIP ICE CREAM

The chunks of chocolate scattered through this rich mixture linger on the palate, extending your pleasure as they slowly melt.

Serves 6–8

400ml full-fat milk

300ml double cream

40g cocoa powder

200g Venezuelan Rio Caribe Superior 72% chocolate, roughly chopped

1 tsp vanilla essence

4 egg yolks

100g caster sugar, plus 2 tbsp extra

80g Indonesian Javan Light Breaking 69% chocolate, chopped into small pieces

Put the milk, cream and cocoa powder in a saucepan and heat gently until just below boiling point. Turn the heat down to very low and add the Venezuelan Rio Caribe chocolate. Stir until the chocolate has melted and the mixture is smooth. Remove from the heat and stir in the vanilla essence.

Whisk the egg yolks with the 100g sugar until pale and creamy. Slowly pour in the warm chocolate mixture, whisking constantly, until well blended. Pour the mixture back into a clean pan, place over a low heat and cook, stirring constantly, until the mixture thickens and coats the back of a spoon. Pour into a large bowl and sprinkle the extra sugar over the top to stop a skin forming. Leave to cool, then chill for several hours.

Tip the chilled mixture and the Indonesian Javan chocolate into an ice-cream maker. Churn, following the manufacturer's instructions, then firm up in the freezer before serving.

To make this without an ice-cream maker, see the instructions at the end of page 87.

CHOCOLATE AND MERINGUE SEMIFREDDO

A semifreddo is a frozen dessert that, unlike most ice creams, doesn't need to be churned while freezing. This makes it easy and quick to make, without the need for an ice-cream maker.

Serves 10

250ml full-fat milk

110g caster sugar

200g Madagascan Sambirano Superior 71% chocolate, roughly chopped

600ml double cream

45g icing sugar

1 tsp vanilla essence

2 tbsp brandy

150g baby meringues or crushed large ones

Equipment: 20 x 10-cm loaf tin

Line the loaf tin with baking paper. Heat the milk and sugar in a pan over a medium heat, stirring until the sugar has dissolved. Remove from the heat and stir in the chocolate until it has melted. Set aside to cool.

Whip the cream until stiff, then whisk in the icing sugar. Mix in the vanilla essence and brandy, then fold in the cooled chocolate mixture. Finally, fold in the meringues.

Spoon the mixture into the lined loaf tin and freeze for at least 4 hours, preferably overnight. Remove from the freezer and leave to stand for 15 minutes before serving. Turn out of the tin, peel off the baking paper and slice. Serve on its own or with a chocolate sauce (see pages 124–5 and 127).

PUMPKIN, QUINCE AND WHITE CHOCOLATE SORBET

The combination of flavours in this sorbet is sublime and it makes a great match for many chocolate desserts when you want the contrast of a light, fruity accompaniment. Use a good-flavoured pumpkin, such as Crown Prince or the little Uchi Kuri variety. Look out for quinces at local markets or good greengrocers from the beginning of October until December.

Serves 6–8

1 pumpkin (to yield 250g flesh when prepared)

450–500g quinces (to yield 250g flesh when prepared)

250ml water

200g granulated sugar

100g white chocolate, roughly chopped

To prepare the pumpkin, peel, then cut open and discard the seeds and pith. Chop the flesh into small chunks. To prepare the quinces, wash the skin well, remove the stalk, then cut open and discard the seeds. Chop into chunks.

Place the prepared pumpkin and quinces in a pan. Add 3–4 tablespoons water (not too much as most of the water should have evaporated by the time the pumpkin and quinces are cooked). Cover and cook slowly over a very low heat for about 20 minutes, or until the pumpkin and quinces are soft. Remove from the heat and set aside.

Place the water and sugar in a pan over a moderate heat and stir until the sugar has dissolved, then bring to the boil. Remove from the heat and stir in the white chocolate, until melted.

Place the cooked pumpkin and quinces and the chocolate syrup mixture in a blender or food processor and blitz until smooth. Tip the mixture into a bowl and chill. Churn and freeze in an ice-cream maker, following the manufacturer's instructions. Firm up in the freezer before serving.

If you don't have an ice-cream maker, simply tip the sorbet mixture into a bowl and place in the freezer for 1–2 hours, or until it starts to freeze around the edges. Remove from the freezer, stir well, then return to the freezer for a further 2 hours. Remove, stir again and freeze for another 2 hours. Repeat this process once more. Finally, return to the freezer and leave until firm. Transfer to a sealable container for longer-term storage. The sorbet will keep well for a 2–3 weeks.

CHOCOLATE SORBET

This is a great recipe to use as a way of exploring the world of chocolate. You can substitute any top-quality dark chocolate, from anywhere in the world for the Madagascan Sambirano, so experiment and have fun following this fabulous flavour trail.

Serves 4

50g caster sugar

420ml water

200g Madagascan Sambirano Superior 71% chocolate, roughly chopped

Place the sugar and the water in a saucepan over a low heat and stir until the sugar has dissolved. Gently simmer for 1–2 minutes, then remove from the heat. Stir in the chocolate until melted. Chill the mixture, then churn and freeze in an ice-cream maker, following the manufacturer's instructions. Place in the freezer to firm up before serving.

If you don't have an ice-cream maker, simply tip the mixture into a bowl and place in the freezer for 1–2 hours, or until it starts to freeze around the edges. Remove from the freezer, stir well, then return the freezer for a further 2 hours. Remove, stir again and freeze for another 2 hours. Repeat this process once more. Finally, return to the freezer and leave until firm. Transfer to a sealable container for longer-term storage.

Serve the sorbet on its own or with fresh strawberries or raspberries and White Chocolate Sauce (see page 125).

VARIATION: Add 200ml strained and sweetened blackcurrant purée and 3 tablespoons crème de cassis to the mixture before freezing as described above.

MOUSSES AND SOUFFLÉS

WHITE CHOCOLATE, RASPBERRY AND KIRSCH MOUSSE

Delicious, delightful and totally decadent, make this whenever you want to wow your guests. It looks stunningly beautiful and the Kirsch gives it a real kick, as well as a touch of luxury that marries well with the raspberries and white chocolate.

Serves 6

300g fresh or frozen raspberries

2–3 tbsp caster sugar

5 tbsp Kirsch

200g white chocolate, roughly chopped

1 tbsp cold water

2 egg whites

Pinch of salt

300ml double cream

6 fresh mint or geranium leaves, to garnish

Set aside 6 of the largest raspberries to use as a garnish and push the rest through a sieve, using the back of a spoon. Stir caster sugar to taste and 1 tablespoon Kirsch into the berry pulp. Set aside.

Melt the chocolate with the remaining Kirsch and tablespoon of cold water in a heatproof bowl set over the pan of gently simmering water, making sure the bottom of the bowl is not in contact with the hot water. Stir until well combined and smooth. Take off the heat and set aside to cool slightly.

Whisk the egg whites with the salt until they form stiff peaks, then set aside. Whisk the cream until it is just starting to thicken, but you can still swill it around in the bowl. Don't overwhip. Working quickly, fold the cream into the melted chocolate until just combined, then carefully fold in the egg whites, also until just combined. If you overwork the mixture, you will have a heavy mousse.

Divide the raspberry sauce between six tall serving glasses. Spoon the mousse mixture over the sauce, which should automatically swirl around the mousse creating a rippled effect. Garnish with a fresh raspberry and a mint or geranium leaf. Chill for at least 2 hours before serving. The dessert keeps well up to 3 days in the fridge.

CLASSIC CHOCOLATE MOUSSE IN A BITTER CHOCOLATE CASE

This is one of my dinner party favourites. The chocolate case adds a bit of flair to the presentation. I've used two very different chocolates here. The Indonesian Javan is light coloured, with hints of caramel and toffee flavours. The Madagascan Sambirano is deep and dark, with subtle notes of summer berries.

Serves 12

250g Madagascan Sambirano Superior 71% chocolate, roughly chopped

300g Indonesian Javan Light Breaking 69% chocolate, roughly chopped

6 eggs, separated

80g caster sugar

450ml double cream, lightly whipped

Equipment: 26-cm tart or shallow cake tin

Lightly oil the tart or cake tin, then take a piece of baking paper, at least 45 x 45cm, and press it into the tin so it sticks firmly to the base and sides and comes up a little above the rim of the tin.

Melt the Madagascan Sambirano chocolate in a heatproof bowl set over a pan of gently simmering water, making sure the bottom of the bowl is not in contact with the water. Pour into the lined tin and spread evenly, with a flexible spatula, over the bottom and up the sides. Chill in the fridge.

Melt the Indonesian Javan chocolate in a heatproof bowl set over a pan of gently simmering water, making sure the bottom of the bowl is not in contact with the water. In a separate bowl, whisk the egg whites with half the sugar until stiff.

In another bowl, whisk the egg yolks with the remaining sugar and stir into the melted chocolate. Fold in the lightly whipped cream, then fold in the egg whites. Tip the mixture into the prepared chocolate case and place in the fridge to chill for at least 2 hours, preferably overnight.

Carefully lift out of the tin and peel the baking paper off the sides. Use a fish slice or spatula to lift off the baking paper on the base and place on a serving plate. Keep chilled until ready to eat and serve with whipped cream or crème fraîche.

MAKING THE CLASSIC CHOCOLATE MOUSSE

EL TESORO MOUSSE CAKE

Here's an early classic from the El Tesoro kitchen. I've taught many of the people who have passed through the hacienda how to make it, so it has now travelled far and wide across the world! The simplicity of the ingredients make it an excellent vehicle for sampling all the complex flavours of cacao at its best.

Serves 12

180g 100% cacao, finely grated

250g unsalted butter, cut into small cubes

5 eggs

200g caster sugar

1 tsp vanilla essence

Equipment: 25-cm springform cake tin

Preheat the oven to 160°C. Lightly grease, then line the cake tin with baking paper.

Melt the cacao and butter in a heatproof bowl set over a pan of gently simmering water, making sure the bottom of the bowl is not in contact with the water. Set aside to cool slightly.

Meanwhile, beat the eggs with the sugar and vanilla essence until pale, thick and fluffy. Pour in the cacao and butter mixture and beat to combine.

Tip the mixture into the lined cake tin and smooth over the top to even out. Stand in a roasting tin, then pour enough freshly boiled water into the roasting tin to come halfway up the sides of the cake tin. Bake in the preheated oven for 30 minutes, or until set. Remove from the oven. Take out of the roasting tin and leave to cool completely in the cake tin on a wire rack.

Chill in the fridge until ready to serve. To help loosen the cake from the tin, insert the warmed blade of a knife all around the edges of the cake just before attempting to remove it.

CLASSIC CHOCOLATE AND ESPRESSO MOUSSE

Although this mousse is extremely rich and indulgent, no matter how large the helping I serve, I have never known anyone leave the tiniest amount behind. It is, however, best after a fairly light main course.

Serves 6

130g Madagascan Sambirano Superior 71% chocolate, roughly chopped

95g unsalted butter

60ml espresso or very strong black coffee

3 large eggs, separated

50g caster sugar

1½ tbsp dark rum

Pinch of salt

Geranium leaf or flower, to garnish

Melt the chocolate and butter in a heatproof bowl set over a pan of gently simmering water, making sure the bottom of the bowl is not in contact with the water. Stir gently until well combined, then remove from the heat and stir in the coffee.

Whisk the egg yolks with the sugar until thick and creamy. Add the rum and whisk again – the mixture should be the consistency of runny mayonnaise. Carefully fold in the melted chocolate mixture. Set aside.

Whisk the egg whites with the salt until they form stiff peaks. Stir a few tablespoons into the chocolate mixture and then gently fold in the remaining egg whites until just combined. Do not overwork or you will have a heavy mousse.

Spoon into individual glasses or ramekins and chill for at least 2 hours, preferably overnight. Garnish with a geranium leaf or flower if you wish. Serve on its own or with whipped cream. This mousse keeps well in the fridge for 2–3 days, but the coffee flavour will gradually lose its intensity.

69 MOUSSE

This rich, boozy mousse is a little heavier than others. The flavours of good chocolate always stay on the palate and here the Indonesian Javan's caramel notes linger beautifully.

Serves 8

180g Indonesian Javan Light Breaking 69% chocolate, roughly chopped

5 egg yolks

½ vanilla pod

60g caster sugar

250ml double cream

50ml Cacao Nib and Vanilla Cognac (see page 34), or good-quality cognac

4 egg whites

Pinch of salt

Equipment: 8 small glass dishes or ramekins

Melt the chocolate in a heatproof bowl set over a pan of gently simmering water, making sure the bottom of the bowl is not in contact with the water.

Place the egg yolks in a large bowl. Split the vanilla pod and scrape the seeds into the bowl of egg yolks. Stir in the sugar and whisk until light and creamy. Beat in the double cream, then stir in the melted chocolate until well combined. Stir in the cognac. Set aside.

Whisk the egg whites with the salt until they form stiff peaks. Stir a few tablespoons into the chocolate mixture, then gently fold in the remaining egg whites until just combined. Don't overwork or you will have a heavy mousse. Divide the mixture between your serving dishes and chill for at least 2 hours, preferably overnight, before serving.

The mixture can also be made into a semifreddo. Simply spoon into a 20 x 10-cm loaf tin that has been lined with baking paper and freeze for at least 4 hours. Remove from the freezer and leave to stand for 15 minutes before serving. Turn out of the tin, peel off the baking paper and slice.

CHOCOLATE SOUFFLÉ

The world's greatest chocolate soufflé by Marco Pierre White at Wheelers of St James (*see overleaf*).

Serves 6

20g unsalted butter

110g caster sugar, plus extra for coating

20g cocoa powder, plus extra for coating

30g plain flour

4 egg yolks

350ml full-fat milk

40g Madagascan Sambirano Superior 71% chocolate, roughly chopped

12 egg whites

FOR THE HOT CHOCOLATE SAUCE:

150ml full-fat milk

30ml double cream

30g caster sugar

200g Venezuelan Rio Caribe 72% chocolate, roughly chopped

30g unsalted butter

Equipment: 6 x 7-cm soufflé dishes, about 6cm deep

Preheat the oven to 180°C. Use half the butter to grease the insides of the soufflé dishes. Place in the fridge until the butter has set hard. Grease the dishes again using the remaining butter, this time also greasing the top edge. Sprinkle the insides with caster sugar to form a light coating, tipping out any excess, then sprinkle with cocoa powder to coat, also tipping out any excess. Set the prepared dishes aside in a cool place.

Sift the 20g cocoa powder and flour together into a bowl. In another bowl, beat the egg yolks with 80g caster sugar until thick and creamy. Stir in the sifted mixture and set aside

Bring the milk to the boil over a medium heat, then pour over the cocoa mixture and stir until well blended. Tip the mixture back into the pan, place over a low heat and bring gently to the boil. Simmer for 5 minutes, stirring continuously, until the mixture thickens and forms a smooth custard. Set aside.

Melt the chocolate in a heatproof bowl set over a pan of gently simmering water, making sure the bottom of the bowl is not in contact with the water. Stir the melted chocolate into the custard mixture until well blended. Set aside and leave to cool.

Whisk the egg whites until they form soft peaks. Fold in the remaining caster sugar and whisk again until the mixture forms soft peaks. Stir 2 tablespoons into the cooled chocolate custard mixture, then carefully fold in the remainder until evenly blended. Do not overwork.

Divide the mixture between the prepared soufflé dishes, placing about 2 tablespoons in each. Level off the tops, and run a finger around the edge of each to push the mixture away from the sides. Bake in the preheated oven for 12–13 minutes, until well risen.

Meanwhile, make the sauce. Place the milk, cream and sugar in a saucepan over a medium heat until just starting to boil. Remove from the heat and stir in the chocolate until melted and evenly mixed. Return the pan to a low heat, add the butter and stir until melted and the sauce is smooth and evenly blended.

Serve the cooked soufflés immediately, with the hot chocolate sauce handed separately in a jug.

INTERNATIONAL CHOCOLATE SPREAD

Standing on the bitterly cold dock of Zaandam port in Holland, outside a vast warehouse stacked with mountainous piles of cacao beans, my gaze was drawn to the huge container ships that were moving in and out of the harbour. As the freezing wind whipped across the water, I thought about all the journeys that cacao has made over the centuries, how it has crisscrossed the globe in jute sacks, from the New World to Europe, to the Caribbean, Africa and Asia.

So much has changed in the world since the first cacao shipments sailed from Veracruz in Mexico to Seville in Spain. Yet cacao is still carried by sea from its country of origin, albeit in huge container ships, and it is still often transported in sacks, although jute sacks were banned in the 1970s because of a contaminant in the jute. The larger cacao processors now seem to prefer what's known as the 'mega-bulk' method, loading their beans loose into containers or directly into the hold.

Today, Amsterdam is the most important cacao port in the world. There are between 500,000 and 600,000 tonnes of cacao in the port at any one time, which is about a fifth of the world's entire supply. So it's not surprising that when my quest for fine beans began to extend beyond first Venezuela and then South America, I was told that Holland was the place to find a quality cacao dealer. That's how I found Daarnhouwer & Co, the company that now supplies me with cacao beans from around the world; that's why I was in Zaandam, a suburb of Amsterdam, standing on the cold docks.

Jan Kips, the company's managing director, had just shown me around a warehouse that contained tens of thousands of tonnes of cacao, some stored in sacks and some lying around in gigantic loose piles that almost reached the ceiling of the cavernous building. It was mind-blowing to see so many beans in one place. There was cacao from countries all over the world in the warehouse, waiting to be sent off to anywhere from Germany to Japan. Much of it was being stored for Daarnhouwer, which sources cacao beans from Madagascar to Nicaragua and supplies cacao (and coffee, tree nuts and dried fruits) to chocolate and confectionery companies internationally.

Back in 2008, when Willem Bolk, my cocoa trader at Daarnhouwer, first sent me a batch of Peruvian San Martin cacao, I was overawed by how delicious it was. This immediately inspired me to make chocolate with beans from other countries. 'What else have you got?' I asked eagerly.

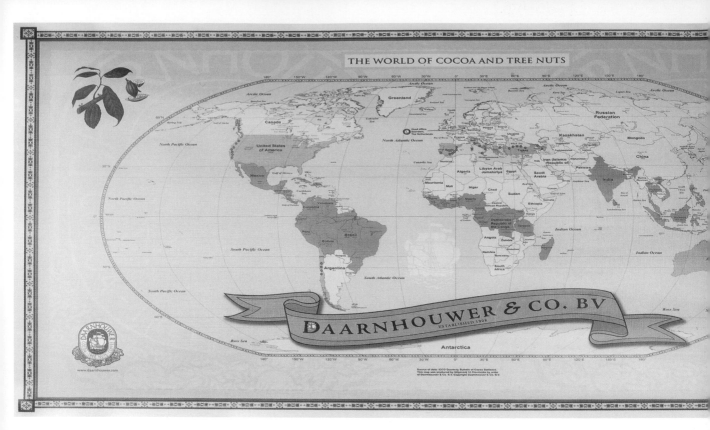

THE WORLD OF COCOA AND TREE NUTS

DAARNHOUWER & CO. BV
ESTABLISHED 1908

He started to send me the most amazing varieties of beans and soon I was making sample batches of chocolate using Indonesian, Colombian, Madagascan and Nicaraguan cacao. It was incredibly exciting. I wanted to know everything about the origins of each batch: the exact variety, the local climate, the farmers' stories and growing conditions. Inevitably, I began to explore the story of how cacao travelled beyond Mesoamerica, the region where cacao was first cultivated, that stretches roughly from central Mexico down to Honduras and Nicaragua.

How and when did cacao first make its way to Spain? Nobody is quite sure. For some reason, Hernán Cortés is often credited with introducing it to the Spanish court, possibly when he sent a ship of booty from Veracruz to Spain in 1519, although cacao isn't mentioned in the list of cargo. During the conquest of Mexico two years later, Cortés issued chocolate to his soldiers and claimed that the men could march all day after drinking just one cup. So did he take cacao with him in 1528, when he arrived at the court of Charles V, bearing an extravagant array of gifts from Mexico, including jaguars, dwarfs, mirrors and bouncing balls? Again, there's no hard evidence.

In 1544, a group of Dominican Friars introduced a delegation of Guatemalan Maya to Prince Philip in Spain. Among the

offerings they brought were clay gourds filled with beaten chocolate, so perhaps this was chocolate's debut in Europe. Either way, it wasn't imported officially until 1585, so it wasn't an overnight sensation. Yet during the first half of the seventeenth century, it became wildly popular at the Spanish court, where it was drunk hot, spicy and sweet.

An expensive import, chocolate was an elite drink among the Spanish, just as it had been for the Maya and Aztecs. The Spanish, however, viewed it as medicinal rather than magical or spiritual; it was thought to aid digestion and circulation, among other things. Meanwhile, by the mid-sixteenth century, chocolate was being drunk by virtually everyone in Mesoamerica, rich and poor, and more than one traveller to the New World noted that in some areas it was becoming a common addiction. Mexico was by far the biggest market for cacao.

There's a famous story about a group of passionate chocoholics who turned nasty when someone tried to get between them and their drinking chocolate. The trouble began when a bishop of Chiapas, Mexico, became irritated with the ladies of his congregation, who insisted that they needed to drink hot chocolate during mass because of their weak stomachs. He banned chocolate from the cathedral and threatened to excommunicate anyone who ate or drank during services. Unwilling to do without their mid-mass fix, the ladies began to attend church in the convents instead of the cathedral. Despite being told about rumours of death threats against him, the bishop stood firm. The cathedral emptied altogether and shortly afterwards the bishop was found dead, having drunk a bowl of chocolate laced with poison. To this day, there's a Mexican proverb that warns: 'Beware the chocolate of Chiapas'.

Because of its dark, rich flavours and pungent aroma, chocolate was an effective way to mask the bitter taste of poison – although this wouldn't work with my chocolate because the poison would flatten out the flavour notes! Chocolate is behind a litany of crimes of passion, revenge and mercy killings – even Pope Clement XIV was allegedly murdered with a cup of bitter tasting chocolate. The Duchess of Portsmouth was convinced that King Charles II had been poisoned with a 'dish' of chocolate at her house in 1685, although he probably died of kidney failure; a spurned mistress of Napoleon is also reported to have added something suspect to his chocolate beverage, hoping to exact vengeance with a deliciously deadly weapon.

Chocolate was often used in love potions and witchcraft spells, according to documents reporting cases that were brought before Inquisition Tribunals in the seventeenth and eighteenth centuries. Over and again, people either confessed to or denounced their neighbours for mixing menstrual blood, crow's heart, human flesh and excrement into hot chocolate and offering it to their chosen victim. It was the ideal vehicle for these concoctions because who in their right mind would turn down a delicious cup of steaming chocolate? But the Inquisition came down hard on these misguided chefs, who risked death for their superstitious experiments. Ironically, chocolate was one of the refreshments served to high-ranking officials, priests and nobles at the *auto-da-fés*, where the Inquisition's victims were publicly and cruelly punished or killed.

With demand for cacao rising rapidly, the colonialists in New Spain saw it as a way to make vast sums of money. At first, they made slaves of the local population and put them to work on the plantations, but then Pope Paul III outlawed the enslavement of Indians in 1537. So they instituted a legal system of forced work called *encomienda*, exacting tribute from the natives in the form of labour in return for teaching them Spanish and Christianity. But that didn't work either because the Indians began to die in alarming numbers from Old World diseases and epidemics against which they had no immunity. Shockingly, disease and maltreatment meant that by the end of the seventeenth century, only about a tenth of the Indian population had survived the hostile takeover of their country.

Cacao production dropped drastically and the price shot up. New sources of cacao were needed to feed the growing national obsession. The answer lay in South America, particularly Ecuador and Venezuela. In Ecuador there were vast forests of wild cacao that the conquistadores had begun to cultivate at the beginning of the seventeenth century, later using African slaves in the place of Indians. This was forastero cacao: hardy, high-yielding and often bitter. The Mexican market didn't like it all that much – it was known as *cacao de los pobres* (poor man's cacao). But given a choice between Ecuadorian forastero and nothing, the addicted Mesoamericans had to make do.

Venezuelan cacao was much more popular because it was predominantly the tastier criollo variety that grew on plantations along the country's Caribbean coast. It's tragic to think that slaves were worked to death on these haciendas. Cacao is life-enriching and should be produced with love, but sadly it has a darker history. Much of Venezuela's crop made its way to Europe, where society ladies and dandies sipped it without a care for the human suffering involved in its production.

One day I chanced upon an ancient cacao hacienda along the coast from my farm. I was there because I'd heard about a nearby river that was stuffed full of crayfish. It was an incredible river. I filled half a bucket in a couple of hours, drawing the crayfish out into the shallows with a bit of coconut on a string, and flicking them out of the water onto the ground.

Later, I went exploring and came across an abandoned seventeenth-century hacienda called Arroha, which had huge deep steps leading up to an entrance so wide that you could have ridden into the building on a horse. Surrounded by tall shade trees, it was still in great condition and, amazingly, the roof was still intact, although most of the cacao trees had died. I wandered around the land and buildings, imagining the days when the storehouses were filled with criollo beans and merchants galloped through the surrounding forest to negotiate prices for the next cacao harvest. It felt like I had travelled back in time for the afternoon.

Italy discovered the wonders of Venezuelan chocolate in the early seventeenth century, shortly followed by France. The first chocolate house opened in London in 1657 and was an instant success. The brilliant diarist Samuel Pepys even mentions that he 'went to Mr Bland's and there drank my morning draft of chocolate'. Serving up hot chocolate in the mornings is no longer very common in Britain, where we think of it more as a milky soporific drink that will lull us into dreamland. But a morning chocolate pick-me-up remains a widespread custom in Europe and South America. Today, the Colombians produce 30,000 tonnes of cacao for the internal market, to quench their thirst for morning chocolate; and the Spanish traditionally drink a dark, sweet elixir made from cacao and sugar that hasn't changed much for over 400 years.

Whole industries grew up around the drinking of chocolate in Europe. First, chocolate-pot lids were pierced with holes to fit the *molinillo* beating stick – a design that is still on sale in Mexican markets today. The French developed silver chocolate pots with built in *molinillos* (or *moussoirs*, as they called them), and porcelain cups and saucers also became popular. Later, when making chocolate became more mechanized, there was an explosion of chocolate-related equipment and merchandise.

One of the most intriguing of the specialized chocolate ceramics was the *trembleuse* stand, devised for people with shaky hands by the Marqués de Mancera, Viceroy of Mexico, himself a palsy sufferer. The *trembleuse* (known as a *mancerina* in Mexico) is a special saucer with a cup holder that steadied the cup, like a reinforced, exaggerated saucer lip. Since chocolate was often administered as nourishment for the old and the sick, it became a standard piece in every chocolate set.

Although chocolate was predominantly a drink, it was also used in desserts to complement candied fruits and ices. It's easy to make a chocolate spread or sauce by adding just a small amount of water to sugar and cacao, and it's a great way to make the chocolate flavours shine. I've always been very conscious of the nasty chocolate spreads that are out there and, not wanting my kids to eat them, I've made a lot of simple chocolate spreads and ice-cream sauces over the years, using organic cane sugar. My Cream Chocolate Sauce (see page 124) is very rich and lush, so I tend to save that for sorbets, while the water-based Dark Chocolate Sauce (see page 125) is ideal for ice cream.

While chocolate was making its way around the world, cacao cultivation spread to other parts of South America, such as Brazil and Paraguay, and several Caribbean islands, including Trinidad, where the trinitario variety was born 30 years after most of the island's cacao trees died out in 1727. At first, the Spanish controlled cacao export from the New World, directing every shipment through the port of Cadiz. But soon the merchants and growers of Venezuela were circumventing this monopoly and illegally selling to Dutch traders. Many sea battles ensued!

Cacao made it to Africa via the islands of Principe and Sao Tomé, west of Gabon, where the Portuguese planted forastero cuttings taken from Brazil. More cuttings were taken to Equatorial New Guinea and the colonies of Portuguese Africa. Then, in 1879, a West African blacksmith took some plants home to Ghana, where the British governor seized upon the idea of growing cacao and encouraged its cultivation. Cacao then journeyed on to Nigeria and to the Ivory Coast, which is now the world's largest producer. Moving east, the Spanish took it to the Philippines, the British to Sri Lanka and the Dutch to Java and Sumatra. By 1991, Africa was the source of just over half of the world's cacao, while Mexico, cacao's birthplace, supplied only 1.5%. I recently found out from Willem at Daarnhouwer & Co

Jan Kips (left) and Willem Bolk (right) in the sample room at Daarnhouwer.

that the beans I use to make my Madagascan 71% chocolate bar are grown from trees that arrived on the island as seedlings from Venezuela 100 years ago! Once Venezuelan criollo, they have now developed their own flavour.

I'm always pleased when the phone rings and I see '+31' come up on the screen because it means that Daarnhouwer is on the line and I'll soon be having an interesting conversation about cacao beans. Jan and Willem would probably deny being chocolate romantics when they have their trader hats on, but they are definitely *secret* chocolate romantics! They know everything there is to know about the international cacao market, not to mention cacao cultivation and chocolate-making.

Chocolate goes through far too many stages, from bean to bar, to taste-test it at work. When it comes to differentiating flavours, life is a lot easier for coffee traders than cacao traders because they can roast, slurp and taste samples of coffee beans in the office. But since the flavour profile can change dramatically during the chocolate-making process, cacao traders would need a mini roaster, grinder, refiner and conching machine just for starters – in which case, they might as well open their own chocolate factory! So Jan and Willem leave the tasting to the

chocolate and confectionery makers, first sending out samples for their clients to approve.

'We don't deal in flavours. We deal in quality beans,' they always insist.

Yet when I had told one of their colleagues that I couldn't stop eating cacao beans, he had said, 'Yes, I had to stop. I was eating so many that I would get stomach ache.'

I thought, 'They don't deal in flavours, but they eat the beans! They must be chocolate romantics!'

Soon it wasn't enough to talk chocolate to someone on the end of a phone line, so in November 2009, I travelled to Zaandam to meet Jan and Willem at their offices. As they showed me around, Jan told me that it takes at least four years to become a competent cacao broker because there's so much to learn. It's a commodity business, so he and his team have to know about contracts, how to hedge and fix future prices, as well as bean quality, origins and fair trade.

There are distinct markets for cacao: the actual or physical markets and the futures or terminal markets. Nearly all cacao, coming from the place it has been grown, is traded on the physical market: there are often middlemen, known as cocoa brokers, who earn commission linking up planters, wholesalers and exporters; Daarnhouwer are cocoa dealers because they actually buy and trade beans at their own risk. Once the beans reach the port of export, they are graded and loaded into containers. Spot trading happens at today's price, once there has been an inspection of the goods.

Cacao futures contracts are generally used to offset the possibility of adverse price fluctuations; the process involves agreeing to a price for a given quantity and a contract that will be settled at a fixed date in the future, when the goods will be exchanged. By counterbalancing transactions in the futures market with what is happening in the cash market, otherwise called hedging, a trader can often reduce the risk of loss. When I visited the massive dockside warehouse where Daarnhouwer stores some of its cacao, I noticed that there were several tonnes of beans stacked up in bags that had been there for more than a decade, acting as security against catastrophic price movements.

When a cacao sample arrives at Daarnhouwer, Jan and Willem look for quality in the beans and examine them for defects: they assess the humidity, bean size and degree of fermentation, count the number of broken beans and check whether there's any mould. The Federation of Cocoa Commerce (FCC) divides beans into two categories: good fermented, which may have a maximum of 5% defective (mouldy or insect-damaged) beans; and fair fermented, which must have less than 10% defective beans. Ideally, the bean sizes of each batch should be the same because a mixture of sizes will cause problems during roasting: the small beans need less roasting than the large beans, so if you roast them all together, inevitably some will get burnt.

At the end of the day, Jan and Willem invited me to a tasting in the board room, where we set out on a journey of flavours – even though they don't deal in flavours! Using a cacao cutter, we sliced up a range of beans from different countries.

First, I nibbled some rare Porcelana beans that Willem said didn't really taste of chocolate because they were so acidic. I had already tried Venezuelan and Mexican Porcelana. Sometimes Porcelana can be overrated, but these beans were light in colour with fruity flavour notes, definitely beans with merit, although they didn't set me on fire.

Next Jan plundered the storeroom and the jars of sample beans that Daarnhouwer kept over the years, from Cameroon to the Solomon Islands. Amazingly, you can store well-fermented and dried beans for 20 years and they will still keep their flavour. Meanwhile, he kept up a continuous stream of information about cacao, which included a description of a beautiful, expensive bean from Belmont in Grenada and the fact that cacao from Cuzco in Peru has the highest fat content in the world at 58%.

He also told me a wonderful story about a passionate cacao lover, an employee of the now defunct East Java plantations that flourished under the Dutch occupation of Indonesia and produced a gorgeous-tasting, high-quality cacao. When the Dutch left in 1948, the plantations were sadly neglected, but this one employee had been determined that the cacao of the region would live on. After he found similar soil in northern Tanzania, he smuggled seedlings out of East Java and planted them in East Africa, going on to grow fantastic cacao there for the next 20 years. That's true devotion!

It felt like two worlds were meeting in the Daarnhouwer boardroom. I got out my chocolate and Jan and Willem had their first taste of what I'd been making with the beans that they had been sending me, as well as beans from elsewhere. There were

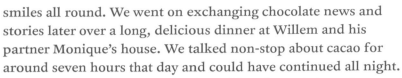

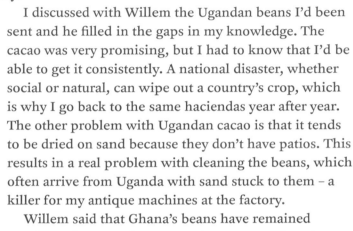

smiles all round. We went on exchanging chocolate news and stories later over a long, delicious dinner at Willem and his partner Monique's house. We talked non-stop about cacao for around seven hours that day and could have continued all night.

I was looking for an interesting African bean. 'It's madness and it breaks my heart that I don't have a bean from the African mainland,' I told them. Africa produces 80% of the world's cocoa, but I simply haven't found one that complements the other flavour profiles in my range, partly because I haven't tasted very many.

I discussed with Willem the Ugandan beans I'd been sent and he filled in the gaps in my knowledge. The cacao was very promising, but I had to know that I'd be able to get it consistently. A national disaster, whether social or natural, can wipe out a country's crop, which is why I go back to the same haciendas year after year. The other problem with Ugandan cacao is that it tends to be dried on sand because they don't have patios. This results in a real problem with cleaning the beans, which often arrive from Uganda with sand stuck to them – a killer for my antique machines at the factory.

Willem said that Ghana's beans have remained consistent because the country is at peace. Ghanaian cacao is a good-quality standard cacao, with an 81% yield. Sierra Leone cacao used to be as good as Ghanaian, but the country's wars have ravaged the plantations, although that's changing now. Nigeria, Togo and Ivory Coast also used to be as good, according to Jan, who has been in the business since the early 1970s. Looking back nearly four decades, he can see many changes.

Natural disasters have a tremendous impact on the supply of cacao. The beans from Bahia in Brazil are very standard these days, because 'witch's brooms' disease almost wiped out the cacao crop. It's on the rise again, but Jan says that it's nothing special yet, although I recently tasted a very promising Brazilian bean. Costa Rican cacao was apparently very good until 1984, when a particularly nasty root rot ravaged the crops. Where Costa Rica once produced 4000 tonnes of cacao annually, now it produces just 200 tonnes.

While I was in Mexico, I saw for myself how disease can ravage a cacao crop. Four years ago, an incurable fungus arrived in Chiapas, probably from Honduras, carried on people's shoes, in their bags and on fruit they had forgotten to leave behind before crossing the border. The effect on Mexican plantations has been devastating, reducing the crop by as much as 80% in some areas. Only the really well-tended plantations with large workforces have remained unaffected; the average cacao farmer in Mexico is really suffering. Experts are investigating the way spores carry fungus and are seeking a cure through the study of cacao genetics, but it's widely felt that many of the affected plantations will have to be completely replanted. However, waiting three to five years for new trees to mature would put many small farmers out of business. It's a huge dilemma.

Problems like these mean that the big cacao processing companies are only interested in disease-resistant hybrids that can be consistently sourced in enormous quantities; they are less concerned with sourcing a variety of flavours or producing high quality chocolate. Things have changed so much in the last few decades. In the 1970s, a box of Black Magic chocolates was made from beans sourced from a variety of countries; chocolate from Jamaica, Grenada and Papua New Guinea were added to the 60% Ghanaian chocolate base, whereas now only a couple of blends are used. I understand that the big companies don't want to take risks, but it's a real shame. The Javan light breaking cacao that I use to make my Indonesian 69 chocolate is difficult to source because it's not consistent. Every year the crop is different. And yet for me it's worth the gamble because the flavour is like no other.

But profit is the bottom line for the big chocolate companies, and this has led them to buy up one another and grow into massive conglomerates. As I stood on the freezing dock at Zaandam, where some of the world's biggest cacao-processing factories lie nearby along the river Zaan, I wondered what would happen if the world's big bean-buyers started making chocolate on a large scale? What if they bought up *all* the chocolate factories of the world, apart from the tiny independents, in the same way that they have swallowed the smaller cacao processors? Is it possible that one day these enormous conglomerates will dominate the industry, perhaps come close to a chocolate monopoly? One thing is certain – the number of specialist-origin bean dealers is dwindling because the demand for high-yielding, fast-growing hybrid cacao with few distinctive flavours is constantly threatening the high-quality cacao market.

Fortunately, there has been a surge in interest in fine-quality and single-estate beans from small chocolatiers and confectionery-makers. Reacting to the market in mass-produced goods, producers and consumers have begun giving more consideration generally to nutrition, flavour and provenance of food, which has boosted interest in single-estate products. Who would have thought that 20 years ago cloudy olive oil would end up being more expensive than clear olive oil? It's just another indication of the way palates have changed.

After 24 hours of non-stop chocolate storytelling and fact-swapping, I left Jan and Willem with a big box of truffles, made from all my different varieties of cacao. Truffles are a great present, as I discovered in Venezuela, where I taught myself to make them on the farm, combining local whipping cream and cacao. They were so easy to make, but felt like the height of sophistication in the wilds of South America. Cream brings out the subtle flavour notes of cacao better than anything else, and people's eyes light up at the very mention of truffles wherever you are in the world.

There are some small companies out there who have touched on the idea of making chocolate with distinct flavour profiles, like wine, but I'm taking it even further. On a recent trip to Venezuela, I visited the farmers of Las Trincheras, whose beans I use to make my nutty Las Trincheras bar. This was the first time that they had tasted the chocolate I've made from their beans and they appeared very proud of the results. Then I got out some Madagascan 71 and explained how the cacao had come from Venezuela a hundred years ago, but had developed its own characteristics. They were amazed by the flavour profile. One of them commented that 'the fruit jumps in your mouth'.

Next they tried the Indonesian 69. Never having done a chocolate tasting before, they were fascinated by the differences between each type of chocolate, which were very apparent to them and really took them by surprise. They immediately noticed the Indonesian bar's light colour; they thought it was slightly acidic, but started talking about the toffee, caramel and fruity flavour notes. Suddenly these local farmers were using words that are used in the trade to describe chocolate, showing that you don't have to be a chocolate connoisseur to distinguish the flavours!

I travelled on to the hacienda El Tesoro. When I arrived, fruit and vegetables were piled high at the back of the house, as

always. The array of bananas was fantastic. They are the stuff of fantasy; they come from the cloud forest in all shapes, sizes and flavours. From the heaps of Manzano, Titiaro and Cullaco bananas, I chose the Manzanos, which have an apple taste, and whipped up a Chocolate and Banana Crumble Tart (see page 139) to test on Ricardo and the others, who are always eager to taste the results of my latest experiments in the kitchen. The combination of the apple-flavoured banana with the chocolate was quite incredible. Ricardo always reacts in the same way when he finds something absolutely delicious; he tilts his head sideways, half closes his eyes and smiles. It's a totally natural thing and it's always a sign of approval, so I was pleased to see it happen again. It reminded me of the time I brought him some of my sweet chocolate from the factory. 'You used the Manzano,' he said dreamily. 'It's beautiful.'

The next day we went looking for pumpkins on the mountain. It's usually quite difficult to grow things up there, but I've found that pumpkin seeds sown in the rainy season will grow and creep all over the forest floor, just below the bananas. Sometimes the pumpkins are eaten by wild animals, but we were lucky to find a couple of huge ones nestling in undergrowth. I took them back to the farm and made Pumpkin and White Chocolate Tart (see page 144). White chocolate is simply cocoa butter, milk powder and sugar, and these ingredients combine fantastically with the sweetness of the pumpkin.

The Venezuelans have a very sweet tooth, so I wondered how Ricardo and the others would react to my Bitter Chocolate Tart (see page 136). The great thing about this delicious dessert is that you don't put too much sugar in it, so the flavour profile of the chocolate really shines. With any chocolate, once you go over the balance and make it too sweet, you mask the flavour profiles, which is why quality dark chocolate is always around 70% cacao. More mainstream chocolates are often so tipped over into sweet that they don't really taste of anything but flavoured sugar; you can't make out any of the back notes at all.

By way of farewell, I served a Bitter Chocolate Tart the day before I left. Right on cue, Ricardo's head tilted sideways and his eyelids fluttered downwards. 'Can you taste the citrus fruity flavours of the Rio Caribe?' I asked everyone. They just smiled and reached for seconds.

SAUCES AND SPREADS

BITTER CHOCOLATE AND COFFEE SAUCE

Simple and delicious, this is very quick to make. Poured over ice cream, it makes a fabulous, almost instant dessert. Coffee is a natural partner for chocolate and gives the sauce a satisfying and surprising lift. Stored in a sterilized sealed container, it will keep well for 2–3 weeks in the fridge.

Makes 600ml

400ml freshly
brewed strong coffee
(not espresso)

50g granulated sugar

25g slightly salted butter

250g Venezuelan
Hacienda Las Trincheras
72% chocolate, roughly
chopped

1 tbsp dark rum

Put the coffee and sugar in a saucepan and warm over a low heat, stirring constantly until the sugar has dissolved. Stir in the butter and chocolate until they are melted and well mixed in. Turn up the heat, bring to the boil and cook for 30 seconds. Remove from the heat and leave to cool slightly, then stir in the rum.

CREAM CHOCOLATE SAUCE

Don't worry if you don't use this immediately, as it will keep for up to 2 weeks in the fridge if stored in a tightly sealed sterilized container. It's great poured over a fresh fruit salad and, of course, ice cream.

Makes 300ml

160ml double cream

50ml water

70g granulated sugar

90g Venezuelan Rio
Caribe Superior 100%
cacao, roughly chopped

Put the cream, water and sugar in a saucepan and bring to the boil over a medium heat. Remove from the heat and add the cacao. Mix well, then chill. Remove from the fridge about 30 minutes before serving.

DARK CHOCOLATE SAUCE

This sumptuous sauce really shows off the full flavour profile of whichever type of chocolate you make it with. I've used Peruvian 70%, but you could experiment with other varieties. You'll never get bored with it. Keep it in a bottle in the fridge, ready to pour at any time.

Makes 500ml

400ml water

160g Peruvian San Martin 70% chocolate, finely chopped

Pour the water into a saucepan and bring to the boil over a medium heat. Lower the heat, add the chocolate and gently bring to the boil again, then simmer for 1 minute to thicken. Decant into a sterilized bottle. Seal and chill. This should keep for 2–3 months in the fridge.

WHITE CHOCOLATE SAUCE

White chocolate sauce is like pulling a white rabbit out of a hat: magic every time.

Makes 300ml

150g white chocolate, roughly chopped

200g crème fraîche

2 tbsp Kirsch

Melt the chocolate in a heatproof bowl set over a pan of gently simmering water, making sure the bottom of the bowl is not in contact with the water. Remove from heat. Stir in the crème fraîche and Kirsch until well blended.

BLACKCURRANT AND CHOCOLATE PASTE

Somewhere between a spread and a savoury jam, this paste is lovely on bread or served as a condiment with a meaty game stew. It's also wonderful made with blackberries picked from the hedgerows in autumn.

Makes 250g

450g fresh blackcurrant purée, sieved

100g caster sugar

25ml good-quality balsamic vinegar

40g Madagascan Sambirano Superior 100% cacao, coarsely grated or chopped

Heat the blackcurrant purée in a saucepan with the sugar and vinegar, stirring until the sugar has dissolved. Cook very gently until it has reached the setting stage – when a little left to cool on a cold plate rapidly forms a skin on top (or use a jam thermometer; the mixture is ready when it reaches 104°C).

Remove from the heat and stir in the cacao until it has melted. Pour into a warm, sterilized jam jar, allow to cool slightly, then seal. This paste should keep well for at least 3 months if stored in the fridge.

CHOCOLATE AND BLACK PEPPERMINT SAUCE

Black peppermint is one of my favourite mints – it makes a lovely herbal tea – but unless you grow it yourself, it is hard to find. You can, however, substitute any other variety of mint in this recipe.

Makes 450ml

100g granulated sugar

330ml water

50g black peppermint or other fresh mint leaves, washed

100g Venezuelan Carenero Superior 100% cacao, finely chopped

Put the sugar and the water in a large saucepan and bring to the boil over a medium heat, stirring constantly until the sugar has dissolved. Remove from heat and stir in the mint leaves. Leave to infuse for 20–30 minutes.

Strain into a fresh saucepan and bring to the boil. Take off the heat and stir in the cacao until dissolved. Return to the boil for a few seconds to emulsify. Using a funnel, pour into a sterilized bottle. Seal and chill. This sauce will keep in the fridge for at least 2–3 months.

CACAO NIB BALSAMIC VINEGAR

Infusing balsamic vinegar with cacao nibs sweetens, thickens and magically ages it, making even a thin young balsamic vinegar taste years older than it actually is. Use this in salad dressings and in sauces and gravies.

Makes 300ml

250ml oak aged balsamic vinegar

100g cacao nibs

Place the cacao nibs in a clean jar and pour over the balsamic vinegar. Seal tightly and leave in a cool place for 6–8 weeks, shaking the jar occasionally.

Strain the mixture through a sieve, then pour into a sterilized bottle and seal.

CACAO, ROASTED PEPPER AND CHILLI HARISSA

I love chillies, but I don't like them so hot that I cannot taste anything else. So I've added roasted sweet red pepper to this sauce to balance the heat of the chillies. However, it is always hard to judge how hot chillies will be as they vary so much. You can reduce the heat of the chillies in this recipe by deseeding about a third of them before using or, if you want the sauce quite mild, halve the amount used. This is a great accompaniment to oily fish, lamb and pork, including sausages. You could also serve it with a Moroccan tagine.

Makes 600ml

16 long red chillies

4 large red peppers

½ teaspoon cumin seeds

150ml extra virgin olive oil

10g Madagascan Sambirano Superior 100% cacao

1 tbsp Cacao Nib Balsamic Vinegar (see page 127), or good-quality balsamic vinegar

Salt

Preheat the oven to 250°C.

Wrap the chillies in a double layer of foil and place on a baking tray. Put the unwrapped red peppers alongside them on the same tray. Roast in the hot oven for about 25 minutes, or until the peppers are slightly blackened and soft. Allow to cool slightly, then peel and deseed the red peppers. Remove the chillies from the foil, but leave whole, just removing any stalks. Put both the chillies and peppers in a blender or food processor and whizz to make a rough purée (don't overwork; leave a little texture). Set on one side.

Toast the cumin seeds in a dry frying pan until they smell fragrant. Tip them into a mortar and crush with a pestle to a coarse powder.

Place the puréed peppers and the chillies in a large saucepan, add the powdered cumin and the olive oil. Bring the mixture to the boil over a medium heat, then simmer gently until the sauce has reduced by about a half. You will find the oil separates out. Remove from the heat, add the cacao, balsamic vinegar and salt to taste and stir until well combined. Spoon the hot harissa into warm sterilized jars, allow to cool slightly, then seal. This sauce should keep for at least 3 months in a cool place.

CHOCOLATE SPREAD

Spread thinly or thickly, this makes a superb snack served on fresh crusty bread or on warm toast (*opposite*). The nutty notes of the Hacienda Las Trincheras chocolate make it a popular choice for this recipe, but you could try experimenting with other chocolates until you find your particular favourite.

Makes 250ml

45g granulated sugar

150ml water

200g Venezuelan Hacienda Las Trincheras 72% chocolate, roughly chopped

Put the sugar and water in a saucepan over a low heat and stir until the sugar has dissolved. Raise the heat slightly and bring to the boil. Stir in the chocolate until just melted and remove from the heat.

Pour into a sterilized jar and seal. Once opened, keep in the fridge and consume within 2 weeks.

CHOCOLATE CUSTARD

This is a light yet thick chocolate custard. Serve hot or cold with ice cream, or use as a base for other desserts.

Makes about 750ml

6 egg yolks

100g caster sugar

700ml full-fat milk

1 vanilla pod, split lengthways

170g Madagascan Sambirano Superior 71% chocolate, finely chopped

Beat the eggs yolks and sugar together in a bowl until light and creamy. Put the milk and vanilla pod in a saucepan and bring to the boil. Remove from the heat and pour over the egg mixture, stirring constantly. Sieve into a clean pan to achieve a smooth consistency and remove the vanilla pod.

Add the chocolate and beat gently until it has melted and is well mixed in. Take off the heat.

PASTRY AND TARTS

BITTER CHOCOLATE AND LEMON TARTS

One of the first things I did when I arrived at the hacienda was to plant more lemon trees. Lemon and chocolate go together brilliantly.

Makes 10

120g Venezuelan Hacienda Las Trincheras 72% chocolate, roughly chopped

4 whole eggs

2 egg yolks

150g granulated sugar

Juice and zest of 4 unwaxed lemons

250ml double cream

Caster sugar, for sprinkling

Equipment: 10 x 8-cm tartlet tins

Lightly grease the tartlet tins and line each with a 16-cm square piece of baking paper. Press the paper firmly on the sides and bottom of the tins, leaving excess paper rising up about 2–3cm above the rim of the tins.

Melt the chocolate in a heatproof bowl set over a pan of gently simmering water, making sure the bottom of the bowl is not in contact with the water. Using a small flexible spatula, spread the melted chocolate evenly over the baking paper in the tins, including over the paper extending above the rim. Don't worry if the edges are uneven; they look better if they are. Place in the fridge to chill.

Meanwhile, whisk the whole eggs, yolks, sugar, lemon juice and cream together in a large bowl until well blended. Pass through a sieve into a saucepan. Stir in the lemon zest, then heat gently over a low heat, stirring constantly until the mixture lightly coats the back of the spoon. Strain into a bowl, sprinkle over a little caster sugar (to prevent a skin forming) and leave to cool.

When the chocolate cases have set, lift them out of the tins and peel off the baking paper. Handle them very carefully, as they can easily break. When the lemon mixture has cooled, spoon or pipe it into the chocolate cases and serve. These tartlets will keep well in the fridge for 2–3 days, or you could freeze them for up to a month.

CHOCOLATE PASTRY

Inspired by my mince pies (see page 232), the chocolate adds a great flavour to the pastry and there's something rather elegant about chocolate-brown pie crust.

Makes 1kg

80g Venezuelan Rio Caribe Superior 72% chocolate, roughly chopped

50g cocoa powder

350g plain flour

175g unsalted butter, cut into small pieces

230g caster sugar

4 large egg yolks

1 tsp milk

2 tsp vanilla essence

Melt the chocolate in a heatproof bowl set over a pan of gently simmering water, making sure that the bottom of the bowl is not in contact with the water. Allow to cool slightly.

Meanwhile, sift the cocoa powder and flour together into a large mixing bowl. Add the butter and rub into the flour and cocoa until the mixture resembles fine breadcrumbs. In a separate bowl, whisk the sugar, egg yolks, milk and vanilla essence together, then stir in the melted chocolate until well blended. Pour onto the flour, cocoa and butter mixture and mix well, first with a knife and then with one hand, until the mixture comes together to make a smooth ball of pastry.

The pastry can also be made by blitzing the butter, sugar, egg yolks and vanilla essence together in a food processor. Add the melted chocolate and pulse to blend in, then add the sifted cocoa powder and flour and blitz again until the mixture forms into a smooth ball of pastry.

Wrap the pastry in cling film or place in a plastic bag and chill for at least 2 hours before using. It keeps well in the fridge for 1–2 days, or you can store it in the freezer for up a month. In both cases, make sure it is well wrapped.

BITTER CHOCOLATE TART

This fine tart, with its sweet pastry base and lovely creamy filling, is an absolute must for lovers of dark chocolate. You'll come back to it again and again. Serve on its own or with whipped cream or crème fraîche.

Serves 10

500ml double cream

1 vanilla pod, split lengthways

400g Madagascan Sambirano Superior, 71% chocolate, roughly chopped

50g unsalted butter

FOR THE PASTRY:

200g plain flour

Pinch of salt

100g unsalted butter, softened

100g caster sugar

4 small egg yolks

1 tsp vanilla essence

Equipment: 23-cm tart tin

First make the pastry. Sift the flour with the salt onto a board or clean work surface, Make a large well in the centre and put the butter in it. Place the sugar, egg yolks and vanilla essence on top of the butter and mix together using the fingertips of one hand until they form a soft paste. Gradually, still using your fingertips, draw the flour into the paste and knead to form a smooth dough. Shape into a ball. You can also make the pastry in a food processor by blitzing together all the ingredients except the flour, then adding the flour and blitzing again to form a ball of dough. Flatten the ball slightly, wrap in cling film and chill for at least 1 hour.

While the pastry is chilling, preheat the oven to 180°C and lightly grease the tart tin.

Roll out the pastry on a lightly floured surface to a thickness of about 3mm and use it to line the tart tin. Prick the base lightly with a fork, then bake in the hot oven for 10 minutes. Lower the heat to 165°C and bake for a further 15 minutes, or until the pastry is a pale golden colour. Remove from the oven and leave to cool in the tin on a wire rack.

Meanwhile, make the filling. Put the cream and vanilla pod in a saucepan over a medium-low heat and bring to the boil. Remove from the heat. Scrape the seeds from the vanilla pod into the cream and stir. Put the chocolate and butter in a heatproof bowl. Strain in the hot cream and stir until the chocolate and butter have melted and are well mixed into the cream. Allow the mixture to cool slightly.

Remove the cooked pastry case from the tin, place on a serving plate and pour in the filling. For a smoother surface, pour the filling into the pastry while the mixture is still hot. Leave until cold before serving.

CHOCOLATE AND BANANA CRUMBLE TART

Whenever I hear the word 'banana', it takes me back to the beach at Choroni in Venezuela. I remember standing there, chatting to an American I had just met. We were eating bananas that I had grown on my farm in the cloud forest. He turned and said: 'I'll never eat another banana at home again. I didn't know what bananas were until I came here.'

Serves 6–8

½ recipe quantity Chocolate Pastry (see page 135)

Cocoa powder, to dust

20g unsalted butter

30g muscovado sugar

3 ripe bananas, thickly sliced

2 tbsp dark rum

180g yoghurt

1 egg

3 passionfruit, sieved pulp only

20g caster sugar

1 tsp vanilla essence

FOR THE CRUMBLE:

125g plain flour

8g cocoa powder

65g slightly salted butter, cut into small pieces

60g caster sugar

Equipment: 22-cm round tart tin, or 11 x 35-cm oblong tart tin

Preheat the oven to 180°C. Lightly grease the tart tin.

Place the pastry on a work surface lightly dusted with cocoa powder and roll out until you have a circle a little larger than the tart tin and about 3mm thick. Use it to line the tin. Place in the fridge to chill for at least 1 hour.

Put the butter and muscovado sugar in a saucepan over a low heat and stir until the butter has melted and the sugar has dissolved. Turn up the heat, add the banana slices and fry until lightly caramelized, turning once. Pour in the rum, remove from heat and leave to cool slightly.

Meanwhile, bake the prepared pastry case in the hot oven for 10 minutes. While it is cooking, make the crumble. Sift the flour and cocoa powder together into a large bowl. Add the butter and rub in until the mixture resembles fine breadcrumbs. Set aside.

Mix together the yoghurt, egg, passionfruit pulp, caster sugar and vanilla essence in another bowl until well blended.

Remove the pastry case from the oven and lower the temperature to 130°C. (If there are cracks in the pastry, brush just enough egg white into the cracks to fill them and return to the oven for a couple of minutes to set.) Spread the caramelized banana slices evenly over the base of the pastry case, then pour in the yoghurt mixture. Return to the oven for 10–12 minutes, or until the yoghurt custard has set.

Remove from the oven again and turn the heat up to 180°C. Sprinkle the crumble mix evenly over the custard and return the tart to the oven for 25 minutes. Allow to cool slightly before serving.

PECAN TART WITH CHOCOLATE PASTRY

Whenever I think of pecans, I always think of America, where pecans are a favourite ingredient in pies and desserts. Their flavour combines beautifully with chocolate.

Serves 8

½ recipe quantity Chocolate Pastry (see page 135)

Cocoa powder, to dust

200g pecan nuts

250ml maple syrup

3 eggs

1 tsp vanilla essence

Equipment: 23-cm tart tin

Preheat the oven to 180°C. Lightly grease the tart tin.

Place the pastry on a work surface lightly dusted with cocoa powder and roll out until you have a circle a little larger than the tart tin and about 3mm thick. Use it to line the tin. Prick lightly and chill in the fridge for at least 1 hour.

While the pastry is chilling, spread the nuts on a baking tray and place in the hot oven for 10-12 minutes, or until lightly toasted. Allow the nuts to cool before using. Leave the oven on.

Line the chilled pastry case with a greaseproof paper and fill it with baking beans or dry rice. Bake for 15 minutes.

Meanwhile, make the filling by mixing together the nuts, maple syrup, eggs and vanilla essence in a bowl.

Take the pastry case out of the oven, remove the paper and beans and turn the oven down to 170°C. Pour the egg mixture into the cooked pastry case and return to the oven for 20-25 minutes, or until the filling is set. Leave to cool on a wire rack before serving.

FIG, MASCARPONE AND CHOCOLATE BRIOCHE

In the autumn, my eyes always wander to my often-forgotten fig tree, looking out for a succulent ripe fruit to pick and eat. Alas, in Britain, figs rarely ripen fully on the tree. They do, however, ripen enough to use in this open tart. You could serve it for breakfast, tea or dessert. It's best warm, but you can also eat it hot or cold (*see overleaf*).

Serves 8

250g strong white flour

1 tsp salt

2 tbsp caster sugar

1 tbsp milk powder

1 tsp easy-blend yeast

2 large eggs, beaten

100g unsalted butter, softened

FOR THE FILLING:

375g mascarpone cheese

12–16 fresh figs

80g Venezuelan Rio Caribe Superior 72% chocolate, chopped into small pieces

75g muscovado sugar

Equipment: 26-cm springform cake tin

Sift the flour and salt into a large mixing bowl and stir in the sugar, milk powder and yeast. Make a well in the centre and drop in the beaten eggs and butter. With the fingers of one hand, gradually mix the dry ingredients into the butter and eggs to form a very soft, but not sticky, dough. Knead on a work surface for about 5 minutes, or until smooth You can also make the dough by placing all the brioche ingredients in a mixer with a dough-hook attachment and working for 5–7 minutes.

Place the dough in a clean bowl, cover with a clean tea towel and leave to rise for at least 4 hours, or until doubled in size.

Grease the cake tin. Knead the risen dough for about 2 minutes, then press onto the base and at least 3cm up the sides of the tin.

Spread the mascarpone over the base of the brioche dough. Remove the stalks from the figs. Cut a cross-shape in the top of each, extending about 2cm down into the flesh. Arrange on top of the mascarpone, then sprinkle over the chocolate pieces and muscovado sugar. Leave in a warm place for 1½–2 hours to allow the dough to rise.

When ready, preheat the oven to 180°C and bake the brioche for 25–30 minutes. To test if cooked, tap lightly on the base – it should sound hollow.

CHOCOLATE PROFITEROLES OR ÉCLAIRS

These are very popular and often bought as a treat, but are always far better when freshly made at home. Remember when making choux pastry to add the final egg very slowly and carefully until the right consistency is reached. If too much is added, the profiteroles will be flat; not enough, and they will be heavy and split at the sides.

Makes 20

FOR THE CHOUX PASTRY:

150g plain white flour

250ml water

100g slightly salted butter

4 eggs

FOR THE TOPPING:

150ml double cream

20g caster sugar

80g Madagascan Sambirano Superior 71% chocolate, roughly chopped

FOR THE FILLING:

350ml double cream

2 tbsp icing sugar (optional)

1 tsp vanilla essence

Equipment: Piping bag with a 2-cm nozzle

First make the pastry. Sift the flour into a bowl. Put the water and butter into a saucepan over a low heat until the butter has melted and the mixture comes to the boil. Take off the heat, quickly tip in all the flour and beat vigorously with a wooden spoon until the mixture becomes thick and smooth and comes away from the sides of the pan. This should happen quite quickly. Set aside until completely cool.

When cool, beat in 3 eggs, one at a time. The mixture might seem to curdle, but beat well and it will become smooth again. Whisk the remaining egg in a cup and beat in just a little at a time until the mixture is soft, shiny and smooth. It should have a dropping consistency and not be too runny. You might not need all of the last egg. Preheat the oven to 190°C. Line a baking tray with baking paper and sprinkle lightly with water.

Fill the piping bag with the choux pastry mixture and pipe your desired shape onto the lined baking tray. For profiteroles, pipe balls about 6cm in diameter; for éclairs, pipe strips 8–9cm long, making the ends slightly fatter than the middle. Bake 15–20 minutes, until golden brown. Turn the oven off. Pierce a tiny hole in each pastry, then return to the oven for 5 minutes. This will prevent the pastries from going soggy. Remove from the oven, take off the tray and leave to cool on a wire rack.

For the topping, put the cream and sugar in a saucepan over a moderate heat, stirring until the sugar has dissolved. Remove from the heat and stir in the chocolate until melted. Set aside.

To make the filling, whip the cream with the sugar, if using, and the vanilla essence until just stiff. With a serrated knife, cut halfway into each pastry along one side and pipe or spoon some of the whipped cream into the centre until full. If you've made profiteroles, pile them onto a plate, pour the chocolate over them and leave to set. If you've made éclairs, dip each into the chocolate so that it comes halfway up the sides. Leave on a wire rack to set.

RELIGIEUSE

Invented in the nineteenth century, these pastries consist of a large profiterole with a small one sitting on top. Choux pastry takes a little care to make, but is really quite easy to master.

Makes 10–12

1 recipe quantity choux pastry (see page 145)

160g Madagascan Sambirano Superior 71% chocolate, roughly chopped

500ml double cream

2 tbsp icing sugar (optional)

1 tsp vanilla essence

Equipment: Piping bag with a 2-cm nozzle

First make the choux pastry and set aside to cool completely.

Preheat the oven to 190°C. Line a baking tray with baking paper and sprinkle lightly with water.

Put the prepared choux pastry into the piping bag. Pipe 10–12 balls about 6cm in diameter onto the lined baking tray, then pipe the same number of 3-cm balls. Bake in the hot oven for 15–20 minutes, or until golden brown. Turn the oven off. Pierce a tiny hole in each choux ball, then return to the still-warm oven for 5 minutes: this will prevent the pastries from becoming soggy. Transfer to a wire rack and leave to cool.

Melt the chocolate in a heatproof bowl set over a pan of gently simmering water, making sure the bottom of the bowl is not in contact with the water. Set aside.

Whip the cream with the sugar, if using, and the vanilla essence until just stiff. With a serrated knife, slice just over halfway into each choux ball. Pipe or spoon in some of the whipped cream until each is full. Dip the filled profiteroles in the melted chocolate so that it comes halfway up the sides. Carefully place a small profiterole on top of each large one while the chocolate is still soft, then chill for at least 30 minutes before serving.

PUMPKIN AND WHITE CHOCOLATE TART

Serve this tart with my Pumpkin, Quince and White Chocolate Sorbet (see page 91) or simply with cream or crème fraîche.

Serves 10

1 pumpkin (to yield 500g flesh when prepared)

250g white chocolate, roughly chopped

150ml double cream

5 eggs

½–1 tsp ground cinnamon, to taste

FOR THE PASTRY:

200g plain flour

Pinch of salt

100g unsalted butter, softened

100g caster sugar

4 small egg yolks

1 tsp vanilla essence

Equipment: 28-cm tart tin

First make the pastry. Sift the flour with the salt on to a board or clean work surface. Make a large well in the centre and put the butter in it. Place the sugar, egg yolks and vanilla essence on top of the butter and mix together using the fingertips of one hand until they form a soft paste. Gradually, still using your fingertips, draw the flour into the paste and knead to form a smooth dough. Shape into a ball, flatten slightly, then wrap in cling film and chill for at least 1 hour. You can also make the pastry in a food processor by blitzing all the ingredients except the flour together, then adding the flour and blitzing again to form a ball of dough.

Meanwhile, peel the pumpkin, then cut in half and discard the seeds and pith. Chop the flesh into small chunks and place in a pan with 250ml of water. Cover and cook over a gentle heat until the pumpkin is soft. Remove the lid and continue cooking until any water left in the pan has evaporated. Remove from the heat and stir in the white chocolate until melted. Tip the mixture into a blender or food processor and blitz to form a smooth purée. Add the cream, eggs and cinnamon and pulse until well blended. Set aside.

Lightly grease the tart tin. Roll out the pastry on a lightly floured surface to a thickness of about 3mm and use it to line the tart tin. Prick the base with a fork, then chill for 20 minutes in the fridge.

Preheat the oven to 180°C, then bake the pastry case for 15 minutes, or until a pale golden colour. Lower the oven to 160°C.

Spoon the pumpkin mixture into the cooked pastry case and smooth over the top. Bake in the hot oven for 20–25 minutes, or until slightly risen and set. Serve warm or cold.

BISCUITS
AND
SNACKS

ALMOND, WHITE CHOCOLATE AND LAVENDER CRESCENTS

It is particularly satisfying to use home-grown ingredients in these lovely little aromatic biscuits. Lavender is very easy to grow, and for cooking is best picked before the last flowers on each stalk are fully open. It provides a delicate perfumed note to the white chocolate and almond pieces.

Makes 18–20

130g slightly salted butter

65g light muscovado sugar

1 tsp lavender flowers, finely chopped

100g plain flour

130g ground almonds

60g whole almonds, toasted and coarsely chopped

180g white chocolate, roughly chopped

Preheat the oven to 170°C. Line a large baking tray with baking paper.

Beat the butter and sugar together in a large bowl until light and fluffy, then beat in half the lavender flowers. Mix in the flour and the ground almonds until well combined. Stir in the chopped toasted almonds and 100g of the chocolate. The mixture should be a soft dough. If it is sticky, gradually blend in more flour until the right consistency is reached.

With floured hands, shape portions of the mixture into crescents about 8cm long and 2cm thick in the middle and arrange on the prepared baking tray. Bake in the preheated oven for 15–20 minutes, until lightly golden. Leave to cool on the baking tray for 10 minutes, then transfer the biscuits to a wire rack to cool completely.

Melt the remaining chocolate in a heatproof bowl set over a pan of gently simmering water, making sure the bottom of the bowl is not in contact with the water. Using a fork, drizzle melted chocolate over the top of each biscuit. Sprinkle with the remaining lavender flowers and leave until the chocolate is set. Store in a cool place in an airtight container.

ORANGE-BLOSSOM CHOCOLATE BISCUITS

These biscuits are topped with dark chocolate and flavoured with orange blossom water. They are lovely dipped in a cup of hot tea.

Makes 24

170g unsalted butter, softened

140g caster sugar

1 tbsp orange-flower water

1 tbsp Kirsch

150g plain flour

150g fine semolina

300g Peruvian San Martin 70% chocolate

Equipment: 6-cm round pastry cutter

Beat the butter and sugar together in a large bowl until light and fluffy. Add the orange-flower water and Kirsch and beat well.

Sift the flour and semolina together into a clean bowl, then mix into the butter mixture to form a soft dough. Wrap in cling film and chill in the fridge for at least 20 minutes.

Preheat the oven to 150°C. Line two large baking trays with baking paper.

Roll out the dough on a lightly floured surface to a thickness of about 1cm. Cut out rounds using the pastry cutter and arrange them, well spaced, on the prepared baking trays. Bake in the hot oven for 18–20 minutes, until only just golden – the biscuits should remain pale. Leave to cool on the baking trays.

When the biscuits are cold, temper the chocolate (see page 10). Dip the upper side of each biscuit in the chocolate, shake well and place back on the lined baking sheets. Leave until the chocolate has set. These biscuits will keep well in an airtight container for up to 2 weeks.

CHOCOLATE LETTERS

You could have great fun piping out the mixture here to spell various letters or names.

Makes about 15

100g icing sugar

200g slightly salted butter

1 egg white

½ tsp vanilla essence

150g plain flour

40g cocoa powder

Equipment: Piping bag with 1.5-cm star nozzle

Preheat the oven to 180°C. Line a baking tray with baking paper.

Beat the icing sugar and butter together in large bowl until light and fluffy. Beat in the egg white and vanilla essence.

Sift the flour and cocoa powder together into a clean bowl, then mix into the butter and sugar mixture until well combined.

Spoon the mixture into the piping bag, then pipe out about 15 biscuit-sized letters onto the lined baking tray. Bake in the hot oven for 12–15 minutes. Transfer to a wire rack and leave to cool completely. The biscuits will keep well in an airtight container for 7–10 days.

CHOCOLATE WAFERS

Wonderfully light and crunchy, these fine wafers go brilliantly with ice cream and are also marvellous sandwiched together with caramel, then dipped into melted 72% chocolate.

Makes 14–16

65g Nicaraguan Waslala Superior 100% cacao, finely chopped

75g lightly salted butter, softened

60g granulated sugar

90g light muscovado sugar

2 large egg whites

80g plain flour

15g cocoa powder

1 tsp ground cinnamon

Equipment: 9-cm round pastry cutter

Melt the cacao in a heatproof bowl set over a pan of gently simmering water, making sure that the bottom of the bowl is not in contact with the water.

Beat the butter with the granulated and muscovado sugars in a large bowl until light and fluffy. Add the egg whites, one at a time, mixing well. Stir in the melted cacao until well combined.

Sift the flour, cocoa powder and cinnamon together into a clean bowl, then stir into the beaten butter and sugar mixture to form a sticky dough. Using a spatula, scrape the mixture onto a large sheet of baking paper and cover with another sheet. Press the mixture between the sheets of baking paper into a 16-cm disc. Wrap in cling film or place in a plastic bag and chill in the fridge for at least 2 hours.

When the dough has sufficiently chilled, preheat the oven to 170°C and line two large baking trays with baking paper.

Place the dough on a lightly floured work surface and roll out to a thickness of 3mm. Using the pastry cutter, cut out circles and transfer to the prepared baking trays by lifting carefully with a metal spatula. Make sure the dough circles are well spaced. Gently press a fork over the top of each one to make a decorative pattern. Bake in the hot oven for 12 minutes. Allow to cool completely on the baking trays. Store in an airtight container for up to 2 weeks, or freeze and keep for up to 6 months.

CHOCOLATE MACAROONS

These are a great stand-by for afternoon tea, especially when you've got guests arriving at short notice. They're very simple and quick to make.

Makes 16–18

170g Venezuelan Hacienda Las Trincheras 72% chocolate, roughly chopped

2 large egg whites

150g caster sugar

Few drops of almond extract

100g ground almonds

Equipment: Piping bag with 2-cm nozzle

Preheat the oven to 150°C. Line a large baking tray with baking paper.

Melt the chocolate in a heatproof bowl set over a pan of gently simmering water, making sure the bottom of the bowl is not in contact with the water. Set aside.

Whisk the egg whites in a clean bowl until they form stiff peaks. Add the sugar, a few tablespoons at a time, whisking well between each addition. Fold in the almond extract with the melted chocolate until evenly mixed, then fold in the ground almonds until just combined.

Fill the piping bag with the mixture and pipe mounds 4cm in diameter onto the prepared baking tray, allowing 2–3cm space between each. Bake in the preheated oven for 12–14 minutes, or until the macaroons are beginning to crisp on the outside and lift easily off the baking paper. Transfer to a wire rack and leave to cool completely. They will keep for up to a week if stored in an airtight container.

CRANBERRY, BITTER CHOCOLATE AND ORANGE BISCOTTI

I love biscotti, whether served with my coffee or with ice cream or sorbet. They are always a favourite. Here the cranberries and orange give the chocolate a tangy punch.

Makes 35-40

125g slightly salted butter

175g caster sugar

2 small eggs

3 tbsp Kirsch

2 tsp vanilla essence

Zest of 2 large oranges

350g plain flour

2 tsp baking powder

120g dried cranberries

120g Venezuelan Rio Caribe Superior 100% cacao, chopped into small pieces

Preheat the oven to 170°C. Line a large baking tray with baking paper.

Beat the butter and sugar together in a large bowl until light and fluffy. Beat in the eggs, one at a time, until well combined. Mix in the Kirsch, vanilla essence and orange zest.

Sift the flour with the baking powder into a clean bowl, then stir into the butter and sugar mixture to form a soft dough. Fold in the cranberries and cacao.

Divide the mixture into three pieces and, on a lightly floured surface, shape each into a rectangle about 24cm long, 8cm wide and 3cm thick. Arrange on the lined baking tray, allowing about 6cm between each piece. Bake in the hot oven for 25–30 minutes, until lightly golden. Leave to cool slightly on the baking tray. Reset the oven to 140°C.

Cut the still-warm pieces at an angle into 1-cm thick slices. Return to the oven for about 30 minutes, turning them after 15 minutes, until crisp and completely dry (otherwise they won't stay crunchy). Transfer to a wire rack and leave until cool.

These biscuits will keep well for 2–3 weeks in an airtight container.

VARIATION: Substitute 120g white chocolate and 120g pine nuts for the cranberries, cacao and orange zest.

SOFT CHOCOLATE AMARETTI BISCUITS

These almond and chocolate biscuits are very easy to make and almost addictive. Whenever I've made a batch, I find myself reaching into the cupboard to grab one every time I have a cup of tea or coffee.

Makes 35

150g whole unblanched almonds

250g Madagascan Sambirano Superior 71% chocolate, roughly chopped

45g unsalted butter

2 large eggs

75g caster sugar

2 tbsp dark rum

1 tsp almond extract

75g medium-ground polenta

½ tsp baking powder

50g granulated sugar

50g icing sugar

Preheat the oven to 160°C. Spread the almonds over a baking tray and toast in the hot oven for about 15 minutes, or until just beginning to brown. Grind to a coarse powder using a pestle and mortar or by blitzing in a blender or food processor. Set aside.

Melt the chocolate and butter together in a heatproof bowl set over a pan of gently simmering water, making sure the bottom of the bowl is not in contact with the water. Set aside.

Place the eggs and sugar in another heatproof bowl and set over a pan of simmering water, again making sure the base of the bowl does not touch the water. Whisk until very light, thick and creamy. Remove from the heat and continue whisking until slightly cooled, then whisk in the melted chocolate, rum and almond extract until just blended (don't overwhip or the biscuits will be dense and heavy).

Mix the ground almonds with the polenta and baking powder and stir into the chocolate batter until well blended. Leave this soft dough to firm up slightly for 10–15 minutes. Meanwhile, line two large baking trays with baking paper.

Place the granulated sugar in one small bowl and sift the icing sugar into another. Roll pieces of the dough into small balls about 2cm in diameter. Roll each ball first in the granulated sugar and then in the icing sugar. Arrange the sugar-coated balls on the prepared baking trays, making sure that there is about 3cm between each ball. Squash down slightly. Bake in the preheated oven for 12 minutes, or until they are just beginning to darken and have a slightly cracked surface. They should feel soft but set. Remove from the oven and leave to cool on the baking trays. The biscuits will keep for 2–3 weeks if stored in a cool place in an airtight container.

FLORENTINES

It's always nice to take a gift along when you're visiting friends or family. A box of these florentines is usually greatly appreciated, and they're much quicker to make than a cake.

Makes 30

80g candied orange peel, roughly chopped

80g raisins

200g flaked almonds

80g pecan nuts, roughly chopped

50g plain flour

50g unsalted butter

150g light muscovado sugar

60ml clear honey

100ml double cream

300g Venezuelan Hacienda Las Trincheras 72% chocolate

Preheat the oven to 170°C. Line two large baking trays with baking paper.

Place the candied peel, raisins, flaked almonds and pecan nuts in a bowl. Add the flour, mix well and set aside.

In a saucepan, combine the butter, sugar, honey and cream. Bring to the boil over a moderate heat and cook for 7 minutes, stirring occasionally. Do not allow the mixture to caramelize and brown. Remove from the heat and stir in the dried fruit, nut and flour mixture.

Place heaped teaspoons of the mixture on the prepared baking trays, leaving at least 6cm between the spoonfuls. Bake in the preheated oven for about 12 minutes, or until golden brown. Leave to cool on the baking trays until set.

Temper the chocolate (see page 10), then spread a thin layer over the underside of each biscuit. Place chocolate side up on a wire rack to cool. When the chocolate is almost set, mark it with wavy lines, using the prongs of a fork. Leave until the chocolate has completely hardened. The florentines will keep for up to a week if stored in a cool place in an airtight container.

TOLL-HOUSE COOKIES

An American classic, the name comes from an eighteenth-century toll house on the east coast of the United States, although the recipe wasn't invented until the 1930s. The chocolate chips are the distinguishing feature and should be small enough to melt away quickly after each bite.

Makes about 20

75g slightly salted butter

70g muscovado sugar

70g caster sugar

1 egg

¼ tsp bicarbonate of soda

1 tsp vanilla essence

100g Madagascan Sambirano Superior 71% chocolate, chopped into raisin-sized pieces

80g chopped walnuts

100g plain flour

Preheat the oven to 190°C. Line 2 large baking trays with baking paper.

Beat the butter with the muscovado and caster sugar until light and fluffy, then beat in the egg until well blended. Mix the bicarbonate of soda with a teaspoon of water and stir into the butter mixture, along with the vanilla essence. Fold in the chopped chocolate, chopped walnuts and flour until evenly mixed through.

Place heaped teaspoons of the mixture onto the prepared baking trays, spacing the spoonfuls about 8cm apart. Bake in the preheated oven for about 8 minutes, or until golden brown. Allow to cool slightly on the trays, then transfer to a wire rack and leave to cool completely. The cookies will keep for up to 2 weeks if stored in a cool place in an airtight container.

CHOCOLATE MADELEINES

Based on a classic French recipe, these little cakes are delicious anytime (*see overleaf*). Try them for breakfast, accompanied by a cup of steaming hot chocolate (see page 30).

Makes 24

60g slightly salted butter

40g Indonesian Javan Light Breaking 69% chocolate, roughly chopped

45g plain flour

1 tsp baking powder

2 tbsp cocoa powder

2 large eggs

70g caster sugar

Equipment: 2 x 12-hole madeleine tins

Preheat the oven to 170°C. Lightly grease the madeleine tins with butter.

Place the butter in a saucepan over a moderate heat until melted and golden brown. Remove from the heat and stir in the chocolate until melted. Set aside to cool.

Sift the flour, baking powder and cocoa powder together into a large bowl, then set aside.

Beat the eggs and sugar together in a large bowl until very thick and creamy. Whisk in the cooled butter and chocolate mixture until well combined, then very carefully fold in the flour and cocoa mixture until it is just evenly mixed through.

Spoon the mixture into the madeleine tin, allowing it to come about two-thirds of the way up the sides of each hole.

Bake in the preheated oven for about 10 minutes or until the madeleines spring back when lightly pressed. Remove from the oven and transfer to a wire rack. Leave to cool completely. They will keep for up to a week if stored in a cool place in an airtight container, although they are best eaten as fresh as possible.

CHOCOLATE BROWNIES

These brownies are flour-free. If you want them to be nut-free, you can replace the walnuts with chopped white or milk chocolate, or a mixture of both.

Makes 60

200g Venezuelan Carenero Superior 100% cacao, coarsely chopped

100g slightly salted butter

4 eggs

200g caster sugar

120g walnuts, roughly chopped

Equipment: Baking tin about 40 x 24cm

Preheat the oven to 170°C. Lightly grease the baking tin and line with baking paper.

Melt the cacao and butter in a heatproof bowl set over a pan of gently simmering water, making sure the bottom of the bowl is not in contact with the water. Set aside to cool.

Whisk the eggs and caster sugar in a large mixing bowl until light and creamy. Fold in the melted chocolate and butter until well combined, then fold in the chopped walnuts.

Spoon the mixture into the prepared tin and bake in the preheated oven for 15–20 minutes, until the centre is just firm to the touch. Remove from oven and allow to cool in the tin. Slice into approximately 4-cm squares. These brownies will keep for up to a week in an airtight tin.

CHOCOLATE SHORTBREAD

This shortbread is slightly softer than the traditional variety. However, it still has that delicious slightly toasted, buttery taste, which melds beautifully with the chocolate.

Makes about 800g

250g slightly salted butter, softened

100g caster sugar, plus 1 tbsp for sprinkling

100g Venezuelan Rio Caribe Superior 72% chocolate, roughly chopped

300g plain flour

50g cocoa powder

Equipment: 22-cm square shallow cake tin

Preheat the oven to 180°C.

Beat the butter and the 100g of sugar in a large bowl until very light and fluffy.

Melt the chocolate in a heatproof bowl set over a pan of gently simmering water, making sure the bottom of the bowl is not in contact with the water. Set aside to cool slightly.

Sift the flour and cocoa powder together into a clean bowl, then stir into the beaten butter and sugar mixture. Add the slightly cooled chocolate and mix until just combined into a smooth paste. Do not overwork.

Press the mixture into the cake tin, sprinkle over the tablespoon of caster sugar and bake in the hot oven for 30 minutes. Leave to cool in the tin for 10 minutes, then, while still slightly soft, cut into the desired shapes. Transfer to a wire rack to cool completely. The shortbread keeps for 2–3 days in an airtight container, or can be kept frozen for up to a month.

TRIPLE CHOCOLATE CHIP COOKIES

These luscious biscuits are extremely chocolaty and moist. They are best eaten on the day they are made, although they can be stored for up to a week in an airtight container.

Makes 20-25

180g Madagascan Sambirano Superior 71% chocolate, roughly chopped

100g slightly salted butter

130g light muscovado sugar

1 tsp vanilla essence

1 large egg, beaten

120g plain flour

1 tsp bicarbonate of soda

125g each of dark, white and milk chocolate, chopped into small chunks

Preheat the oven to 180°C. Line 2 large baking trays with baking paper.

Melt the Madagascan Sambirano Superior 71% chocolate in a heatproof bowl set over a pan of gently simmering water, making sure the bottom of the bowl is not in contact with the water.

Beat the butter and sugar together until light and fluffy. Blend in the vanilla essence, beaten egg and melted chocolate until well combined.

Sift the flour and bicarbonate of soda together into a large bowl, then mix into the butter, sugar and chocolate mixture. Stir in the small chunks of chocolate until evenly mixed through.

Spoon heaped teaspoons of the mixture onto the prepared baking trays, spacing the spoonfuls about 6-8cm apart. Bake in the preheated oven for 10-12 minutes. Allow to cool slightly on the trays, then transfer to a wire rack and leave to cool completely.

FINANCIERS WITH A MINT CHOCOLATE GLAZE

These lovely, buttery little almond cakes are said to have acquired their name because of their popularity among French bankers in Paris in the 1890s. I've added a rich chocolate glaze infused with fresh mint.

Makes 12

125g slightly salted butter

3 egg whites

70g icing sugar

50g ground almonds

½ tsp vanilla essence

15g flour

FOR THE GLAZE:

60g Madagascan Sambirano Superior 71% chocolate, roughly chopped

60g unsalted butter

30 fresh mint leaves

Equipment: 12 small oval or rectangular cake tins, about 30ml each

Preheat the oven to 200°C.

Heat the butter in a small saucepan over a moderate heat until melted and a rich golden brown. Remove from the heat and strain through a fine sieve into a clean measuring jug, discarding the browned milk solids left behind. Use a little of the melted butter to lightly grease the insides of the cake tins, reserving about 100ml for the cakes themselves. Set aside to cool.

Lightly beat the egg whites until just starting to become foamy. Add the icing sugar, ground almonds, vanilla essence and flour and beat until well combined. Fold in the melted butter, then spoon the mixture into the prepared tins so that it comes almost to the top.

Arrange the filled tins on a baking tray and bake in the preheated oven for 8–10 minutes, or until golden brown and springy to the touch. Remove from the oven and allow to cool for about 5 minutes in the tins, then transfer to a wire rack and leave to cool completely.

Prepare the glaze by melting the chocolate in a heatproof bowl set over a pan of gently simmering water, making sure the bottom of the bowl is not in contact with the water. Set aside.

In a clean saucepan, melt the butter over a moderate heat. Take off the heat, add the mint leaves and leave to infuse for 15 minutes. Remove and discard the mint leaves, then stir the butter into the melted chocolate. Allow to cool slightly, but do not let the mixture set.

Carefully place a teaspoon of the mint and chocolate mixture on the top of each cake. Using the back of a spoon, spread the mixture evenly to form a thin glaze. Leave the cakes on a wire rack until the glaze is set. They will keep for up to a week if stored in a cool place in an airtight container.

CHOCOLATE DOUGHNUTS

When I was a child, I loved freshly made doughnuts. I could hardly wait to create a recipe for them with chocolate added. Here they are – light and delicious!

Makes 24

500g plain flour

1 tsp salt

40g granulated sugar

7g easy-blend yeast

250ml warm milk

2 eggs, lightly beaten

40g unsalted butter, melted

200g Chocolate Spread (see page 130) or 24 Truffles (see page 198)

Sunflower oil, for deep-frying

Caster sugar, for coating

Sift the flour and salt into a warm bowl. Stir in the sugar and yeast, then make a well in the centre of the mixture and pour in the milk, eggs and butter. Using your fingertips, gradually mix the flour into the wet ingredients to form a smooth soft dough. If the dough is sticky, add a little more flour, but make sure it is still soft. Turn out onto a lightly floured surface and knead for about 10 minutes, until smooth and elastic. Alternatively, the dough can be prepared by placing the ingredients in the bowl of an electric mixer and working together for about 10 minutes using a dough-hook attachment. Whatever method you use, place the prepared dough in a large bowl, cover loosely with cling film or a clean tea towel and leave to rise in a warm place for at least 6 hours, or overnight.

Turn the dough out onto a lightly floured work surface and knock back to its original size. Divide into 24 equal pieces. With lightly floured hands, roll each piece into a ball, then flatten to form a round about 1cm thick and 7cm across. Place a teaspoon of chocolate spread or a truffle in the centre of each round of dough. Wet around the edges with a little water, then fold the dough over the chocolate, pinching the edges together firmly to make sure the chocolate filling is firmly sealed inside. Carefully re-form each piece of chocolate-filled dough into an evenly shaped ball. Arrange on a large, paper lined baking tray, lined with baking paper, about 4cm apart. Leave in a warm place until doubled in size. This can take 2–3 hours.

Heat sufficient sunflower oil to deep-fry the doughnuts in a large pan or deep-fat fryer until it reaches 180°C, or is hot enough to brown a small cube of day-old bread in about 30 seconds. Fry small batches of the doughnuts in the hot oil for 3–4 minutes until golden brown. Using a slotted spoon or spatula, lift the doughnuts out of the hot fat and drain on kitchen paper. Dredge with caster sugar until well coated and eat, preferably while still warm, on the day they are made.

CHOCOLATE FRENCH TOAST

If my kids are ever bored with pancakes, I whip up French toast as an alternative. It is very simple and quick to make. You could add a topping of fresh fruit compote and some whipped cream for an extra special treat.

Per person

1 small egg, beaten

1 tsp caster sugar

1 tbsp milk

2–3 drops vanilla essence

25g Madagascan Sambirano Superior 71% chocolate

2 slices of brioche, or any other type of white bread

Butter, for frying

Caster sugar, for sprinkling (optional)

Beat the egg, sugar, milk and vanilla essence together in a shallow bowl and set aside.

Melt the chocolate in a heatproof bowl set over a pan of gently simmering water, making sure the bottom of the bowl is not in contact with the water. Spread the melted chocolate on one of the slices of brioche or bread, leaving a good centimetre clear around the edge. Place the other slice of brioche or bread on top to form a chocolate sandwich.

Dip the sandwich in the egg mixture until well coated on both sides. Heat a small knob of butter in a frying pan over a moderate heat until melted and starting to sizzle. Add the chocolate sandwich and cook for 1 minute. Lower the heat a little and cook for another minute, or until the sandwich is golden on the underside. Turn over and cook for 2–3 minutes on the other side, or until it is also golden. Remove from the pan, sprinkle lightly with caster sugar, if desired, and serve immediately.

MAKING CHOCOLATE

Just before the Terry's of York factory closed in 2005, I went along to take a look at the chocolate-making machines there. Passing through its heavy iron gates, I stood in front of the vast red-brick building and stared up at its imposing Victorian clock tower, where letters spelling 'Terry's of York' adorned the clock face in place of numerals.

Inevitably, I found myself imagining how things had been when this once mighty chocolate empire had opened in 1926, when the smell of roasting cacao beans had filled the now empty courtyard. This was where some of the twentieth century's biggest confectionery brands were born: Chocolate Apples, soon to be followed by the more popular Terry's Chocolate Oranges; and Terry's All Gold, so named because the great Aztec leader Montezuma drank his chocolate from gold vessels. A plaque on the Terry's café in town informed chocolate lovers that the Latin name for cacao, *theobroma*, meant 'food of the gods'. This was once a place that celebrated chocolate.

I stopped to chat to the small group of security guards at the entrance to the factory. Most of them had worked there for their entire adult lives. But Kraft bought Terry's in 1993, and production has since relocated to Sweden, Belgium, Poland and Slovakia. There was a sense of real sadness in the air. As I cruised around the deserted buildings, staring up at silos so huge you couldn't see the top of them, I came across the one remaining production line that was still running. Fascinated, I watched the last conveyor belt as it snaked its way through the ghost factory carrying a never-ending file of Terry's Chocolate Oranges. It was a poignant sight, and a slightly eerie one, but at the same time it felt like a privilege to witness the last breaths of the factory before it closed forever, to be present at the end of an era.

On my way home, I passed the site of the old Rowntree factory in the centre of York, which was housed next to the River Ouse at Tanner's Moat until 1895. Founded by benevolent Quakers in 1869, Rowntree offered company employees relatively good working conditions in an era of mass exploitation, but still imposed strict rules. Apparently, if they were a few minutes late, they lost two hours' pay. They also had to work on Saturdays and launder their own overalls.

Chocolate was still very expensive back then, and the workers couldn't afford to buy it. Instead, they found an ingenious way of ensuring they didn't go without. Every Saturday at work, they splashed their overalls with as much chocolate as they possibly could, layer upon layer. Then, when they got home, they scraped it off, shared it out and ate it!

Chocolate-making only began to change with the Industrial Revolution. Until then, it was a hugely labour-intensive process. In 1701, an English traveller called Ellis Veryard wrote a lengthy description of how chocolate was made in Spain. First, he said, the beans were dried over a gentle fire in an iron pan pierced with holes, while being stirred continuously. When the 'kernels' crumbled under pressure, but without turning to dust, they were placed in a box over the fire and turned every two hours.

The following day, the beans were gently rolled on a slab of stone, or metate, to remove the shells, and then winnowed, sieved and ground on the stone, which was now heated by a fire beneath it. Sugar was then added, along with cinnamon, which were mixed up and ground forcefully until incorporated in the cacao mass. The grinding continued, involving a huge amount of effort; vanilla, musk and achiote went into the mix. Eventually the cacao mass was formed into rolls, blocks or cakes and left to dry, then mixed with hot water and beaten with a stick to make a frothy drink. By that time the person doing all the work would definitely need a pick-me-up!

In the 1750s, Joseph Fry in Bristol began producing chocolate for the UK market, all of it handmade. It wasn't until the end of the century that he patented a grinding machine powered by a James Watt steam engine. Even then, chocolate was still predominantly a drink. There was a trend for adding milk to it, but this didn't mask the bitterness of the cacao and only added fat to what was already a fairly fatty concoction. More than 50% of the bean is made up of cacao butter, which would float to the surface when melted in hot water and make the cacao particles hard to disperse.

Things began to move forward in the nineteenth century, when food pioneers experimented with ways of extracting the cacao butter from the nibs, turning cacao into powder and removing the bitterness by treating it with heat or alkali. The crucial breakthrough came in 1828, when the Dutch chemist and chocolate-maker Conrad Van Houten built a hydraulic press that separated cacao butter from the liquor and left a dry solid that could be pulverized into powder, which he then treated with alkali salts to neutralize the acidity and make it easier to mix with water. This process became known as 'Dutching'. Hot chocolate suddenly became twice as digestible and a lot easier to prepare. Dutching makes the chocolate darker – which dispels the idea that the darker the chocolate, the better it is, because it also strips out some of the goodness. Needless to say, I don't Dutch. It's a process used mainly by large manufacturers.

Now that cacao butter could be extracted from the beans, 'eating' chocolate became a possibility because the butter could be used to bind and coat a mix of milled sugar and cacao nibs to make a chocolate bar. Joseph Fry made this discovery in 1847 and went on to open the first chocolate bar factory; by now, roasting, winnowing and grinding had all become mechanized. In 1875, the Swiss chocolatier Daniel Peter launched a milk chocolate bar after his neighbour Henri Nestlé developed condensed milk. Too much water in chocolate adversely affects its shelf life and texture, so Nestlé's dehydrated milk formula was key to the future of the milk chocolate bar.

But chocolate was still grittier and more bitter than it is today because there was one more important nineteenth-century innovation to come: a process known as conching, which involves heating and grinding the cacao solids to make them smoother and more integrated. Conching was apparently the result of a happy accident in the factory of Rodolphe Lindt, after one of Lindt's employees left a grinding machine running all night. It's not recorded whether the worker was sacked before he was promoted, or simply sacked so that Rodolphe Lindt could take the glory for a new invention. Either way, chocolate factories all over Europe were soon resounding to the deafening rhythm of row upon row of conching machines.

Conching is still a huge part of chocolate-making today; it's just that the machines at the big processing factories now hold 20 tonnes (yes, 20 tonnes!) of soft-state cacao, instead of the Victorian standard of four tanks, each containing 125 kilos, which is the capacity of my beautiful antique conching machine at the factory in Devon.

Is it possible to make chocolate in such large quantities and still retain the great flavour profiles? It's very difficult. Big volumes always seem to dilute flavour. So there's a dilemma for the quality chocolate manufacturer who wants to make chocolate in large quantities and spread the word about great chocolate far and wide. The only way around it is to diversify and make chocolate from many different types of beans so as not to lose out on flavour as your volume expands. It makes the business more complicated because you're using scores of different beans.

Peter Cooke, Mike Gray and Stephen Beckett: the chocolate romantics of York.

I already produce five different chocolates and nine different 100% cacao cylinders; there are eight experimental chocolate liquors in my factory fridge at the time of writing.

The big chocolate confectionery manufacturers use very advanced technology, but the industry is obsessed with price point and the drive to produce a cheap bar and increase profits. What you end up with is the cheapest sweet from the most diluted form of liquid cacao. But at the fine end of the chocolate market, you can't cut corners. It takes me around ten days to go from bean to bar, whereas some confectionery-makers roast quickly on a high heat and perhaps conche too briefly sometimes.

My dream is to make the ultimate confectionery bar – something healthy, tasty and beautiful. I want everyone to experience the poetry of chocolate, everywhere from corner shops to supermarkets. I've always considered myself 'Mr Homemade', making everything from the raw material. Brought up in a remote part of Ireland, my sisters and I even made our own sweets and lemonade when we were kids!

Like everybody, I often find myself at a petrol station wanting a delicious little chocolate snack, only to look despondently through the confectionery displays and go away empty-handed. So when I started making chocolate, I dreamed of creating something like Willie's Walnut Whip (see page 206), which could offer everybody a lovely chocolate morsel. I experimented with a naughty marshmallow base and a beautiful chocolate ganache until it was just how I had imagined it. Then I popped a nut on top and dipped it in the finest chocolate. From there, the possibilities of making wholesome confectionery seemed endless. My mum's (Anna's) Jewel Bites (see page 190) couldn't be a simpler or healthier treat: a 100% cacao mixed with fruits and nuts and cast into a bar; or what about Apples Dipped in Chocolate (see page 191)?

I was always trying to think up healthy sweets for my kids. I wanted to teach them that making food with pure ingredients is always a better option, just as I had learned as a child. I was in the garden with Evie one summer mulling it over when I looked up at the damson tree and had a brainwave. 'Let's make jelly babies out of the damsons!' I said. That's how my Damson, Chocolate and Star Anise Jellies (see page 194) were born.

Filling chocolates was my next step when playing with confectionery. I found some antique moulds on the Internet and felt like an alchemist as I stooped over my little cooking pot, concocting the most beautiful flavours by combining orange-flower water, orange peel and saffron. I knew I'd got it right when I felt a relay of flavours across my tongue. I had the basis for my White Chocolate, Saffron and Orange Blossom-Filled Chocolates (see page 202).

Making sweet chocolate was the natural step for me to take after I had introduced the flavours of real chocolate to the UK market with my 100% cacao bar. It was another challenge. I wanted to continue spreading the word about real chocolate and I had the great fortune of having a television show follow me as I did. Still, my plans didn't make a lot of business sense. I was probably going to have to invest in expensive machinery and work even harder than before.

What is involved in making sweet chocolate? I knew very little about it. Then I started to think about what is involved in outsourcing it. Since a good businessman would investigate both avenues and see which worked best, I had to try to be a good businessman. Yet in my heart, my dream was to make my own chocolate, especially as I knew that England didn't have a really fine bean-to-bar chocolate manufacturer.

I went up to Classic Couverture, chocolate manufacturers in Liverpool, where I met a great bunch of guys. But I soon realized that it would be too expensive to have them make up my cacao liquor into chocolate, only to send it off to somebody else to be barred up and then pay for it to be stored. The figures were absurd. I would have had to charge a fortune for my chocolate and I wasn't prepared to do that.

I then visited other chocolate manufacturers to see if anyone could make, bar and store my chocolate for me, but it never seemed viable. Everywhere I went, people said, 'Whatever you do, don't get into manufacturing.' It made me suspicious. Why didn't they want me to make my own chocolate? It could only be because they felt threatened in some way. Perhaps I had something they didn't.

I asked my friend Marco Pierre White for his advice. He pointed out that I already was a manufacturer, so that answered

that. People were warning me off because chocolate is a billion-dollar industry; the large companies keep buying up their competitors in order to control the market. When profit is the bottom line, romanticism gives way to ruthlessness. Chocolate becomes nothing more than business, as I realized when I visited a factory where they were still producing chocolate eggs a few days after Easter. It seemed very peculiar. The Easter season lasts for two or three months at the most, but they make eggs 12 months a year!

I thought about the film *Chocolat*, starring Juliet Binoche: there was romanticism; there was love! The chocolate in that film wasn't coming down enormous tubes in a gigantic factory. It struck me that I had to make my own chocolate, my way. But how? First I needed a conching refiner, which refines and makes the chocolate after I've roasted it. In snatched moments at the factory, between running my round-the-clock, one-man, cacao-making operation, I started looking for kit.

I visited a machine manufacturer in the UK, where they make top-of-the-line conching refiners. As I was shown around the factory, I realized that I was looking at machines that cost more money than I could even imagine spending. Still, what choice did I have? To make sweet chocolate, I needed to go several hundred thousand pounds into debt. It was very daunting.

The UK company drove such a hard bargain that I decided to look elsewhere, to Lloveras in Spain, which makes equally high-end conching refiners. I emailed Jordi Torres at Lloveras and received a response the same day. He sent me brochures and answered my questions promptly, so I flew down to Spain. I was impressed with what I found there. These guys have spent a lot of money developing their machines, making parts that are easy to get and maintain on site. This meant that I could do most everyday repairs myself without the need for expensive engineers. With machines like this, it's the after-service that counts. I definitely felt that they were keen at Lloveras.

But the Lloveras conching refiner, with all the extra bits, was still going to cost nearly 100,000 euros – a killing amount of money! And that wasn't all the kit I needed to make sweet chocolate. Here's how the process works: once I've defined the flavour of my beans by roasting them in a traditional batch-way with my turn-of-the-century roaster, I put them into a conching refiner to refine them into a coarse liquid; then I part-conche the cacao liquor, after which I add sugar and some of the cacao butter. I re-refine the mass until it reaches the required smoothness, then re-conche, adding the last of the cacao butter once the flavour is right.

Next, I pump the liquid chocolate into a holding tank, from where it goes into a tempering machine, which gives the chocolate its shine and snap. Tempering also prevents bloom, which is when the butter and solids separate and the chocolate develops an uneven colour and texture. Then it goes through a depositor, which deposits exactly the right amount of chocolate into each mould. Now it needs to be cooled quickly in a cooling tunnel, which shrinks it and allows it to come out of its mould easily. Finally, it is wrapped.

I had machines for roasting, grinding, refining and conching, and a small tempering machine to make my cacao **cylinders**, but now I needed a conching refiner, a pump, a holding tank, a depositor and a cooling tunnel. Buying all those machines, including a packing machine to wrap the bars of chocolate, would be very expensive. But I had to do it. I started to have suicidal thoughts. I was going to spend any money I'd made from my cacao bars and the taxman's money as well!

At one point, I came across a secondhand Macintyre conching refiner and made enquiries. But as soon as I said that it was for use in the UK, I was told that it was only for an overseas sale. When I asked why, it became apparent the seller didn't wish someone else to make chocolate in this country. It was more evidence of the protectiveness of the chocolate industry.

What kept me going was knowing that I had something unique in the industry – I created my own chocolate and flavours from different beans. This was something that nobody else had done, so I believed that there was enormous potential for my business. In my mind was that great expression 'good dogs come from behind'. I first heard it from Marco, and always thought that I wanted to be one of those dogs!

Thankfully, my path crossed with that of another chocolate romantic just at the right time. This was Arthur Westbrook, who invented the 'one-shot', a way of depositing the outer shell and the filling of a chocolate at the same time; he sold the patent and now his invention is used all around the world. I heard that Arthur was having a sale up in York. Van Meer, his chocolate factory, was closing down and he was retiring. The sale had been running for a year and most of the machines had gone, but I went anyway.

I was keen to meet Arthur, who is a charming gentleman and very knowledgeable about the chocolate industry. He has the gift of the chocolate gab and a twinkle in his eye. From what I understand, as well as being a chocolate-maker, he was a consultant who flew around the world solving problems for people in the industry.

Van Meer turned out to be a sophisticated version of my factory. The first thing that caught my eye was one of the first machines Arthur had ever made – the Arthur Westbrook Junior, which must have been 30 years old. It was a 'one-shot' – a depositor – and there were bits hanging off it and wires everywhere. That's my kind of machine, I thought. I could see how I could fix it and keep it running, within reason.

I didn't need a 'one-shot', but I was already thinking of the future, something I have gradually learned to do. In business you have to think about where you're going to be in five years' time. The depositor also made chocolate eggs, which meant that I could add cream eggs to my line at a later date. I also bought a tempering machine.

The Arthur Westbrook Junior probably wasn't worth the money he was asking for it, but it was going to get me started. I paid the going rate for the tempering machine, which was an Arthur Westbrook special. He made it himself and it's a pretty good machine. While I was in the factory, I saw two other fantastic machines for wrapping eggs. Racing along in my chocolate dreams, I started thinking about other things I could do. I am a machinery addict! But I needed to remember that I'm not like other chocolate companies, which seem to spread themselves and make a bit of this and a bit of that. I've got something special, so I'm going to stick to making bars for now.

'I saw your TV programme,' Arthur told me. 'At first I thought, "That's mad!" Then I thought, "That guy has found a niche."'

We went into a shed outside to look at a compressor, which produces air to run the depositor. On our way out, Arthur turned around and flashed me his cheeky smile. 'Have you got a cooling tunnel machine?' he asked. I said I didn't. 'Well, you can have this,' he said, pointing to a big old rusting tube.

His daughter looked horrified. 'Dad, you can't just give it away!' she said.

'Of course I can,' he replied, patting the machine. 'This will get him started.' Since he was leaving the chocolate industry and I was just starting out, he knew exactly what I needed.

Back in the factory, he asked, 'Do you want any containers?'

Well, everybody who makes chocolate needs trays. 'Yes, great!' I said. He helped me get so many things going. He even came to the factory a couple of months later to give me advice on how things were running.

As my truck was leaving his factory, laden high with plastic containers, he said, 'You know you like those egg-wrapping machines?'

I winced. 'I've got to be realistic about budgets and what I really need,' I said. But the next minute, I found myself offering him half of what he was asking for them, and he accepted! I think we both realized that one of them would probably end up as spares for the other. Still, there I was with two unexpected egg-wrapping machines. So one day I will be able to wrap those cream eggs...

Arthur gave me some great advice. 'Don't make milk chocolate,' he said. 'It will bring all sorts of problems with it.' There would be tempering problems because of the ratio of cacao butter to the solids, he explained. There would be health

and safety issues in having milk in the factory. 'You're not competing against anybody else at the moment, but if you make milk chocolate, the competition is fierce,' he reminded me. It's true: the mainstream milk chocolate market is enormous. What's more, the premium milk market is worth a lot less than the premium dark market.

I still had a big gamble ahead of me. By now, I had bought the Lloveras conching refiner. I had a tempering machine. I had a pump from Arthur. I had a cooling tunnel. I had a depositor. But I didn't have a holding tank, which is needed to hold the chocolate before it is moulded, and I didn't have a wrapping machine. Still, I went ahead.

I found a company that said it could provide a wrapping machine. I thought the owner was a chocolate romantic, but unfortunately that wasn't the case. The saga went on for four months and when the machine finally arrived, it wasn't working very well; they sent an engineer and it started to rattle even more. It was hilarious. When the engineer pulled the wire and the socket off the wall because he didn't know that it was a three-phase plug, my staff and I all looked at each other in amazement. 'Hang on!' we said. 'Everyone knows that you have three-phase electricity in a factory.' It was time to return the wrapping machine and get my money back.

I realized as I went along that there was no easy route to making my own sweet chocolate. There appeared to be tacit agreements between the big companies; no one could make, bar and wrap my chocolate for me. Everyone was saying, 'Don't be a manufacturer. Don't get involved. It's messy.' It was very fishy.

Then I couldn't get any holding tanks, even though I searched through newspapers and listings for secondhand chocolate dealers, made loads of phone calls and emailed people around the country. Eventually, I saw a couple of tanks in Spain that needed to be refurbished. They were in much worse condition when they arrived than I had imagined they would be, but I had them fixed by a local welding firm.

Hang on, what was I going to do about wrapping my bars? I had no choice but to wrap the chocolate by hand until I found a machine. In the end, I employed six people to wrap 2000 bars a day each; that meant 12,000 bars wrapped every day and 36,000 bars in three days. Since humans are not machines, this wasn't always the most reliable way of getting the bars wrapped. But it had to do for the time being.

Now that the mechanics were in place, it was time to experiment with ingredients, flavours and consistency. I was determined to develop a pure, natural chocolate with the simplest, best ingredients. While other so-called quality chocolate contained fatty substances like milk powder (even in dark chocolate!) and other bulking agents to replace costly cacao butter, mine would contain only cacao, cacao butter and sugar.

It didn't take me long to find Ragus Sugars. (I love the fact that Ragus is 'sugar' spelt backwards.) Ragus supplied me with an array of exciting raw cane sugars from around the world and I spent days testing them out to see which combined best with the flavours of the cacao. Interestingly, the natural flavours of some of the sugars, though very tasty, were just too strong; delicious organic raw Cuban sugar won the day.

Next, I needed to find out the exact moment at which to add the sugar to the cacao and butter. You wouldn't think that it would make a difference to the flavour notes, but it really does. Adding the sugar to the cacao mass early on means that the cacao particles will be fully coated with sugar.

The balance of sugar is hugely important in the making of any confectionery, especially my truffles. Too much sugar and the sweetness will mask the flavour; not enough and it won't complement it fully. This is why dark chocolates are commonly around the 70% point, because this is the perfect balance between the sugar and the cacao mass.

I've whiled away so many evenings making ganaches, experimenting with getting the balance of flavours right. There's something supreme about fat, juicy raisins soaked in rum; lavender in truffles, on the other hand, approaches the flavour notes from a different perspective, adding a garden fragrance to the strong cacao. And then, of course, nuts and chocolate are a dream combination. I love the way my White Chocolate and Hazelnut Truffles (see page 200) have a gentler, softer flavour than my dark chocolate truffles (see pages 198–9).

I found another chocolate romantic to help me develop my sweet chocolate: Stephen Beckett, who wrote *The Science of Chocolate* (Royal Society of Chemistry), encouraged, supported and advised me all the way. Stephen is a brilliant scientist; he worked in the research and development department at Rowntree for several decades and knows everything about the chocolate-making process, from the chemical components of cacao to the way fat crystallizes when chocolate cools.

Stephen told me that he and his colleagues in the R&D department at Rowntree once made a chocolate purely out of cacao shell! About 10% of the cacao bean is shell and that means 10% of the bean is wasted; Stephen wondered whether there was any way to make use of the waste. His shell bar tasted a lot better than expected, but in those days there was a legal limit on how

much shell was allowed in chocolate. That limit has now been scrapped and you can have as much shell in there as you want, but I remember letting some through one day and the results weren't great. Stephen advised against it anyway. Shells can wear the conching refiner because they sometimes contain small mineral deposits, collected when drying, and can reduce the machine's lifespan by as much as 6000 hours.

One of Stephen's friends invented something called an extruder, a machine that produced chocolate in a spaghetti-like form that could be moulded into extraordinary shapes before it set fifteen minutes later. It was featured on *Tomorrow's World*. How I would love to get my hands on an extruder! Think of what I could do!

Four times a year, Stephen gathers a group of chocolate experts in York 'to put the world of chocolate to rights'. Stephen and his gang have seen a lot of changes in the chocolate industry over the last few decades. According to them, the halcyon days of mass-produced chocolate were the 1960s and 1970s. Since then, there has been a huge amount of cost cutting. One problem is that when cacao goes up in price, the big companies increase the milk content of their confectionery bars and vice versa. Another problem is that every time a change is made, it is only compared with the previous change, rather than with all the changes that have been made since the cuts began. In business, this is known as the salami effect. Ten thin slices equal a large chunk; ten small cuts equal a huge cut.

Stephen is a fount of interesting chocolate information. He can explain to you exactly how the bubbles are put into a bar of Aero and why the size of those bubbles has altered over the last few decades because of the change in viscosity and quality of the chocolate used. While he was at Rowntree, he made a replica sample of the Aero that was made 20 years before and did a taste test on a range of chocolate lovers. To his surprise, he found that people preferred what they were used to over the old-style Aero that they had previously felt nostalgic for.

Hershey's chocolate in America, with its slightly rancid milk base, is a great example of people liking what they know. Hershey's originated in the days before refrigeration: the milk that went into the company's milk chocolate bars was often several days old when it was condensed and combined with cacao. Still, America went wild for Hershey's, and the US market prefers chocolate made with slightly curdled milk to this day. It's a world away from the flavour I was aiming for with my dark chocolate!

I'll never forget the day I finally made sweet chocolate for the first time. It was incredibly frantic! Up to then, I had run all the machines individually, but not together, so it was touch and go whether I would get the production line up and running. Meanwhile, I had supermarket orders to fill and it was the final day of filming for the second series of *Willie's Wonky Chocolate Factory*, a week before the first programme aired. So it was vital that nothing went wrong.

The day before, the TV crew had turned up wanting to shoot me with some pigs as part of the story. 'I'm going to be really honest with you,' I said. 'I don't think I'm going to have time.' I felt like I was on the verge of losing it. 'I've got 11 guys coming to work at the factory tomorrow and my life on the line.'

The following day, the wrapping wasn't working, the tempering wasn't working; the whole thing was just falling apart. I was very worried; it was a really low point because I'm so emotionally involved with my chocolate.

Finally, I decided to get Arthur Westbrook on the phone. 'How much water is going through the tempering machine per minute?' he asked. 'How cold is it? How hot? At what speed is the chocolate pumping?' Thanks to him, we managed to sort out the problems within a couple of hours. The tempering machine began to work and, finally, everything started. At last, I was riding the chocolate wave!

Meanwhile, the TV crew had gone off to shoot the pigs without me, leaving me to pull my hair out. But by the time they came back, I was up and running. There was a lot of jubilation that day. I was crazy like a fox and flying like an eagle – and the chocolate was zinging with flavour.

CONFECTIONERY

ANNA'S JEWEL BITES

One day my mum mentioned in passing how she had been making some great fruit and nut bites using cacao. I didn't think much more about it until I tasted them. They're the best energy snack going – delicious, healthy and full of zing!

Makes about 40

180g 100% cacao, roughly chopped

100g walnuts, hazelnuts or Brazil nuts, roughly chopped

100g sultanas or raisins, or a mixture

100g crystallized ginger, roughly chopped

1 tsp ground cinnamon

2 tsp vanilla essence

1 tbsp honey (optional)

Splash of rum or cognac (optional)

Equipment: Shallow baking tin about 18 x 27cm

Line a shallow baking tin with cling film so that several centimetres hang over the sides of the tin.

Melt the cacao in a large heatproof bowl set over a pan of gently simmering water, making sure that the bottom of the bowl is not touching the water. Remove from the heat.

Stir the nuts, sultanas or raisins and ginger into the melted chocolate until well coated. Add the cinnamon, vanilla essence, honey and rum or cognac, if using, and stir until well combined. Spoon the mixture into the prepared tin and smooth the top. Leave overnight in the fridge.

Gripping the overhanging cling film and lift the set chocolate block out of the tin. Peel off the cling film and chop the block into bite-sized pieces. If stored in a cool place in an airtight container, these keep well for about a month.

APPLES DIPPED IN CHOCOLATE

These are great fun to make with the kids at Halloween. Use the smallest apples you can find. I like using a variety that my mum grows, called the Pitmaston pineapple apple. These are little golden apples with a hint of honeyed pineapple flavour, which goes beautifully with the chocolate.

Per person:

1 apple, preferably with a long stalk

20–30g chocolate (depending on the size of the apple) – use white, milk or a fruity dark chocolate, such as Indonesian Javan Light Breaking 69%

Line a baking tray with baking paper. Wash and dry the apples well.

Temper the chocolate (see page 10).

Holding the apple by the stalk, dip it into the bowl of tempered chocolate to within about 1cm from the top of the apple. Lift out and tap gently against the side of the bowl to remove any excess chocolate. Place the chocolate-dipped apple on the prepared baking tray and leave until the chocolate has set before eating.

STRAWBERRIES DIPPED IN CHOCOLATE

Kids love helping to make these, as well as eating them. They are so simple to prepare, and make great decorations for a cake or dessert too.

Makes 350g

200g large ripe, firm strawberries

150g chocolate, dark, milk or white, or a mixture

Line a large baking tray with baking paper. Wash the strawberries and dry well.

Temper the chocolate (see page 10).

Holding onto the green stalk, dip each strawberry into the bowl of tempered chocolate, until just over halfway up the fruit. Lift out and shake gently to remove any excess chocolate, otherwise it will pool under the strawberry as it sets. Place carefully on the prepared baking tray. Leave until the chocolate has set.

These are best eaten on the day they are made.

CACAO NIB PRALINE

I see this as a sophisticated nut brittle. Back on the hacienda this was my first experiment with roasted nibs. It makes a great snack, but can also be used in the Willie's Cacao Bean Ice Cream (see page 85), Cacao Praline Panna Cotta (see page 288), Marjolaine (see page 278) or the Cacao Nib Praline, Rum and Custard Cake (see page 276).

Makes 200g

100g cacao nibs

100g granulated sugar

Line a baking tray with baking paper.

Heat the cacao nibs and sugar together in a saucepan over a moderate heat, stirring constantly until the sugar has dissolved. Continue cooking until the mixture is a dark nut brown in colour, taking care not to burn it. Tip onto the lined baking tray and spread out thinly, separating the nibs as much as possible. Leave to cool completely.

Once cool, break into large pea-sized pieces. Store in an airtight container. The praline will keep for several months.

CHOCOLATE FUDGE

When I was a child, I used to make fudge with varying results. Usually I would end up with toffee or a sort of caramel. But now, many years later, I have invested in a sugar thermometer and it means making fudge is consistently easy.

Makes 1.3kg

400ml full-fat milk

1kg granulated sugar

Pinch of bicarbonate of soda

1 vanilla pod

120g slightly salted butter

180g Nicaraguan Waslala Superior 100% cacao, roughly chopped

Equipment: Sugar thermometer; 24-cm square shallow baking tin or silicon mould

Lightly grease the baking tin or silicon mould with a little butter.

Place the milk, sugar and bicarbonate of soda in a large saucepan. Split the vanilla pod lengthways and scrape the seeds into the pan. Bring to the boil over a moderate heat, stirring regularly until the sugar has dissolved. Stir in the butter and cacao until melted. Place a sugar thermometer in the mixture and continue cooking, stirring constantly, until the temperature reaches 116°C. Remove from the heat and leave to cool for 5 minutes.

Beat the mixture with a wooden spatula, rubbing off and blending in any that has started to crystallize on the sides of the pan. As soon as the mixture starts to become granular, pour it into the baking tin or silicon mould and smooth over the surface while it is still warm.

Leave for 1–2 hours, or until just set, then cut into bite-sized squares or small slices. The fudge will keep for up to 2 months in a cool dry place if well wrapped or in an airtight container.

DAMSON, CHOCOLATE AND STAR ANISE JELLIES

You could also make these jellies with any type of fruit that you have available, varying the flavouring to match. Try using mangoes with vanilla essence – as we would at El Tesoro – or raspberries with rose essence, or strawberries with orange-flower water.

Makes 30–35

400g damsons

3g whole star anise

220g granulated sugar

100ml liquid glucose

17g pectin

50g Venezuelan Rio Caribe Superior 72% chocolate, roughly chopped

2 tsp lemon juice

FOR THE COATING:

50g granulated sugar

50g caster sugar

Equipment: 16-cm square shallow baking tin

Lightly oil the baking tin and line with baking paper.

Place the damsons and star anise in a saucepan with half the sugar over a moderate heat and bring to the boil, stirring until the sugar dissolves. Lower the heat, cover the pan and simmer very gently for 10 minutes, or until the damsons are soft. Remove from the heat and leave to cool. Push through a sieve into a clean pan.

Stir in the remaining sugar, the glucose and pectin and place over a moderate heat, stirring constantly until the sugar dissolves. Continue to cook, still stirring constantly, until the mixture is thick and comes away from the sides of the pan. Remove from the heat and stir in the chocolate until it is melted and well mixed in, then stir in the lemon juice. Tip into the prepared tin, smooth the surface and leave in a cool place to set.

Mix the sugars for the coating together in a shallow dish. Once set, cut the jellies into little triangles or squares and dip in the sugar mixture to coat lightly. These jellies will keep well for 2–3 weeks if stored in an airtight container.

CHOCOLATE MARSHMALLOWS

Scented with vanilla and dipped in a thin layer of dark chocolate, these marshmallows are a sophisticated version of those pink and white spongy things you might have toasted on the fire as a child. They are also easy and fun to make with the kids.

Makes 40-45

20g leaf gelatine

300g granulated sugar

110g dextrose, plus extra for sprinkling

130ml water

110g golden or corn syrup

1 vanilla pod

FOR THE COATING:

300g Madagascan Sambirano Superior 71% chocolate

Equipment: Sugar thermometer; electric beater

Place the gelatine in a shallow dish. Cover with cold water and leave to soak for 10 minutes. Line a large baking tray with baking paper.

Put the sugar, dextrose and water in a saucepan over a moderate heat and bring to the boil, stirring constantly, until the sugar and dextrose have dissolved. Place a sugar thermometer in the mixture and continue cooking until it reaches 127°C. Remove from the heat. Squeeze any excess water out of the soaked gelatine and slide into the pan of hot sugar syrup. The syrup will bubble up, so take great care. Pour into a metal or heatproof jug. Set aside.

Place the golden or corn syrup in a heatproof bowl. Split the vanilla pod lengthways and scrape the seeds into the bowl. Slowly pour in the hot syrup from the jug while whisking with an electric beater, set first at a slow speed until all the ingredients are well combined, then increasing to full speed. Continue beating until the mixture has tripled in volume and is stiff enough to hold its shape on the whisk, but is still soft.

Pour the mixture onto the lined baking tray so that it forms a thick, even layer about 3cm deep. Smooth off the edges and surface, then sprinkle a little dextrose over the top. If the mixture is uneven, cover with a sheet of baking paper and a heavy board. Leave for at least 1 hour, until cold and set. Once set, slice into small rectangles about 3 x 2cm.

Temper the chocolate (see page 10). Using a two-pronged fork or a skewer, pick up and dip each marshmallow piece into the warm chocolate. Shake well to remove any excess chocolate, then return to the lined baking tray. Leave to set for at least 1 hour before eating or storing. The marshmallows will keep for 2–3 months if kept in an airtight container in a cool place.

SEA SALT AND PICKLED LEMON CHOCOLATE CARAMELS

As a child, I remember watching my father sprinkle salt on slices of fresh pineapple before he ate them. It always made me pull a face. Now I understand why he did it – the salt tempers the sweetness of the fruit. Here I have also added pickled lemons to further balance the sweetness and add a sour note, which along with the bitterness of the chocolate gives these caramels an unexpected complexity of flavours.

Makes 100

65g pickled lemons, preferably homemade

500g caster sugar

500g golden or corn syrup

400ml double cream

130g unsalted butter

4 tsp sea salt flakes

300g Madagascan Sambirano Superior 71% chocolate

Equipment: Sugar thermometer; 20-cm square shallow baking tin.

Lightly oil the baking tin and line with baking paper.

Prepare the pickled lemons by removing and discarding the pith and pulp. Rinse well, pat dry and chop into very small pieces.

Place the caster sugar, syrup and cream in a large saucepan over a moderate heat and stir until the sugar has dissolved and the mixture is well blended. Bring to the boil, place a sugar thermometer in the mixture and continue cooking until the temperature reaches 115°C, then add the butter and stir well to combine. Continue cooking until the temperature of the mixture reaches 140°C. Stir in the chopped pickled lemons and cook for just 1 minute more. Remove from the heat, stir in half the salt, then pour into the prepared tin. Leave to cool and set at room temperature. When the caramel has almost set but is still slightly soft, cut into 10 strips widthways and lengthways to make 100 pieces.

Line two large baking trays with baking paper.

Temper the chocolate (see page 10). Using a pair of wooden skewers or a two-pronged fork, dip each caramel piece into the melted chocolate. Shake well to remove any excess chocolate, then place carefully on the lined baking trays.

Before the chocolate has set, sprinkle a flake or two of the remaining sea salt onto each caramel, then leave to set completely. Store in a single layer in an airtight container. The caramels will keep well in the fridge for 2–3 weeks. Remove from the fridge about an hour before eating.

Clockwise: Willie's Walnut Whips, Rum and Raisin Truffles, Sea Salt and Pickled Lemon Chocolate Caramels, and Damson, Chocolate and Star Anise Jellies.

TRUFFLES

When I was searching for new types of cacao, I travelled with my cast-iron pot from hacienda to hacienda, making cacao and then truffles to find the flavour notes I was looking for. Truffles are a fantastic way of sampling the many flavour sensations offered up by the different varieties of cacao.

Makes 40–45

250ml double cream

150g caster sugar

180g 100% cacao, finely grated

Cocoa powder, for dusting

Heat the cream and sugar in a small saucepan over a low heat, stirring constantly, until just below boiling point. Do not let the mixture boil. Stir in the cacao until melted, then remove the pan from the heat. Transfer the mixture to a bowl. Cover and place in the fridge until cold and firm.

Line a baking tray with baking paper or greaseproof paper.

To shape the truffles, scoop up teaspoonfuls of the mixture and quickly roll between your palms to form small balls. Place on the prepared tray, then put in the fridge to firm up. Alternatively, put the truffle mixture into a piping bag fitted with a 2-cm nozzle and pipe out long strips. Chill until firm, then slice the strips into 3-cm lengths and chill again until firm. Lightly dust the chilled truffles with cocoa powder.

For a truly professional finish, you could also coat the shaped truffles in 350g tempered chocolate (see page 10). Leave to set on a paper-lined baking tray, then dust with cocoa powder.

Store the truffles in an airtight container in the fridge until ready to serve. They will keep well for up to 1 week.

LAVENDER TRUFFLES

The lavender gives a wonderful flavour to these truffles, especially when combined with the punchy Rio Caribe chocolate. They make a superb combination. Be careful, however, not to choose a lavender that is too pungent or it might overpower the chocolate.

Makes 35-40

250ml double cream

Pinch of fresh or dried lavender

250g Venezuelan Rio Caribe Superior 72% chocolate, finely chopped

20g unsalted butter, softened

FOR THE COATING:

300g Venezuelan Rio Caribe Superior 72% chocolate

Lavender flowers for garnish (fresh if possible)

Heat the cream with the pinch of lavender in a saucepan over a moderate heat until just beginning to boil. Remove from the heat and leave to infuse for 5 minutes.

Place the chocolate in a heatproof bowl. Strain the hot cream over the chocolate, discarding the lavender flowers left behind in the sieve. Stir until the chocolate has melted and is well combined, then leave the mixture to cool a little.

Meanwhile, beat the butter for a few minutes in a small bowl, then stir into the warm chocolate and cream mixture. Leave the mixture to cool, then chill in the fridge until firm.

Line a baking tray with baking paper or greaseproof paper.

To shape the truffles, scoop up teaspoonfuls of the mixture and quickly roll between your palms to form small balls. Place on the prepared tray, then put in the fridge to firm up. Alternatively, put the truffle mixture into a piping bag fitted with a 2-cm nozzle and pipe out long strips. Chill until firm, then slice the strips into 3-cm lengths and chill again until firm.

Line a large baking tray with baking paper. Temper the chocolate for the coating (see page 10). Using a pair of wooden skewers or a two-pronged fork, dip each truffle in the melted chocolate and place on the prepared tray. Place one lavender flower on top of each truffle before the chocolate sets.

If stored in an airtight container, these truffles will keep in the fridge for up to 2 weeks.

WHITE CHOCOLATE AND HAZELNUT TRUFFLES

Truffles up in seconds! There's no secret to these. They are simply instant confectionery – roasted nuts rolled in melted white chocolate. Hazelnuts go brilliantly with every kind of chocolate.

Makes about 24

225g whole hazelnuts

225g white chocolate, roughly chopped

Icing sugar, to dust

Preheat the oven to 180°C.

Spread the hazelnuts on a baking tray and toast in the hot oven for about 12 minutes, or until just beginning to brown. Remove from the oven and allow to cool a little. Gently rub off and discard the skins, then roughly chop the nuts so that you still have some coarse pieces. Leave to cool completely.

Meanwhile, melt the chocolate in a heatproof bowl set over a pan of gently simmering water, making sure the bottom of the bowl is not in contact with the water. Remove the melted chocolate from the heat and stir in the chopped hazelnuts.

Allow the mixture to cool and firm up a little. While still malleable, roll into small balls using your hands, lightly dusted with icing sugar to prevent the truffles from sticking to them.

To finish, tip the icing sugar into a shallow dish and roll each truffle in it until lightly dusted on all sides. If stored in an airtight container in a cool place, the truffles will keep well for up to 2 weeks.

RUM AND RAISIN TRUFFLES

Having spent many years in South America, I've discovered that it's hard to beat fine rum as a partner to good chocolate. I make these truffles using lovely fat raisins soaked in Venezuelan rum. The raisins absorb the rum and burst in your mouth when you eat them, producing an amazing cacophony of flavours.

Makes 64

100g raisins

1½ tbsp dark rum

170ml double cream

80g caster sugar

180g Rio Caribe Superior 100% cacao, coarsely grated

20g unsalted butter, softened

FOR THE COATING:

160g Venezuelan Rio Caribe Superior 72% chocolate, very coarsely grated

Equipment: 20-cm square shallow baking tin

Soak the raisins in the rum for 48 hours.

Lightly oil or butter the baking tin and line with baking paper.

Heat the cream and sugar in a saucepan over a moderate heat, stirring until the sugar has dissolved. Bring almost to the boil, then remove from the heat and stir in the cacao until it has melted and is well combined. Stir in the raisins with 1½ tbsp of the rum they were soaked in. Add the butter and mix well. Finally, pour the mixture into the prepared tin, smooth the top and chill until firm.

Fill a jug with freshly boiled water. Heat a sharp knife by dipping it into the water, then wipe dry. Use the knife to cut the firm truffle mix into 8 rows widthways and lengthways to make 64 pieces.

Spread the grated chocolate for the coating on a plate. Take each truffle piece and press into the grated chocolate until coated on all sides. If stored in an airtight container in the fridge, the truffles will keep well for up to 2 weeks.

WHITE CHOCOLATE, SAFFRON AND ORANGE BLOSSOM-FILLED CHOCOLATES

These chocolates are exquisite and the filling is a particular favourite of mine. I love saffron and when paired, as here, with the floral notes of orange blossom, it is sublime. Using crème fraîche in the filling helps to cut through the sweetness of the white chocolate.

Makes 30–40

½ tsp saffron threads

100ml crème fraîche

2 tbsp orange blossom honey

5cm piece unwaxed orange peel

180g white chocolate

1 tsp orange flower water

FOR THE COUVERTURE:

500g Indonesian Javan Light Breaking 69% chocolate

Equipment: 30–40 chocolate moulds; piping bag with a 3–5-mm nozzle

Soak the saffron for the filling in a tablespoon of boiling water.

Meanwhile, put the crème fraîche and honey in a saucepan. Add the orange peel and bring to the boil over a moderate heat. Remove and discard the orange peel, then take off the heat and stir in the white chocolate until it has melted. Stir in the soaked saffron and orange flower water. Leave this ganache mixture on one side to cool.

Temper the chocolate for the couverture (see page 10).

Pour a little of the couverture into each chocolate mould, then turn them upside down so that the insides are fully coated and the excess drips out. Wipe off any chocolate from around the edges of the moulds. Chill until set.

Place the cool ganache filling in the piping bag and pipe into the chilled chocolate moulds until they are almost filled to the top. Give the moulds a shake to even the surface of the filling. Chill again, then cover the filling with more of the tempered couverture. While the chocolate topping is still runny, draw a palette knife over to smooth the surface.

Leave the chocolates in a cool place to set, then release them from their moulds. They will keep well stored in an airtight container in the fridge for up to 2 weeks.

WILLIE'S WALNUT WHIP

I remember the first batch I ever made of these. People said, 'Wow, where did you get these from?' The cardamom in the ganache has since become a favourite spice of mine in desserts. Here its fragrance lifts the filling from the exciting to the exotic and balances the sweetness of the marshmallow.

Makes 40–50

300ml double cream

12 cardamoms, lightly crushed

Finely grated zest of 1 lemon

200g Indonesian Javan Light Breaking 69% chocolate, chopped into small pieces

1 tbsp Chocolate Nocino (see page 34), or brandy

½ recipe quantity set marshmallow mixture (see Chocolate Marshmallows, page 195)

40–50 walnut halves

FOR THE COATING:

500g Madagascan Sambirano Superior 71% chocolate

Equipment: 4-cm round pastry cutter; piping bag with 1.5-cm nozzle

Place the cream in a saucepan with the cardamoms over a moderate heat and bring almost to the boil. Remove from heat. Add the lemon zest, cover the pan and leave to infuse for 1 hour.

Place the chopped chocolate in a heatproof bowl. Heat up the cream again to just below boiling point, then strain over the chocolate, stirring until it has melted. Stir in the chocolate Nocino. Set aside in a cool place to firm up for at least 1 hour. The mixture should still be soft enough to pipe easily.

Using the pastry cutter, cut 40–50 rounds of marshmallow and arrange them on a baking tray lined with baking paper. Fill the piping bag with the firmed-up chocolate and cream mixture. Pipe a small mound onto the top of each marshmallow so that it almost reaches the edge. Place a walnut half centrally on the top of each, pressing it lightly into the filling to secure. Leave in the fridge to firm up.

Temper the chocolate for the coating (see page 10).

Skewer two cocktail sticks into either side of each chilled mound of filling and hold these while carefully dipping the lower half of the marshmallow into the bowl of tempered chocolate until well coated. Turn over and dip the upper half of the mounds in the same way until also completely coated. Shake lightly to remove any excess chocolate. Return to the lined baking tray and remove the cocktail sticks. Leave in a cool place to set completely.

These walnut whips will keep in the fridge for up to 2 weeks if stored in a sealed container.

CELEBRATIONS

I love the rhythms of my factory in Devon: the whirrs and growls of the roaster and grinder, the steady flow of chocolate rivers running through the refiner, the regular pulsations of the conching machine and the precision jerks of the depositor. They fill the air with a kind of music that mingles with the heavy, rich scent of cacao as it rises into the atmosphere and circulates the building. From the storeroom, piled high with beans from around the world, to the kitchen, where experimental samples of chocolate cool in the fridge, the factory is my kingdom and it's alive with energy, noise and gorgeous smells. It's where the rainforest meets the supermarket and flavours reign supreme.

Our busiest time is Christmas, when the nation goes mad buying chocolate, and chocolate-makers all over the country do a lot of key business. In the frantic weeks leading up to Christmas Eve, I get to work at seven in the morning and stay until at least nine in the evening. Almost everyone eats chocolate at this time of year, and not just in the UK. For instance, the Italians wolf down millions of panettone cakes dipped in chocolate, the Brazilians suck brigadeiro sweets made of condensed milk and chocolate, and the Maltese guzzle a chocolate and chestnut drink. Other religious festivals are also marked by chocolate-giving. In many Jewish circles, it's traditional to give chocolate coins or *gelt* at Hanukkah, while Muslims and Hindus can buy Eid and Diwali chocolate hampers.

A few of our present-day Christmas traditions are known to date back to ancient times. Holly and ivy decorations, symbols of everlasting life, were probably part of pagan rituals, while Christmas carols were first sung in fourth-century Rome. In the thirteenth century, nativity scenes were popularized by St Francis of Assisi, and Christmas trees caught on in eighteenth-century Germany.

But it was the Victorians who really shaped the traditional Christmas we know in Britain today, and the 1840s were a key decade. It was then that the first commercial Christmas card was produced, Christmas crackers were invented, 'O Come All Ye Faithful' and 'Once in Royal David's City' were written, and Charles Dickens published *A Christmas Carol*, which played a major role in portraying Christmas as a time of family gatherings and goodwill. This iconic tale also had a big influence on the traditional Christmas dinner. Roast beef and goose had been the usual Christmas fare until then, but after reading about how Scrooge sends a prize turkey to Bob Cratchit's home, suddenly

everybody began eating turkey for Christmas dinner. Within 20 years, it was a Christmas essential, according to the renowned cook Mrs Beeton.

In 1848, a drawing of Queen Victoria, Prince Albert and some of their children gathered around a brightly lit, beautifully decorated Christmas tree caught the public imagination, triggering a widespread trend. The idea of Christmas being a time of gifts and giving also became more common, partly because factories and mass production meant that games and toys no longer needed to be expensively handmade. By now, bars of chocolate were being produced at the Fry's factory in Bristol, so it's no surprise that chocolate became the ultimate Christmas treat. Chocolate bars were given as presents, put in stockings and hung from the branches of Christmas trees. It wasn't long before chocolate was as much a festive prerequisite as turkey and plum pudding.

At Christmas, I always think back to my childhood in Ireland and the year we went to stay with our great friends the Luke family at Inglebrook, a house they rented in Skibbereen, west Cork. I'll never forget the winding road along the river that led to this beautiful old house, which was tucked away in the woods, surrounded by pine trees. We spent a fantastic Christmas together. Of all the treats on offer, the best were their Christmas crackers, which were a foot wide and three feet long. They were filled with real presents, not just trinkets, and lots and lots of chocolates. It couldn't have been better for us kids.

The festive season at the Hacienda El Tesoro was a funny time. Spending Christmas in the tropics seemed quite bizarre, almost surreal. Bathing in the river on Christmas Day felt out of place, lovely as it was. One year we had friends staying and we all had a late night on Christmas Eve. While I was having a coffee out the back the following morning, I heard Tania calling, 'Willie, the Christmas lunch is still running around!' I still hadn't killed the turkey, perhaps because I'd grown fond of it, but I couldn't put it off any longer.

I killed it quickly and down it came, but I neglected to tie its legs, and with a few bold movements, it had its vengeance and scratched my stomach. For the next couple of days I was reminded of that moment every time the salt from my sweat stung the wound. Never mind – it was the best turkey ever, with the juiciest meat, because it had grazed on mangoes and avocados throughout the year.

I usually made a Chocolate and Chestnut Terrine (see page 222) for Christmas lunch in Venezuela, using local chestnuts, known as *castañas*, which grow on trees that look nothing like a chestnut tree but have very similar fruit. I used to collect them when I went to eat in my favourite meat restaurant in Valencia, which was run by the Association of Cattle Farmers and offered delicious grilled meat served on slabs of wood. For years there was a live leopard in a cage at the entrance, which had been caught eating cows on one of the cattle farms. It's no longer there, thankfully. I hope they set it free.

The restaurant was on an avenue lined with *castaña* trees, which had football-sized fruit. The shells would break into three segments to reveal between 50 and 60 large nuts, softer and sweeter than French chestnuts, but strongly reminiscent of them. Since Christmas, however hot and steamy, just wouldn't be Christmas without turkey and chestnuts, every time I went to Valencia I would collect carrier bags full of *castañas* to take home to freeze and keep until December.

Every year I used cacao in all kinds of Christmas food. Grating it into the gravy added a wonderful richness and it also made my brandy butter doubly delicious (see page 218). It seemed natural to put cacao into the mince pie filling, and then I got really excited and decided to wrap them in my Chocolate Pastry (see page 135). These dark brown mince pies made the most brilliant presents. We took a batch with us every time we went on Christmas visits. And when I was experimenting with sugar-free recipes, Chocolate Mincemeat (see page 233) suddenly seemed an ideal candidate, with great results.

Easter is the other really busy time for chocolate-makers, especially the ones that produce Easter eggs. In pre-Christian times, the egg was an emblem of spring and the rejuvenation of nature after the long, dark winter. Later the Christians adopted it as a metaphor for the resurrection of Jesus. Along with meat and other dairy products, eggs were traditionally banned during Lent, which was another good reason for their proliferation at Easter.

Painting and decorating eggs in springtime was a popular custom long before the birth of Christ, but the first chocolate Easter eggs didn't appear until the early 1800s, when eggs made from a crude, crunchy cacao paste went on sale in Germany and France. It was a great idea that really took off when chocolate manufacture was revolutionized later in the century. Fry's produced Britain's first chocolate Easter eggs in 1873, followed by Cadbury's in 1875, who filled their smooth dark eggs with sugared almonds. Chocolate eggs decorated with marzipan flowers and chocolate piping came next. By the end of the century, the Cadbury's product list included 19 varieties of Easter egg, each designed with different finishes and contents.

One day I hope to make chocolate eggs, especially as I've now got the machinery to make a complete set of cream eggs, including a wrapping machine. My dream is to make a dark truffle egg with a rich, creamy filling that blows people away. But in the meantime, I'm happy to make my Easter eggs at home by hand with the kids.

A few years ago, I started making Simnel cake, which is the only really traditional Easter cake. It has been around in different versions since medieval times. Originally made for Mothering Sunday by young female servants, who took a cake home to their mums on their day off, it went on to develop a religious symbolism, with 11 marzipan balls on top to represent the 11 good apostles (Judas was excluded). I added cacao to the marzipan because almonds and chocolate are such a great combination. The lightness of the sponge contrasts beautifully with the dark, rich covering of chocolate marzipan.

In the past, people ate a lot of chocolate and other rich foods at Easter as a reaction to strict Lent fasting. However, after the conquest of Mesoamerica and the discovery of cacao, Spanish monks fought a long battle with puritanical clerics and the pope to be allowed to drink chocolate during fasts. Eventually Pope Alexander VII issued an edict stating *'Liquidum non frangit jejunum'* ('Liquids do not break the fast'). But the militant wing of the church rebelled against his decision and the wrangling over whether chocolate was acceptable to the truly devout continued for centuries.

I think I can see it from both points of view. Chocolate is without doubt a nourishing substance and it's also a great appetite suppressant, so I can totally understand why the monks felt that it helped them get through long fasting periods. But perhaps it is kind of cheating to consume gallons of chocolate if your aim is self-denial. Chocolate is, and has always been, a treat, after all. Also, cacao was incredibly expensive until the nineteenth century, so it was a bit like the pope agreeing that they could drink champagne or eat caviar. I bet there were a lot of happy monks the day his ruling was announced!

CHRISTMAS
AND
EASTER

CHOCOLATE CHRISTMAS PUDDING

Most traditional Christmas puddings are too rich and heavy to eat after a big Christmas lunch, so here is a recipe for a lighter version. No butter, suet, sugar or flour is added – only a little olive oil and honey – and it still manages to taste superb. The chocolate combines with and enhances the flavours of the dried fruit beautifully.

Serves 14–16

250g dried unsuplhured apricots

200g pitted prunes

145g whole almonds, roughly chopped

145g ground almonds

1 tsp ground cinnamon

1 tsp ground allspice

1 tsp nutmeg

750ml prune juice

90g Venezuelan Rio Caribe Superior 100% cacao, chopped or grated

300g sultanas

300g raisins

200g apples, peeled, cored and grated

4 tbsp concentrated apple juice

Zest of 3 large oranges, grated

4 large eggs

180ml sherry

50ml brandy

Splash of olive oil

Equipment: 1.8-litre heatproof pudding bowl, or 2 x 900-ml heatproof pudding bowls

Chop the apricots and prunes and place in a large bowl with the chopped and ground almonds, the cinnamon, allspice and nutmeg. Set aside.

Bring the prune juice to the boil in a saucepan over a moderate heat. Lower the heat slightly and simmer until reduced by about two-thirds. Remove from the heat and stir in the cacao until it has melted. Leave to cool for 5–10 minutes.

Stir all the remaining ingredients, except the splash of olive oil, into the prune juice and chocolate mixture, then tip into the bowl of apricots, prunes, nuts and spices. Cover the bowl and leave in a cool place for 1–2 days, stirring occasionally.

Lightly grease the pudding bowl(s). Fill almost to the top with the prepared pudding mixture. Lightly oil the top of the pudding with the olive oil and cover the bowl with a double layer of greaseproof paper. Tie the paper firmly in place with a length of string, allowing enough extra string to form a handle reaching over to the other side of the bowl.

Place the pudding bowl(s) in a large pan. Add enough freshly boiled water to reach about halfway up the sides of the bowl(s). Place over a low heat, cover the pan and leave to simmer gently for 2½–3 hours, topping up with extra boiled water if necessary. The longer you cook the pudding, the darker it will become.

Using the string handle, lift the pudding out of the pan and set aside to cool. When cold, remove the greaseproof paper and replace with a fresh piece tied firmly in place. Store in a cool, dry place for up to 6 months. Reheat to serve by steaming again in a large pan of simmering water for 2 hours.

CHOCOLATE BRANDY BUTTER

If traditional brandy butter isn't rich enough for you, this delectable variation certainly will be. It is the perfect accompaniment to Christmas pudding and mince pies, or can be used as a filling for Chocolate Macaroons (see page 154).

Makes 250g

180g Peruvian San Martin 70% chocolate, roughly chopped

250g unsalted butter, softened

100g icing sugar

5 tbsp brandy

Melt the chocolate in a heatproof bowl set over a pan of gently simmering water, making sure the bottom of the bowl is not in contact with the water. Remove from the heat and leave to cool slightly.

Beat the butter in a large bowl until light and fluffy. Add a tablespoon of icing sugar and beat well to combine. Now beat in a tablespoon of the brandy also until well blended. Continue in this way, beating the icing sugar and brandy alternately into the mixture until both are used up.

Add the slightly cooled chocolate and mix well. Make sure the chocolate is not too hot or it will melt the butter. If uncertain, add a tablespoon first and if it starts to melt the butter, wait until it is a little cooler before adding the rest.

Place in a sealed container and store in the fridge. It will keep well for 2–3 weeks. Remove from the fridge 1–2 hours before serving to allow to soften slightly.

CHOCOLATE LEAVES

Give your cakes and desserts that professional touch by decorating them with a few of these leaves (see page 254). You can use all sorts of leaves to make them, but firm waxy ones are easiest to peel off the chocolate. In fact, bay leaves are an ideal choice.

Makes 20

80g dark chocolate

20 bay leaves

Wipe the leaves over with a clean, damp cloth. Line a baking tray with baking paper.

Temper the chocolate (see page 10). Dip the underside of each leaf into the chocolate, then remove, shaking off any excess and taking care not to get any chocolate on the upper side of the leaf. Place chocolate side up on the lined baking tray. Leave to set in the fridge.

When ready, remove from the fridge and gently peel off the bay leaves. The chocolate leaves will keep for up to 2 weeks if stored in an airtight container in the fridge.

QUINCE CHEESE CHOCOLATES

These are very quick and easy to make if you buy the quince cheese. Homemade quince cheese is of course far superior, but does involve standing for about an hour over a hot stove while the mixture spits back at you!

Makes 12

250g quince cheese

100g Madagascan Sambirano Superior 71% chocolate

Line a baking tray with baking paper.

Cut the quince cheese into 12 rectangles about 3cm long, 2cm wide and 2cm thick.

Temper the chocolate (see page 10).

Skewering each piece of quince cheese on the end of a fork, dip into the chocolate. When well coated, shake lightly to remove any excess drips and, with another fork, push onto the lined baking tray. Allow to cool slightly.

While the chocolate is still soft, run a fork or skewer over the top of each piece to create a ripple effect. Leave in a cool place until completely set. Stored in an airtight container in the fridge, the chocolates will keep well for up to a month.

CHOCOLATE MUSHROOMS

These are magical decorations for a cake. They are fun and light and, when made well, will have all your friends doing double-takes. The best bit is when people circle around them, then start picking them up to see if they are really mushrooms!

Makes about 50

110g Venezuelan Rio Caribe Superior 72% chocolate, roughly chopped

3 large egg whites

Pinch of cream of tartar

165g caster sugar

1 tsp vanilla essence

Cocoa powder, to dust

Equipment: Piping bag with a 2-cm nozzle

Preheat the oven to 130°C. Line two large baking trays with baking paper.

Melt 50g of the chocolate in a heatproof bowl set over a pan of gently simmering water, making sure the bottom of the bowl is not in contact with the water. Set aside to cool slightly.

Whisk the egg whites with the cream of tartar until they form stiff peaks. Gradually whisk in the caster sugar to form a stiff meringue mixture. Add the vanilla essence, then carefully fold in the melted chocolate until just combined. Don't overmix or you will deflate the meringue.

Fill the piping bag with the chocolate meringue mixture. For the mushroom caps, pipe out about 50 round mounds 3–4cm across on one of the lined baking trays. For the stalks, pipe out about 50 x 2-cm lengths on the other lined baking tray. Allow roughly 2cm between each piece of meringue as it will swell slightly during cooking. Use a barely wet finger to smooth over any trails left by the piping bag on top of the meringue pieces. Bake in the preheated oven for about 1½ hours, or until the meringues lift off the paper easily and are dry and crisp. Remove from the oven and leave to cool on the trays.

Melt the remaining 60g of chocolate in a heatproof bowl set over a pan of gently simmering water, making sure the bottom of the bowl is not in contact with the water. Remove from the heat and leave to cool slightly.

Line a clean baking tray with baking paper. Dip the underside of each mushroom cap into the chocolate so that it is evenly coated. Arrange chocolate side up on the prepared tray. Stick a meringue stalk upright in the middle of the wet chocolate on each cap. Leave in a cool place to set.

Just before you use the mushrooms, dust the domed caps very lightly with cocoa powder. They will keep for about 2–3 weeks if stored in an airtight container in a cool place.

CHOCOLATE CHRISTMAS CAKE

The chocolate in this deliciously moist cake subtly enhances the aroma of the fruit and spices. The cake is best made a couple of weeks or even months before it is needed and kept well wrapped in a cool place. You could marzipan and ice the cake in the traditional manner, or simply glaze it lightly with apricot jam and garnish with Chocolate Candied Orange Peel (see page 234).

Makes 1 large cake

300g dried unsulphured apricots, roughly chopped

300g raisins

500g sultanas

250ml full-bodied sherry, such as amontillado

50g plain flour

100g ground almonds

250g light muscovado sugar

250g slightly salted butter, softened

5 eggs

125g Madagascan Sambirano Superior 71% chocolate, roughly chopped

150g undyed glacé cherries, rinsed and dried if very sugary

Grated zest of 3 oranges

Equipment: Deep 22 cm springform cake tin

Place the apricots, raisins and sultanas in a large bowl. Pour over the sherry, cover the bowl and leave for 2 days, stirring the fruit from time to time.

When ready to make the cake, sift the flour into a bowl and stir in the ground almonds. Beat the sugar and butter together in another bowl until light and fluffy. Beat in one of the eggs, followed by a tablespoon of the flour mixture. Continue beating in the eggs and flour mixture in this way until they are all well combined. Set aside.

Preheat the oven to 140°C. Lightly grease the cake tin and line with baking paper.

Melt the chocolate in a heatproof bowl set over a pan of gently simmering water, making sure the bottom of the bowl is not in contact with the water. Stir the melted chocolate into the butter, flour and egg mixture, followed by all the sherry-soaked dried fruit, the cherries and the orange zest. Mix until evenly combined.

Spoon the mixture into the prepared tin. Bake in the hot oven for 2 hours. Turn the oven down to 130°C and bake for a further 1–1½ hours, or until a skewer inserted into the centre of the cake comes out clean. Remove from the oven and leave to cool in the tin. When cold, wrap well in greaseproof paper and store in a cool place in an airtight container until you're ready to decorate it.

CHOCOLATE AND CHESTNUT TERRINE

When Europeans first arrived in South America, they gave trees and fruits that resembled their native ones back home the same names. As a result, the Venezuelan *castaño* was named after the chestnut. It comes in a football-sized fruit, with a case that divides in three and has scores of nuts inside. These nuts are twice the size of European chestnuts, and make a good alternative to them.

Serves 12–14

250g Peruvian San Martin 70% chocolate, roughly chopped

40g unsalted butter

450g unsweetened chestnut purée

100g unrefined icing sugar

2 tbsp cognac

1 tsp vanilla essence

100ml double cream

Equipment: 18 x 10-cm loaf tin

Lightly grease the loaf tin and line with baking paper.

Melt the chocolate with the butter in a heatproof bowl set over a pan of gently simmering water, making sure the bottom of the bowl is not in contact with the water. Set aside.

Beat the chestnut purée, icing sugar, cognac and vanilla essence together in a large bowl until well blended and smooth. Beat in the melted chocolate and butter until well combined. Add the cream and continue beating until evenly mixed through.

Spoon the mixture into the prepared tin and smooth the surface. Place in the fridge to chill for 2–3 hours, or until firmed up.

Turn the terrine out onto a serving plate. Slice thinly and serve topped with whipped cream, a scattering of raisins soaked in cognac or rum, and a spoonful of Bitter Chocolate and Coffee Sauce (see page 124).

ORANGE, ALMOND, GINGER AND BITTER CHOCOLATE CAKE

There is a real festive feel to this cake, and I think it is a good alternative for those who don't like Christmas cake. You could cover it with candied or fresh kumquats to dress it up.

Serves 8–10

200g slightly salted butter, softened

200g caster sugar

250g ground almonds

1 tsp vanilla essence

3 eggs

Grated zest of 3 oranges

Juice of ½ orange

75g medium-ground polenta

½ tsp baking powder

½ tsp cream of tartar

50g candied orange peel, roughly chopped

60g ginger, preserved in syrup, roughly chopped

80g Venezuelan Hacienda Las Trincheras 100% cacao, roughly chopped

FOR THE SYRUP:

Juice of 2 oranges

2½ tbsp ginger syrup (from the preserved ginger)

¼ vanilla pod

Equipment: 28-cm cake tin (preferably with sloping sides)

Preheat the oven to 160°C. Lightly grease the cake tin and line with baking paper.

Beat the butter and sugar together in a large bowl until light and fluffy. Blend in the ground almonds and vanilla essence, then beat in the eggs one at a time. Mix in the orange zest and juice, then fold in the polenta, baking powder and cream of tartar. Finally, mix in most of the candied peel, preserved ginger and cacao, keeping back a little of all three to decorate.

Tip the mixture into the prepared tin, smooth the top and sprinkle over the pieces of reserved candied peel, preserved ginger and cacao. Bake in the preheated oven for 40 minutes, or until a skewer inserted into the centre of the cake comes out clean. Leave the cake to cool in the tin, then turn out onto a serving plate.

Prepare the syrup by placing the orange juice, ginger syrup and vanilla pod in a saucepan over a medium heat. Bring to the boil, lower the heat and cook until reduced to about 65ml liquid. While still hot, brush the syrup all over the cake, using a pastry brush. Allow the syrup glaze to cool completely before serving. This cake will keep well for just over a week if kept in a cool place in an airtight container.

PANETTONE

Homemade panettone is so much nicer than the shop-bought version. If you can't get hold of a panettone tin, wrap a double layer of foil or greaseproof paper around a deep cake tin so that it sits about 12cm higher than the rim and tie firmly in position. This allows the cake to rise above the top of the tin without collapsing and also protects the cake from overcooking.

Makes 1

300g strong white flour

190g unsalted butter, softened

2 large eggs plus 2 yolks

1 tbsp vanilla essence

Finely grated zest of 2 large lemons

75g caster sugar

½ tsp salt

100g sultanas or raisins, soaked in 75ml dark rum for 2 days

90g candied lemon or orange peel, roughly chopped

80g Indonesian Javan Light Breaking 69% chocolate, roughly chopped

FOR THE STARTER:

100g strong white flour

125ml crème fraîche

125ml milk

1 tsp easy-blend yeast

Equipment: 16-cm panettone tin about 9cm high, or 16-cm cake tin, wrapped as described above

First mix the ingredients for the starter together in a bowl. Cover and leave for 2 hours in a warm place. Lightly grease the panettone or cake tin and line with baking paper.

Sift the flour for the dough into a large bowl. Make a well in the centre and tip in the starter mixture, 150g of the butter, the eggs and egg yolks, the vanilla essence, lemon zest, sugar and salt. With your fingertips, mix the ingredients in the well together, gradually incorporating the surrounding flour into the mixture to form a soft dough. Knead the dough on a lightly floured work surface for about 10 minutes, or until smooth and elastic. If it is sticky, knead in a little extra flour. If it is too dry, knead in a little milk.

Place the kneaded dough in a clean bowl, cover loosely with cling film or a clean tea towel and leave in warm place for 2–3 hours, or until it has doubled in volume. Knead again for 2–3 minutes on a lightly floured work surface, return to the bowl, cover again and leave in a warm place for another 1–2 hours, until it has again doubled in size.

Knead the dough once more for 2–3 minutes on a lightly floured work surface, then flatten out slightly.

Drain the sultanas or raisins of any excess liquid and mix with the candied peel and chocolate in a small bowl. Sprinkle this mixture over the flattened dough and knead gently to mix them evenly throughout the dough.

Shape the dough into a ball and place in the prepared tin, carefully tucking the edges down into the sides and gently levelling the top. Cut a cross, about 1.5cm deep and 8cm wide in the top. Leave in a warm place to rise for about 2 hours, or until doubled in volume.

Preheat the oven to 200°C.

When the panettone is sufficiently risen, place the remaining 40g butter in the centre of the cross and bake in the preheated oven for 20 minutes. Turn the oven down to 180°C and continue baking for a further 25–30 minutes, or until a skewer inserted in the centre of the panettone comes out clean. Remove from the oven and leave to cool in the tin on a wire rack for about 5 minutes. Remove from the tin and leave to cool completely on the wire rack.

Wrap well or store in an airtight container. The panettone will keep well for 3–4 days.

STOLLEN

Stollen is a traditional German Christmas treat – a cross between a pastry and a cake. Slightly less sweet than our traditional cake, it can also be made without any sugar and is still very good.

Makes 1

FOR THE FILLING:

75g dried apricots, roughly chopped

100g flaked almonds

75g candied lemon peel, roughly chopped into small chunks

100g Madagascan Sambirano Superior 71% chocolate, roughly chopped into small chunks

50g raisins

100g sultanas

½ tsp garam masala

½ tsp ground cardamom seeds

75ml dark rum

1½ tsp vanilla essence

Finely grated zest of 1 large lemon

FOR THE STARTER:

125ml crème fraiche

100g strong white flour

125ml milk

1 tsp easy-blend yeast

Mix together all the filling ingredient in a large bowl. Leave to stand for at least 3 hours, preferably for 24 hours, stirring occasionally, or until all the liquid is absorbed by the fruit and nuts.

Mix the ingredients for the starter together in a bowl. Cover and leave for 2 hours in a warm place.

When ready to make the stollen, sift the flour for the dough into a large bowl, then stir in the yeast, caster sugar and salt until evenly mixed through. Make a well in the centre and tip in the starter mixture, eggs and butter. With your fingertips, work the starter, eggs and butter together, gradually incorporating the surrounding flour to form a soft dough. Knead the dough on a lightly floured work surface for about 10 minutes, or until smooth and elastic. If it is sticky, knead in a little extra flour. If it is too dry, knead in a little milk.

Place the kneaded dough in a large clean bowl, cover loosely with cling film or a clean tea towel and leave to rise in a warm place for 2–3 hours, or until doubled in volume. Knead again for 2–3 minutes on a lightly floured work surface, return to the bowl, cover again and leave in a warm place for another 2 hours, until it has again doubled in size.

Knead the dough again for 2–3 minutes on a lightly floured work surface. Roll out into a 36 x 20-cm rectangle.

Place the prepared filling mixture in a wide strip down the middle of the rectangle. Fold the sides of the dough over the filling to encase it. Press all the edges firmly together to seal the filling inside. With a heavy rolling pin, roll along the length of the stuffed dough and from side to side to press the fruit and nuts into the dough. Do this carefully, making sure the filling does not break through. Fold the left-hand end of the stuffed dough over to the middle, then fold the right-hand end over to meet it. Press down gently, shaping the dough again, if necessary, to form a neat rectangle.

FOR THE DOUGH:

225g strong white flour

1 tsp easy-blend yeast

50g caster sugar

½ tsp salt

2 large eggs, lightly beaten

125g unsalted butter, softened

FOR BASTING AND FINISHING:

180g unsalted butter, melted

Icing sugar, to dust

Preheat the oven to 170°C. Line a large baking tray with foil, then place a sheet of greaseproof paper on top. Put the shaped stollen on the paper, cover loosely with cling film or a clean tea towel and leave in a warm place to rise for about 2 hours, or until doubled in size.

Lift the sides of the greaseproof and foil to partially cover the stollen and bake for 20 minutes. Lower the temperature to 160°C and bake for a further 20–25 minutes, or until golden brown and a skewer inserted into the centre comes out clean.

Remove from the oven and brush all over several times with about a third of the melted butter, until it has been absorbed. Leave to cool completely, then wrap the greaseproof paper and foil around the stollen and store in a cool place for 24 hours.

The following day, preheat the oven to 160°C, then unwrap the stollen and warm in the oven for 15 minutes. Remove from the oven, brush all over with another third of the melted butter until has been absorbed, rewrap and store in a cool place for another 24 hours. The next day, unwrap and warm the stollen as before, then brush over the remaining melted butter until it is absorbed. Leave to cool completely. When cool, dust very heavily with the icing sugar. Wrap in fresh greaseproof paper and place in an airtight container. Leave to mature for at least a week before eating. The stollen will keep well for up to a month.

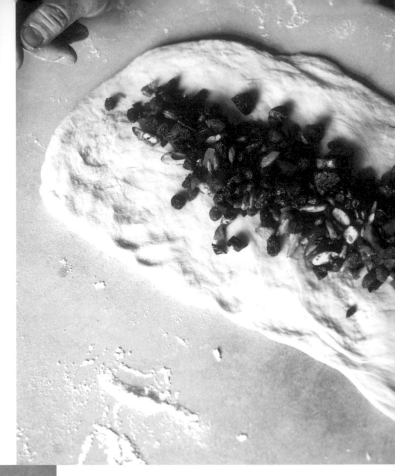

MAKING STOLLEN

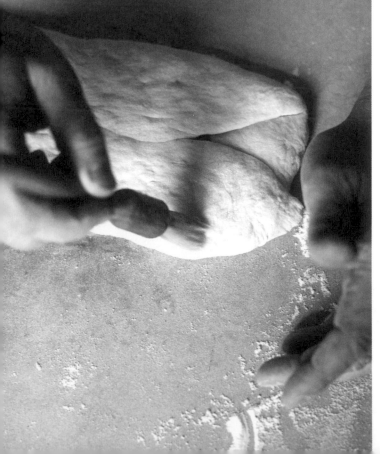
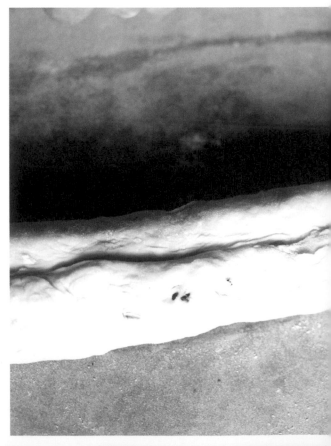

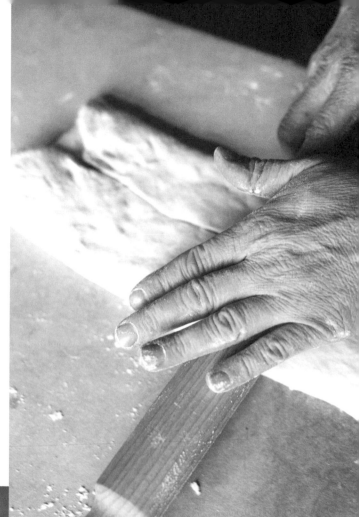

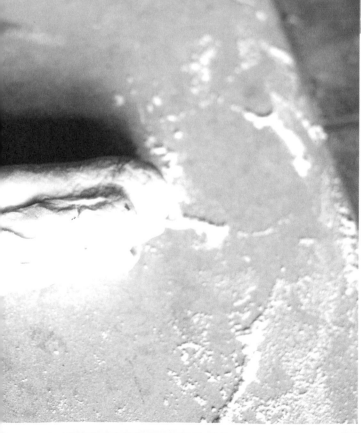

MINCE PIES IN CHOCOLATE AND ORANGE PASTRY

The chocolate and orange flavours combined with sugar-free mincemeat will make these pies real favourites.

Makes 24

30g Venezuelan Hacienda Las Trincheras 72% chocolate, roughly chopped

20g cocoa powder

150g plain flour

125g unsalted butter, chilled and cut into small cubes

25g ground almonds

50g caster sugar

Finely grated zest of 1 large orange

1 large egg yolk, lightly beaten

1 tbsp milk

FOR THE FILLING:

½ recipe quantity Sugar-free Chocolate Mincemeat (see opposite)

Equipment: 2 x 12-hole muffin tins; 7.5-cm and 6.5-cm round pastry cutters

Melt the chocolate in a heatproof bowl set over a pan of gently simmering water, making sure the bottom of the bowl is not in contact with the water. Set aside to cool slightly.

Meanwhile, sift the cocoa powder and flour together into a large mixing bowl. Add the butter and rub in with your fingertips until the mixture resembles fine breadcrumbs. Stir in the ground almonds, sugar and orange zest. Make a well in the centre and place the egg yolk, milk and melted chocolate in it. With a knife, gradually mix the flour into the wet ingredients until well combined and you have a smooth ball of soft, but not sticky, pastry. If it is too wet, add a little more flour. If too dry, add a little more milk. The pastry can also be made in a food processor if you wish.

Wrap the pastry in cling film and leave to chill in the fridge for at least 1 hour.

Lightly grease the muffin tins. Roll out the chilled pastry on a lightly floured work surface to a thickness of about 2mm. Cut out 24 rounds with the 7.5-cm cutter and 24 rounds with the 6.5-cm cutter, re-rolling the pastry if necessary. Carefully press the larger rounds of pastry into the prepared tins so that they fit well into the holes. Fill each pastry case with a heaped teaspoon of the mincemeat.

Using a pastry brush dipped in a little water or milk, dampen around the edge of the smaller pastry rounds and place one on top of each filled pastry case, pressing around the edge to seal. With the point of a sharp knife, pierce or cut a cross in the top, then leave to chill in the fridge for 30 minutes (you can freeze them at this stage for up to a month, then defrost and cook them whenever you wish).

Preheat the oven to 180°C and bake the chilled pies for 10 minutes. Turn down the oven to 170°C and bake for a further 10–12 minutes, until the pastry is crisp and golden. Leave to cool in the tins for 10 minutes. Eat warm or leave to cool completely on a wire rack. The mince pies can also be frozen at this stage, then served after warming through in the oven at 160°C for 10 minutes.

SUGAR-FREE CHOCOLATE MINCEMEAT

My sister Sein gave me this recipe many years ago, and now I would never make my mincemeat any other way. The cacao beautifully complements all the deep, rich flavours of the other ingredients.

Makes 750g

50g 100% cacao, finely grated

3 apples, such as Russets or Coxes, peeled, cored and grated

100g dried apricots, roughly chopped

100g sultanas

100g raisins

100g currants

50ml date syrup

1 tsp each ground cinnamon, grated nutmeg and mixed spice

Zest and juice of 2 lemons or oranges

5 tbsp rum, calvados, or Grand Marnier

5 tbsp cognac

2 tbsp olive oil

Mix the cacao and grated apple in a large bowl. Set aside.

Place the apricots, sultanas, raisins and currants in a food processor and pulse several times to break the fruit up slightly. Add to the cacao and apple in the bowl, along with all the remaining ingredients, and stir until well combined. Place in sterilized jars and seal. Keep in the refrigerator and use within 1 month.

CHOCOLATE CANDIED ORANGE PEEL

Wait until late November or early December, when you see lovely big oranges in the shops, before making this preserved fruit. Once you have made your own peel, you'll never want to go back to using the ready-made variety. Homemade peel keeps well for several months in the fridge and can be used for decorating cakes, biscuits and desserts, as well as for making this fabulous festive snack.

Makes about 250g

6 large unwaxed oranges

1 vanilla pod

4 cloves

150g granulated sugar

FOR THE COATING:

Venezuelan Carenero Superior 100% cacao (for a more bitter peel), or Venezuelan Rio Caribe Superior 72% chocolate (for a sweeter peel) – see method for quantity

Remove a thin slice from the top and bottom of each orange. Cut the fruit into quarters, them remove and set aside most of the pulp, leaving just a small amount attached to the pith.

Bring a large pan of water to the boil. Add the prepared orange quarters and leave to bubble over a medium heat for 5 minutes. Drain into a sieve, then place under cold running water for about 5 minutes. Return to the pan, cover with more boiling water and boil for another 5 minutes. Again drain into a sieve and rinse under cold water for 5 minutes. Repeat the boiling, draining and rinsing once more. This process removes any bitterness from the pith.

Squeeze the juice from the reserved orange pulp into a clean pan. Add the boiled and rinsed orange quarters, the vanilla pod, cloves and sugar. Add just enough cold water to cover, then bring to the boil over a medium heat. Lower the heat, cover the pan and leave to simmer very gently for 1 hour. Remove the pan lid and cook for another 30 minutes. The mixture should be very thick and sticky.

Preheat the oven to 100°C. Place a wire rack on a baking tray lined with baking paper. Tip the candied orange quarters onto the rack, then place in the oven for 1–2 hours to dry out.

Slice the candied orange into strips 5mm thick. Weigh them and for every 250g peel, measure out about 100g of your chosen chocolate. Line a baking tray with baking paper.

Temper the chocolate (see page 10). Skewering the strips of candied orange on a fork, dip them into the chocolate until well coated. Shake off any excess chocolate, then push off the fork onto the lined baking tray and leave in a cool place to set. Store in an airtight container in the fridge for up to a week.

EASTER EGGS

The key pleasure in making your own Easter eggs comes at the moment when you remove them from their moulds and there they are – perfect and beautifully shiny. You can fill them with whatever homemade truffles you wish (see pages 198–201). Take great care when tempering the chocolate. If not done properly, it will not shrink and will stick to the mould.

Makes 2

500–600g chocolate of your choice

Homemade truffles or other sweets, to fill

Equipment: 2 Easter-egg moulds, about 10 x 6cm

Place a wire rack over a large baking tray lined with baking paper.

Temper the chocolate (see page 10). Pour about a quarter of the chocolate into each half of the egg moulds and swirl around until they are evenly coated. Turn each half-mould upside down and place on the wire rack set over the lined baking tray. Leave for 1–2 minutes, then turn over and leave to cool.

If you have a lot of chocolate left over, it probably means that the eggshells are too thin. If so, as soon as the chocolate has set, pour more over the first layer, swirl to spread evenly, then again leave upside-down on the wire rack for 1–2 minutes before turning over and leaving in a cool place until completely set.

If using rigid moulds, gently knock the outside of each one to release the chocolate shell. If using flexible moulds, peel them back to ease out the chocolate.

Fill one half of each chocolate egg with the truffles or sweets of your choice, then place the other half on top and carefully paint a little melted chocolate over the join. Press the half-shells very carefully together to help seal them, then leave until the painted join is completely set. Wrap in cellophane and tie with a ribbon. Store in a cool place for up to 2 weeks.

SIMNEL CAKE

The origins of this traditional Easter cake go back to medieval times. It is a light fruit cake, with a layer of marzipan inside and on top, plus a decoration of 11 balls of marzipan to represent the good apostles – Judas being excluded. The one difference in my recipe is that I have added chocolate to the marzipan. Since Easter and chocolate are inseparable, I thought it a very fitting addition.

Makes 11 slices

125g slightly salted butter, softened

100g light muscovado sugar

2 large eggs

60g self-raising flour

40g ground almonds

200g dried unsulphured apricots, chopped

200g raisins

1 tsp garam masala

1 tsp ground cinnamon

Grated zest of 1 lemon

1 tbsp lemon juice

1 tbsp honey

FOR THE MARZIPAN:

150g Venezuelan Hacienda Las Trincheras 72% chocolate, roughly chopped

100g icing sugar, plus extra for dusting

200g ground almonds

1 egg

½ tsp almond extract

1 tbsp almond oil or melted butter

Equipment: 18-cm springform cake tin

First make the marzipan. Melt the chocolate in a heatproof bowl set over a pan of gently simmering water, making sure the bottom of the bowl is not in contact with the water. Set aside to cool slightly.

Sift the icing sugar into a bowl and mix in the ground almonds. Set aside. Mix together the egg, almond extract and almond oil in another bowl. Stir in the melted chocolate until well blended. Add to the sugar mixture and beat briefly with a wooden spoon. Turn onto a work surface, lightly dusted with icing sugar, and knead to form a smooth paste. Don't overwork or the marzipan will be oily. Put into a clean bowl, cover and set it aside.

Preheat the oven to 160°C. Lightly grease the cake tin, then line with baking paper.

To make the cake, beat the butter and muscovado sugar in a large mixing bowl until light and fluffy. Beat in one of the eggs followed by half the flour. Repeat with the other egg and remaining flour. Stir in the ground almonds, chopped apricots, raisins, garam masala, cinnamon and lemon zest and juice until evenly mixed through. Spoon half of the cake mixture into the prepared tin.

Lightly dust a work surface with icing sugar and roll out one-third of the marzipan into a round just over 14cm in diameter. Place this on top of the cake mixture in the tin. Spoon the remaining cake mix over the top. Level the surface and bake in the preheated oven for 50 minutes, or until a skewer, inserted into the centre, comes out clean. Remove the cake from the oven and leave to cool completely in the tin.

Turn the cool cake out of the tin and place on a cake board. Roll out about two-thirds of the remaining marzipan into a round a little bigger than the cake. Cut to neaten if necessary. Warm the honey in a saucepan over a gentle heat until very runny and liquid. Brush this all over the cake, then place the round of marzipan on top of the cake and press down gently. Roll the remaining marzipan into 11 equal-sized balls, about the size of a small walnut. Arrange in a circle around the top of the cake, pushing them slightly into the marzipan topping so that they don't roll off. If you wish, tie a wide ribbon around the sides of the cake to decorate. Wrap well in greaseproof paper and store in an airtight container.

FOR THE LOVE OF CHOCOLATE

The moment I saw the Hacienda El Tesoro, I knew I wanted to live there. It was such a magical place, a beautiful, natural oasis. The colours and colliding scents of the forest overwhelmed me and I was speechless as I took in the gentle stream beside the house, the ripe fruit on the overladen trees and the view of the lush valley sloping down from the emerald green lawn, which was dotted with nutmeg trees. The landscape seemed enchanted. It took my breath away.

The farm's owner, Fernando Perreira, felt that the time had come to sell, but he was still very emotionally attached to it. He had fallen in love with the farm as a boy and vowed to buy it when he grew up. Later, he and his family had lived there until his children went away to school. I sensed that he was keen to sell it to someone who would love it as much as he did. How could I persuade him that I was that person?

Meanwhile, we had met two Italian architects in Choroní and they had told us about their great friend Franco, who had a holiday house in the village that perhaps we could rent. We soon became friends with Franco and moved into his house. He took us under his wing. When I set up my second meeting with Fernando to discuss buying the farm, I called Franco in the city.

'This is how we'll do it,' he said excitedly. 'I'll bring five kilos of filet steak and you buy two bottles of whisky.'

The following weekend, we found ourselves on the patio of the hacienda at twilight, looking out at the beautiful forested valley. More than anything, I realized, Fernando Perreira wanted to talk about his love and passion for the farm. So that's what we did, over a barbecue, with a glass of whisky in our hands. The evening sealed my future at El Tesoro. At the end of the meal, Fernando said, 'Willie, I'm going to sell the farm to you!' That's a great example of how sharing food encourages friendship and intimacy.

Sharing chocolate goes even further, perhaps. Among the Maya, who saw chocolate as an alternative to alcohol, there was a specific word for drinking chocolate together at special events – *chokola'j*. Aristocrats in eighteenth-century France and Spain held chocolate parties, known as *chocolatadas*, where drinking chocolate was considered every bit as convivial as drinking punch. And today people belong to chocolate societies and hold chocolate-tasting evenings, taking their devotion to the fruit of the *Theobroma cacao* tree to the level of wine connoisseurs. Quite simply, chocolate makes people feel happy. That's why I serve up

a 'choc-shot' at the end of a dinner party in place of an espresso. It's a great way to round off a sociable evening.

Chocolate also has age-old associations with romance. It was drunk at elite Maya marriage ceremonies, like champagne is today, and cacao beans were exchanged between couples at betrothals. I was reminded of this when a woman rushed up to me in a supermarket in Newbury and told me that she had personally made 27 Cloud Forest Cakes for her own wedding. I could really see why. My recipe (see page 264) is a great for all occasions – moist and rich, and covered with a delicious ganache. In truth, cakes are only as good as their ingredients, so it made me very happy to think that someone had chosen to make my cacao into cakes for such an important, romantic day.

The Cloud Forest Chocolate Cake was one of the first recipes I invented using my Hacienda El Tesoro cacao. I've taught all my friends how to make it. My great friend Tom Vogel used to take it to parties in New York, where he claimed women would virtually faint with joy when they tasted it.

I discovered the happiness that chocolate can spread in my late teens, when I began buying it for girls, hoping they would think of me when they ate it. I discovered they liked truffles best, maybe because they are such a great way to taste chocolate.

Is there something within the female genetic coding that makes women more susceptible to cravings for chocolate? And does it trigger a specific kind of feminine sensory reaction? The debate about the pleasure-enhancing effects of chocolate, especially its effects on women, has been going on for centuries.

In the early days of chocolate production, most Mayan and Aztec women missed out on cacao because it was reserved for priests, and the warrior and merchant classes. But things changed with the conquest of Mesoamerica. In his memoirs, the sixteenth-century conquistador Bernal Díaz describes a banquet in Mexico City in 1538, where the ladies drank *cacahuatl* out of golden goblets. By 1590, according to another traveller, Spanish women in the New World had become totally addicted to chocolate. Since the *señoras* had control of their hacienda kitchens, this may partly be why it went on to become so popular among the settlers and their creole descendants.

The Spanish used cacao medicinally for many different ailments, from bruises and cuts to respiratory problems. As time went by, it began to gain credibility as a treatment for 'feminine complaints', and by 1815, women in England were being encouraged in medical pamphlets to mix chocolate with 'iron water' (whatever that was!) when they felt 'out of sorts'.

Modern research into the cravings of the female sex has shown that chocolate increases libido and counteracts mood swings in women. It contains magnesium and iron, so female chocolate cravings might signal a physical need for these nutrients because magnesium levels rise and fall during the menstrual cycle and iron may become depleted. Chocolate also contains phenylethylamine, another chemical that is found naturally in the body; it releases a dopamine in the brain that stimulates physical pleasure. It has been suggested that this is why some women say they prefer chocolate to sex, although this is probably oversimplifying things. After all, men love chocolate too.

Perhaps part of chocolate's appeal is that it contains a molecule called anandamide, which is said to activate cellular receptors and make you feel happy and high. I am the living proof of this theory! Whenever I experience a dip in energy at the factory, I whip up a quick hot chocolate booster, or just grab a bite of unsweetened cacao if I'm pressed for time. Within minutes, I'm buzzing and energized again. My chocolate never fails to uplift me.

I'll always remember the day my local electrician, Chris, came to do some work at the factory. It was obvious by his expression when he arrived that he was feeling low. 'I've had the worst day,' he told me. 'I feel terrible.'

When someone is in a really bad mood, the last thing they want is to be patronized, so instead of saying, 'Oh, you poor thing...' I said, 'I know exactly what you need.'

I happened to have half a Chocolate Torta (see page 252) in the factory kitchen that I'd brought from home, so a few minutes later I placed a piece of cake and a cup of tea on the floor beside him. A little later, as I walked past him feeling slightly guilty that he was having to work when he felt so bad, he stopped me in my tracks and flashed me a huge grin.

'It's incredible!' he said. 'I came in here feeling really bad, but now I can't find the terrible.' It was a great way of describing how the torta had taken him somewhere else. What's more, it's a very fast and easy cake to make.

The theobromine in chocolate is a substance similar to caffeine; it's a stimulant, which is another reason why high-quality chocolate often gives people an energy boost. The rich antioxidant flavonoids it contains could also be a contributing factor. There are twice as many antioxidants in dark chocolate as there are in red wine.

I remember making Chocolate Truffle Cake (see page 253) for a photographic crew at our house, and despite my warnings about eating too much of it, most of them couldn't resist having an extra slice or two before bed. The next day, several people told me that they'd had trouble sleeping; one guy told me that he had been up virtually the whole night.

'I thought you were joking when you warned us off the cake!' he said blearily.

'You'd better have some more for breakfast!' I laughed.

Conversely, chocolate also contains the amino acid tryptophan, which plays a vital role in the production of serotonin, a calming neuro-transmitter that leaves you feeling relaxed and fulfilled. Everyone is familiar with the contented feeling that chocolate can bring. However, tryptophan, along with all the other substances in chocolate, is broken down by the digestive system before it can reach the brain or blood system. How much actually gets through is unknown, so the effects when taken in chocolate may be anecdotal. We're still learning; investigating the 700 different chemical components in chocolate is a huge task. Still, the evidence is mounting that chocolate is good for you in more ways than one.

Could the research as it stands amount to proof that chocolate is an aphrodisiac? It's a claim that has constantly resurfaced throughout the centuries, and it just won't go away. Cacao was revered for its aphrodisiacal properties among the Maya and the Aztecs in ancient times. The conquistador Bernal Díaz describes seeing the Aztec emperor Motecuhzoma consume vast quantities of a cacao drink, which he was told was for success with women.

The Spanish were very taken with the idea of chocolate as a love potion. Although the Church usually allowed it to be drunk by priests and monks during fasting, a number of Inquisition documents reveal a deep suspicion of its alleged power to excite the venereal appetite, citing examples of men who sought out 'knowledgeable women', or witches, to cook up seductive chocolate drinks with which to debauch their targets. Equally, women would mix their blood with chocolate in order to seduce unwilling men.

In the eighteenth century, the notorious Marquis de Sade was implicated in a scandal involving the known aphrodisiac Spanish fly, with which he is alleged to have spiked the chocolate pastilles on offer at one of his balls, provoking a spontaneous, frenzied orgy. The marquis was a huge fan of chocolate. Not only did he consume it in coffee, biscuits, cakes and drinks, but he swore by cacao butter suppositories for his piles! Casanova was another chocolate devotee. He fervently believed it to be an aphrodisiac, often drinking it to enhance his love-making.

I asked my supplier Juan Franceschi where he stood when it came to chocolate's aphrodisiacal reputation. 'I don't know if it's true,' he said with a smile. 'All I know is that cacao gives you a lot of energy and you need energy to make love!' Good point!

I've read that a fifth of all chocolate is consumed between 8 p.m. and midnight. Perhaps this is why After Eights are so successful! At El Tesoro, we used to offer night-time chocolate goodies to guests staying in a particular room at our house because couples who stayed there always seemed to end up fighting! It was hard to know if it worked or not, but people seemed very happy to take chocolate to bed with them. Venezuela is such a hot country that chocolate has an added sensual dimension, because it melts so quickly in the heat, and there's something very hedonistic about melting chocolate.

Traditionally, it was always women who seemed most susceptible to the seductive powers of chocolate and this was seized upon by early marketeers in the UK. When Terry's of York produced chocolate 'conversation lozenges' in the late 1820s, they were daringly stamped with teasers such as, 'Do you flirt?' One wonders what the correct response was: to maintain eye contact while it melted languorously on your tongue, or pop it in, lower your gaze and suck like hell?

Unlike Terry's, Fry's, Rowntree's and Cadbury's were founded and run by staunch Quaker families who went on to play a leading role in the Temperance Movement. So when J.S. Fry & Sons won sole rights to supply chocolate and cacao to the Royal Navy in the mid-nineteenth century, one of their aims was to wean sailors off grog. Again chocolate was being seen as a healthy alternative to alcohol.

But despite their puritanical beliefs, Fry's appealed to their target market by playing on the female fondness for chocolate, a marketing ploy that has endured ever since. Early posters advertising Fry's Milk Chocolate show sailors wooing married women with tempting bars of confectionery. More than a century later, one of the most famous advertising slogans of the 1970s and 1980s was Cadbury's 'All because the lady loves Milk Tray'.

Cadbury's were always miles ahead of their time when it came to marketing their chocolate. In 1868 they produced the world's

first box of chocolates, containing chocolate-coated candied sweets. Soon afterwards, Richard Cadbury cleverly played on the romance of chocolate by creating the first heart-shaped chocolate box for Valentine's Day. What a genius! Hershey's Kisses in the USA and Perugina's Baci (also 'kisses') in Italy were simply an extension of this idea. Love and chocolate remain inextricably linked to this day.

The tradition of giving chocolate to women as a romantic gift soon spread around the world. For many years in Japan, it was only women who ate chocolate, which often had an important role to play in courtship rituals. In fact, Valentine's Day is peak season for chocolate sales there. The Japanese import 40,000 tonnes of cacao every year, and there's a huge demand for quality beans. On my last visit to the Franceschi's hacienda in San José, I watched some of the workers loading a massive lorry with sacks of high-grade criollo that was bound for Tokyo.

I heard a funny story recently about a cacao powder boom in Japan a few years back, which was triggered when the founder of a well-known cacao company reached 100 years of age. Asked about the secret of his longevity, he said, 'I drink a cup of chocolate every day.' When his words were reported, there was an immediate rush on cacao powder in Japan. Suppliers were flying it in on planes to answer demand. Everyone with stores of cacao powder anywhere near Japan made a killing by charging premium prices for it.

Chocolates with 'exotic' fillings are the most recent trend in Japan: the upmarket chocolate shops of Tokyo charge a fortune for chocolates containing foie gras and royal jelly! Gourmet chocolate there is the sole preserve of the rich, just as it was in seventeenth- and eighteenth-century Europe, when it cost three times as much as coffee. In Europe, though, it has long been an affordable luxury that can be enjoyed by everyone.

Sixteen of the top 20 chocolate-consuming countries are European. The Swiss come first, followed by Austria, Ireland, Germany and Norway, and the British aren't far behind. China is an emerging market, although currently only a tiny proportion of Chinese people seem remotely interested in eating chocolate. But we're talking about a country with a population of around 1.3 billion people, so all eyes are on developing chocolate habits in China, where the majority of sweets and desserts are based on rice, fruit and nuts. All they need to do is substitute chocolate for the rice and a world of delicious options will open up to them!

You can be endlessly innovative with cacao and chocolate. My 100% cacao bar in particular seems to inspire people because it's something new. People who enjoy cooking and eating find their own uses for it, and I'm always amazed at how imaginative they are. I answered the phone one day to an elderly lady who told me how every morning when she wakes up, she looks forward to grating my cacao onto her cornflakes. I got off the phone and thought, 'That's such a great story.' I myself love cacao grated on my fried eggs in the morning, with a splash of chilli oil!

It's so lovely how many people have visited the factory and sent me emails about my recipes, and photographs of things they've cooked. It's great to think that I provide the raw material for people to put their passion to work in the kitchen. I feel very lucky to work with chocolate because it's something that everybody loves.

One man sent me a card to say that he sprinkles cacao on his porridge. I wrote back to ask whether he cooks his porridge with salt or sugar, and I'm still waiting to hear. Someone else told me that he mixes cacao into his mashed potato. A friend rang and told me how good it is simply grated on a freshly chopped fruit salad because the cacao complements the fruit of the sugar; she loves it with plain yoghurt too, and her father adds it to his lamb curries and swears by it. The owner of a smart coffee shop in London wrote to tell me that he grates it on the top of his cappuccinos. Marlena, who works in my factory, took it back to Poland with her last Christmas and gave it to all her friends and family. Apparently, they're still raving about it; they ground it up finely and used it in place of cocoa powder in their cakes and puddings.

Cakes don't have the romantic associations of truffles and chocolate, but they are all about sharing. I'm always sending cakes to my friends and family for birthdays and other special occasions. My Chocolate, Hazelnut and Espresso Cake (see page 266) is a big favourite. It's another great recipe born at El Tesoro hacienda when I was looking for a way to combine cacao with the Blue Mountain coffee that grew high up in the cloud forest. The beans of this creole-type coffee had a blueish glow to them and a deep, rich flavour that combined beautifully with my cacao. The white chocolate and mascarpone topping sends the cake rocketing into pure indulgence, a place we all want to go! Speaking of indulgence, I've also made some pretty enormous Black Forest gateaux (see page 274) in my time, using a giant spatula to smooth the ganache and cream over the top before I cover it in huge chocolate flakes.

At the other end of the spectrum, I was always aware of people going for another piece of Cloud Forest Chocolate Cake because it was gluten-free. This spurred me on to experiment with a cake that would tick more than one box for people with food allergies. The result was The Ultimate Flourless, Sugarless Chocolate Cake (see page 271), a way of combining the natural richness and sweetness of date syrup with cacao.

I was also keen to tone down the taste of rich, dark chocolate for the kids, and that's how I came up with Chocolate and Blackberry Lava Cakes (see page 263). These also made good use of the excess blackberry coulis I had in the freezer after autumn gathering sprees. The first time I made the lava cakes, it turned into a bit of a chemistry experiment because I overcooked them slightly, causing the jam to boil over and burst out of the top like a volcano. My kids can't get enough of them, so I cheat sometimes and substitute the blackberry coulis for any good jam that happens to be in the cupboard.

In summer, when a lighter dessert is more appealing, I sometimes give them a creamy Chocolate Roulade (see page 298), if I can keep it away from our dog Bentley for long enough! Bentley is famous for eating my cakes. There was one particularly annoying episode when my sister Sophie and her boyfriend Rory invited us to the beach near their house on the north Devon coast. Before leaving home, I took a couple of rolls of cacao with me, thinking that it would be good to knock up a dessert.

Back at their house after the beach, I made a quick, beautiful Chocolate Roulade and left it on the side for a couple of minutes, only to return to find that Bentley had indulged in one half. Bentley seems to be immune to the effects of theobromine, which are potentially very hazardous to most household animals. I don't know why. Perhaps it's because he's grown up with chocolate all his life! Fortunately, there was just enough left over for the kids after I had neatly chopped off the end, so I wasn't too cross with Bentley, and I used the leftover cacao to make a chocolate sauce for the rest of us to eat with ice cream.

Whenever I think back to the origins of a recipe, particularly if it's a pudding or a cake, my mind fills with images of chocolate splashed on the kitchen table, the kids licking the mixing bowl and people gasping with delight as they taste their first mouthful. It makes me realize how lucky I am to be a chocolate farmer and maker. It makes the long, hard journey of growing, harvesting, importing and processing absolutely worth it. Good chocolate really does spread happiness and love, which is why I'm proud to put my name on it. I might not be the greatest business man alive, but as long as the chocolate is good, I feel good. Viva cacao!

CAKES

CHOCOLATE TORTA

**It's Italian, it's simple and it takes just 15 minutes to prepare.
I like it served with crème fraîche and seasonal soft fruit.**

Serves 8–10

250g Madagascan
Sambirano Superior
71% chocolate, roughly
chopped

120g butter, cut into
small cubes

6 eggs, separated

150g caster sugar

2 tbsp plain flour

Equipment: 30-cm
springform cake tin

Preheat the oven to 140°C. Grease the inside of the cake tin with a little butter, then dust lightly with flour.

Melt the chocolate and butter in a heatproof bowl set over a pan of gently simmering water, making sure the bottom of the bowl is not in contact with the water. Set aside.

Whisk the egg yolks and sugar together until pale and fluffy. Fold in the flour until just mixed through, then stir in the melted chocolate and butter. Set aside.

Whisk the eggs whites in a clean bowl until they form soft peaks. Stir 2 tablespoons of egg white into the chocolate mixture to loosen it, then carefully fold in the remaining egg white until just evenly mixed through. Take care not to overwork.

Tip the mixture into the prepared tin, smooth the top to even out and bake in the preheated oven for 40 minutes. Remove from the oven and leave to cool in the tin on a wire rack. When cold, turn out and cut into slices to serve.

CHOCOLATE TRUFFLE CAKE

A classic truffle cake, you can vary the type of chocolate you use to change the flavour profile. This is a must for any chocolate connoisseur (*see overleaf*).

Serves 8–10

1 recipe quantity
Chocolate Génoise
(see page 270)

70g granulated sugar

70ml water

3 tbsp dark rum

FOR THE TRUFFLE:

2 sheets leaf gelatine

80ml water

45ml liquid glucose

275g Madagascan
Sambirano Superior
71% chocolate, roughly
chopped

500ml double cream

Cocoa powder,
to sprinkle

Equipment: 20-cm
springform cake tin

Preheat the oven to 170°C. Lightly grease the cake tin and line the base and sides with baking paper.

Prepare the chocolate génoise mixture and tip into the prepared tin. Smooth the top and bake in the preheated oven for about 20–25 minutes, or until the edges have shrunk back slightly and the centre is springy to the touch. Leave to cool in the tin for 10 minutes, then turn onto a wire rack and leave until cold. Reline the sides and base of the cake tin with fresh baking paper.

While the génoise is baking, heat the sugar and water in a saucepan over a moderate heat, stirring until the sugar dissolves. Bring to the boil, then remove from the heat and stir in the rum. Set aside.

Slice the cooled chocolate génoise in two horizontally and place one of the halves in the prepared cake tin (you can freeze the other half for up to 3 months for later use). Sprinkle over the rum syrup and set aside.

Soak the gelatine in cold water for 10 minutes. Heat the 80ml water with the glucose in a saucepan until hot but not boiling. Remove from the heat. Drain the gelatine and stir into the hot glucose mixture until dissolved. Set aside.

Melt the chocolate in a heatproof bowl set over a pan of gently simmering water, making sure the bottom of the bowl is not in contact with the water. Remove from the heat, then stir in the warm gelatine syrup until well combined. Set aside to cool.

Lightly whip the cream until just beginning to thicken – it should still be quite sloppy. Gently fold the cream into the cooled chocolate mixture. Spoon over the syrup-soaked layer of génoise in the tin. Smooth over the top to even out. Sift cocoa powder evenly over the top and place in the fridge to set.

When set, remove from the fridge, ease out of the tin and carefully peel the baking paper from the sides and base. Place on a serving plate and keep chilled. About an hour before serving, remove from the fridge and leave in a cool place to soften slightly. Serve on its own or with cream or crème fraîche.

PEACH, CHOCOLATE AND ALMOND GALLETTE

Galettes are one of the oldest forms of cake, dating back centuries. Traditionally, they are flat, round and crusty, and can be sweet or savoury. This moist cake makes a brilliant dessert.

Serves 6–8

100g Madagascan Sambirano Superior 71% chocolate, roughly chopped

20g cocoa powder

130g plain flour

120g light muscovado sugar

180g slightly salted butter

2 small eggs, lightly beaten

90g ground almonds

3 tbsp dark rum

FOR THE FILLING:

40g granulated sugar

50ml water

4 large peaches, ripe but firm

4 tbsp unrefined icing sugar

1 tsp vanilla essence

250g mascarpone cheese

Equipment: 20-cm springform cake tin; piping bag with 2-cm nozzle (optional)

Preheat the oven to 180°C. Lightly grease and line the base and sides of the cake tin with baking paper.

Start preparing the filling by placing the granulated sugar and water in a large saucepan. Bring to the boil over a moderate heat, stirring until the sugar has dissolved. Set aside.

Bring a large pan of water to the boil. Plunge each peach into the boiling water for about 10 seconds, then peel and discard the skin. Cut each peach in half, discard the stone, then add to the sugar syrup. Cover, bring to a simmer and cook for 1–2 minutes. Carefully lift out the peaches and place in a single layer on a large plate or in a shallow dish. Reduce the remaining syrup to about 2–3 tablespoons, pour over the peaches and leave to cool. When cool, slice each peach-half into three. Set aside.

To make the cake, melt the chocolate in a heatproof bowl set over a pan of gently simmering water, making sure the bottom of the bowl is not in contact with the water. Set aside to cool slightly.

Sift the cocoa powder with the flour into a bowl and set aside. Cream the muscovado sugar and butter in another bowl until light and fluffy, then stir in the melted chocolate until evenly combined. Stir in half the beaten eggs, followed by 2–3 tablespoons of the flour and cocoa mixture. Stir in the remaining egg, then blend in the remaining flour mixture, the ground almonds and the rum until evenly mixed.

Finish off the filling by mixing the icing sugar and vanilla essence into the mascarpone until well combined. Gently fold in the peach slices, making sure not to break them up.

Spoon or pipe just over half of the chocolate cake mixture evenly over the bottom of the prepared tin, then spoon or pipe a layer around the sides of the tin. Spoon the mascarpone and peach filling on top of the cake mixture, then spoon or pipe the remainder of the cake mixture over the filling to completely cover it. Bake in the preheated oven for 30 minutes. Remove from the oven and leave to cool completely in the tin before turning out and serving.

BLACK FOREST GATEAU

There have been many interpretations of this magnificent cake. The one given here contains all the usual treats – chocolate, cream, Kirsch and cherries.

Serves 12–14

1½ recipe quantities Chocolate Génoise (see page 270)

FOR THE FILLING:

1 can or jar pitted black cherries in syrup, about 250g drained weight

9 tbsp Kirsch

130g Peruvian San Martin 70% chocolate, roughly chopped

220ml double cream

3 egg yolks

45g caster sugar

40ml water

FOR THE TOPPING:

600ml double cream

100g Madagascan Sambirano Superior 71% chocolate

Equipment: 3 x 24-cm sandwich tins

Preheat the oven to 170°C. Lightly grease the sandwich tins with a little butter, then line them with baking paper.

Make the chocolate génoise mixture and divide between the prepared sandwich tins. Bake in the preheated oven for 13–15 minutes, or until the edges have shrunk back slightly and the cakes feel springy. Remove from the oven, leave to cool in the tins for about 10 minutes, then turn out onto a wire rack and peel off the paper. Set aside to cool completely.

Drain the cherries, reserving about 9 tablespoons of the syrup. Place the drained cherries in a bowl. Stir in a tablespoon of the Kirsch and set aside.

Melt the chocolate in a heatproof bowl set over a pan of gently simmering water, making sure the bottom of the bowl is not in contact with the water. Turn off the heat, but leave the bowl of chocolate over the water to keep warm.

In another bowl, whisk the cream until it is just starting to thicken but is still pourable, then set aside.

In a clean bowl, whisk the egg yolks until thick and creamy, then set aside.

Heat the sugar and water together in a saucepan over a moderate heat, stirring until the sugar has dissolved. Bring to the boil and cook for 1 minute, then remove from the heat.

Carefully pour the hot sugar syrup onto the whisked egg yolks in a slow stream, whisking all the time until evenly blended. Whisk in the warm melted chocolate, followed by the whipped cream and mix until evenly combined. Place in the fridge to firm up slightly.

Mix the remaining 8 tablespoons Kirsch with the 9 tablespoons of reserved syrup from the cherries and sprinkle over the three cooled chocolate génoise sponge cakes. Whip the cream for the topping until thick.

Place one of the sponges on a serving plate or cake board and spread half the chilled chocolate mixture over the top, followed by a third of the whipped cream. Press about half of the Kirsch-soaked cherries into the layer of cream, then place another sponge cake on top. Spread the remaining chilled chocolate mixture over this, followed by another third of the whipped cream. Press the remaining cherries into this layer of cream and top with the third sponge. Spread the remaining whipped cream all over the top and sides of the cake. Set aside in a cool place.

Melt the chocolate for the topping in a heatproof bowl set over a pan of gently simmering water, making sure the bottom of the bowl is not in contact with the water. Pour a thin layer onto a cool flat surface, such as a marble or granite chopping board or a metal baking tray, and leave to set. Once set, hold a knife at right angles to the chocolate and push the blade away from you to make chocolate shavings. Use to decorate the top and sides of the cake. Cover and keep refrigerated until ready to serve. Eat within 2–3 days.

CHOCOLATE, LEMON AND ALMOND CAKE

This cake makes a stunning finale to any dinner party. It involves several stages, but the effort of making it will be well rewarded. Layers of almond cake, rich ganache and tangy lemon cream topped by a sumptuous chocolate glaze mean it certainly won't go unnoticed by your guests.

Serves 10

FOR THE LEMON CREAM:

1 sheet leaf gelatine

4 egg yolks

5 tbsp freshly squeezed lemon juice

Zest of 2 unwaxed lemons, finely grated

60g caster sugar

75g unsalted butter, cut into small pieces

80ml double cream

FOR THE ALMOND CAKE:

6 egg whites

200g caster sugar

200g ground almonds

FOR THE GANACHE:

225ml double cream

240g Madagascan Sambirano Superior 71% chocolate, roughly chopped

First make the lemon cream. Cover the gelatine with cold water and leave to soak. Put the egg yolks, lemon juice and zest, caster sugar and butter in a heatproof bowl set over a pan of gently simmering water, making sure the bottom of the bowl is not in contact with the water. Whisk until the mixture thickens, then remove from the heat. Drain the gelatine, squeeze dry and stir into the lemon mixture until it has dissolved and is evenly mixed. Chill in the fridge for 2 hours. Whip the double cream until it just starts to thicken, then fold into the chilled lemon mixture until well combined. Set aside in a cool place.

Lightly grease the baking tin with butter, then line with baking paper. Preheat the oven to 190°C.

Whisk the egg whites for the cake until they form stiff peaks. Add the sugar and whisk again until stiff. Carefully fold in the ground almonds, taking care not to overwork. Tip the mixture into the prepared tin and spread out evenly. Bake in the preheated oven for 15 minutes, until lightly golden and set. Remove from the oven and leave to cool in the tin for 10 minutes, then turn out onto a wire rack and leave to cool completely.

While the cake is baking, bring 50ml of the cream for the ganache to the boil in a pan over a moderate heat. Remove from the heat and stir in the chocolate until melted and evenly mixed through. Set aside to cool. Whip the cream until thick, then fold into the cooled chocolate and cream mixture. Set aside to firm up slightly before using.

Slice the cooled almond cake in half **horizontally.** Place one half on a plate or board. Spread about a quarter of the ganache evenly over it, then spread all the lemon cream over that, not quite to the edge. Carefully place the other half of almond cake on top, then spread the remaining ganache evenly over the top and sides of the cake. Leave in the fridge to chill for about 2 hours.

FOR THE GLAZE:

180g Madagascan Sambirano Superior 71% chocolate, roughly chopped

90g unsalted butter, cut into small pieces

2 tbsp glucose syrup

1 tbsp cocoa butter

Equipment: 25 x 38-cm baking tin

To prepare the glaze, melt the chocolate in a heatproof bowl set over a pan of gently simmering water, making sure the bottom of the bowl is not in contact with the water. Stir in the butter, glucose syrup and cocoa butter until evenly combined, then remove from the heat and leave to cool slightly.

Stand the chilled cake on a wire rack over a sheet of baking paper to catch any drips. Spoon the chocolate glaze over the cake to cover it. Shake gently to even out the glaze, then leave in a cool place to set completely. Slide the cake carefully onto a serving plate or board and store in the fridge, where it will keep for up to 4 days. Remove from the fridge and leave to stand at room temperature for about 30 minutes before serving.

DEVIL'S FOOD CAKE

With its origins in eighteenth-century America, this cake was sometimes thought to be made of beetroot and cocoa. Here I've made it with paprika to give it that authentic reddish colour and a little bit of extra zing.

Serves 10

150g plain flour

1 tsp baking powder

1 tsp bicarbonate of soda

100g cocoa powder

1 tbsp paprika

180g slightly salted butter

250g caster sugar

1 tbsp vanilla essence

3 large eggs

125ml plain yoghurt

About 250ml warm water

FOR THE GANACHE:

600ml double cream

300g Madagascan Sambirano Superior 71% chocolate, roughly chopped

100g milk chocolate, roughly chopped

1½ tbsp clear honey

Equipment: 2 x 16-cm sandwich tins

First make the ganache. Heat the cream in a saucepan over a low heat until just beginning to boil. Remove from the heat and stir in both chocolates and the honey until completely melted and well blended. Cover and set aside to cool at room temperature while you make the cake.

Preheat the oven to 160°C. Lightly grease the sandwich tins and line with baking paper.

Sift the flour, baking powder and bicarbonate of soda together into a large bowl. Set aside. Sift the cocoa powder into a separate bowl, then stir in the paprika and set aside.

In another bowl, beat the butter until soft. Add the sugar and vanilla essence and beat again until the mixture is light and fluffy. Beat in the cocoa powder mixture, a tablespoon at a time, until evenly mixed through. Finally, beat in the eggs one at a time until well combined.

Stir in the flour mixture in two or three batches, blending well between each addition. Mix in the yoghurt, then gradually add enough warm water to bring the mixture to a soft dropping consistency. Divide evenly between the two prepared tins and bake in the preheated oven for about 30 minutes, or until a skewer inserted in the centre comes out clean.

Remove the cakes from the oven and leave to cool in the tins for about 15 minutes. Turn out onto a wire rack, peel off the baking paper and leave to cool completely.

When the cake layers are completely cold, place one layer upside down on a serving plate or cake board and spread about a third of the ganache over the top. Cover with the other layer of cake, then spread the remaining ganache evenly over the sides and top. Cover the cake and keep in a cool place until ready to serve. Do not place in the fridge or it will become too hard. It will keep well for up to 2 days.

CHOCOLATE AND BLACKBERRY LAVA CAKES

My kids just love these puds, so I always keep a stock of blackberry purée in the freezer. Simply blitz the berries in a food processor, then strain out the seeds by forcing the pulp through a sieve with the back of a spoon. Boil the resulting purée until reduced and really thick. If you don't have any blackberry purée to hand, you can use jam with the seeds seived out instead.

Serves 6

90g Venezuelan Rio Caribe Superior 100% cacao, roughly chopped

75g slightly salted butter

2 large eggs

90g caster sugar

1 tsp vanilla essence

20g ground almonds

1 tbsp Kirsch (optional)

100g blackberry purée, sweetened to taste, or good-quality blackberry jam

Equipment: 6 x 75-ml ramekins

Preheat the oven to 170°C. Butter the insides of the ramekins well and arrange on a baking tray.

Melt the cacao and butter in a heatproof bowl set over a pan of gently simmering water, making sure the bottom of the bowl is not in contact with the water. Remove from the heat. In a clean bowl, whisk together the eggs, caster sugar and vanilla essence until light, thick and creamy. Gently fold in the melted cacao and butter until evenly mixed, then fold in the ground almonds.

Stir the Kirsch, if using, into the blackberry purée. Place 2 teaspoonfuls of the purée in the bottom of each ramekin, then divide the cake mixture between them. Bake in the preheated oven for 10–15 minutes, until the cake mixture is set and the purée is bubbling up around the sides.

Remove from the oven and allow to cool for about 5 minutes. Serve immediately with cream, crème fraîche or ice cream.

VARIATION: If you have a piping bag, trying piping jam into the centre of the cake mixture. Slip a knife around the edge of each cake to release it from the ramekin and invert onto a plate.

CLOUD FOREST CHOCOLATE CAKE

I've taught all my friends how to make this cake. It's the king of cakes and simply sexy, the way to everyone's heart. You can cut out the icing if you wish, and simply serve the cake lightly dusted with icing sugar or cocoa powder.

Serves 12

180g 100% cacao, finely grated

250g unsalted butter

6 eggs

50g light muscovado sugar

125g caster sugar

100g ground almonds

FOR THE ICING:

250ml double cream

75g golden caster sugar

90g cacao, finely grated

Equipment: 25-cm springform cake tin

Preheat the oven to 170°C. Lightly grease the cake tin, then line with baking paper.

Melt the cacao and butter together in a heatproof bowl set over a pan of gently simmering water, making sure the bottom of the bowl is not in contact with the water. Remove from the heat and set aside.

Beat the eggs with the muscovado and caster sugar in a large bowl until pale and doubled in volume. Stir in the melted cacao and butter mixture, then carefully fold in the ground almonds until evenly mixed through.

Tip the mixture into the prepared cake tin and bake in the preheated oven for 35 minutes, or until slightly risen and a skewer inserted into the centre comes out clean. Remove from the oven and leave in the tin on a wire rack to cool.

To prepare the icing, place the cream and sugar in a pan over low heat and bring just to the point of boiling. Remove from the heat and stir in the grated cacao until melted and evenly mixed through. Set aside to cool.

When the cake is completely cold, place on a serving plate or cake board and spread the cooled icing evenly over the top and sides. Keep at room temperature until ready to serve. Don't store in the fridge as the cake and icing can become too hard.

CHOCOLATE BUNDT CAKE

The term 'bundt', first used in the United States around 1900, simply describes a ring-shaped cake baked in a tin of the same name. Some bundt cake tins have straight sides, while others are fluted or ridged, but you can also get them in elaborate styles, shaped perhaps like a flower or a fairytale cottage.

Serves 12–14

225g plain flour

50g cocoa powder

1 tsp baking powder

125ml double cream

200g Venezuelan Rio Caribe Superior 72% chocolate, roughly chopped

125ml natural yoghurt

1 tsp vanilla essence

250g slightly salted butter, softened

200g caster sugar

5 eggs

FOR THE GLAZE:

160ml double cream

160g Indonesian Javan Light Breaking 69% chocolate, roughly chopped

2 tbsp clear honey

Equipment: 22-cm bundt tin, about 8cm deep

Preheat the oven to 160°C. Lightly grease the inside of the bundt tin with a little butter.

Sift the flour, cocoa powder and baking powder together into a large bowl and set aside. Heat the cream in a saucepan over a moderate heat until just boiling. Remove from the heat and stir in the chocolate until melted and evenly mixed through. Stir in the yoghurt and vanilla essence, then set aside to cool to room temperature.

Beat the butter and sugar together in a bowl until light and fluffy. Add the eggs one at a time, beating well between each addition. If the mixture looks like it is starting to curdle, beat in a spoonful of the flour and cocoa mixture.

Carefully fold in half the flour and cocoa mixture, followed by half the cooled chocolate mixture. Add the remaining flour mixture, then the remaining chocolate mixture and stir well.

Spoon the mixture into the greased bundt tin. Smooth over the top, and bake in the preheated oven for 50–60 minutes, or until a skewer inserted into the cake comes out clean. Remove from the oven and leave to cool completely in the tin. When the cake is cool, invert onto a serving plate or cake board.

Prepare the glaze by heating the cream in a saucepan over a moderate heat until just boiling. Remove from the heat and stir in the chocolate until melted and evenly combined. Add the honey and mix until smooth. Allow the glaze to cool slightly, then pour over the top of the cake, letting it dribble down the sides rather than smoothing it over evenly. Leave in a cool place until the glaze has set. Cover and keep at room temperature until ready to serve. To store, keep in an airtight container in the fridge for up to 3 days and bring to room temperature before serving.

CHOCOLATE, HAZELNUT AND ESPRESSO CAKE

There's no doubt that I am obsessed with the quality of chocolate, and I have a similar obsession with coffee too. Biodynamic Brazilian Floresta coffee has to be one of the finest available, and makes all the difference when used in a recipe such as this.

Serves 12–14

200g Venezuelan Hacienda Las Trincheras 72% chocolate, roughly chopped

250g dark muscovado sugar

225g slightly salted butter

2 tsp vanilla essence

2 large eggs

200g hazelnuts, toasted, skinned and coarsely chopped

150g plain flour

1 tsp bicarbonate of soda

180ml hot black coffee

FOR THE TOPPING:

150g white chocolate

150g mascarpone cheese

1½ tbsp cold espresso coffee

4 whole hazelnuts, toasted and skinned, for decoration

Whole coffee beans, for decoration

Equipment: 23 x 13-cm loaf tin, about 7cm deep

Preheat the oven to 170°C. Lightly grease the loaf tin with butter, then line with baking paper.

Melt the chocolate for the cake in a heatproof bowl set over a pan of gently simmering water, making sure the bottom of the bowl is not in contact with the water. Remove from the heat and set aside to cool slightly.

Beat the sugar, butter and vanilla essence together in a bowl until soft and fluffy. Beat in the eggs, one at a time, then stir in the melted chocolate, followed by the chopped hazelnuts.

Sift the flour with the bicarbonate of soda into another bowl. Fold about a third of the flour mixture into the chocolate mixture, followed by about a third of the hot coffee, taking care not to overmix. Repeat until all the flour mixture and coffee have been combined.

Tip the mixture into the prepared loaf tin, smooth the top and bake in the preheated oven for about 50–55 minutes, or until a skewer inserted in the centre comes out clean. Remove from the oven and leave to cool in the tin. When the cake is cold, turn out of the tin, peel off the baking paper and place on a serving plate.

Make the topping by melting the white chocolate in a heatproof bowl set over a pan of gently simmering water, making sure the bottom of the bowl is not in contact with the water. Remove from the heat and stir in the mascarpone and coffee until evenly blended. Spread the mixture over the top of the cake. Using a fork, mark wavy lines through the topping. Finally, decorate with the toasted hazelnuts and a scattering of coffee beans. To store, keep in an airtight container in the fridge for up to 3 days.

CANDIED CITRUS AND PINE NUT RISOTTO CAKE WITH A BITTER CHOCOLATE GLAZE

If you like rice pudding, this lovely moist cake is going to knock your socks off. It has quite a Christmassy feel, so you might want to serve it as a seasonal treat.

Serves 8

200g risotto rice

1 litre full-fat milk

227ml double cream

30g caster sugar

Zest of 2 large unwaxed lemons or oranges, coarsely grated

80g granulated sugar

60ml water

50g pine nuts, lightly toasted

2 eggs, separated

2 tsp vanilla essence

Pinch of salt

3 tbsp Kirsch

FOR THE GLAZE:

150g Venezuelan Hacienda Las Trincheras 72% chocolate, roughly chopped

70g unsalted butter, at room temperature

Equipment: 22-cm ring mould

Preheat the oven to 170°C. Light grease the inside of the ring mould with butter and line with baking paper.

Place the rice, milk, cream and half the caster sugar in a thick-bottomed pan over a moderate heat. Bring just to the boil, then lower the heat and cook gently, stirring occasionally, until the rice is soft but still has some bite to it. Remove the pan from the heat and set aside to cool.

Put the grated citrus zest, granulated sugar and water in a pan over a moderate heat and stir until the sugar has dissolved. Lower the heat and cook very slowly until citrus zest has candied, adding more water if necessary to stop the mixture from drying out and burning. When ready, it should be very thick and sticky. Set aside to cool.

When the candied citrus is cool, add to the cooled rice mixture, along with the toasted pine nuts, egg yolks and vanilla essence and mix until evenly combined. Whisk the egg whites with the remaining 15g caster sugar and the pinch of salt until they form stiff peaks. Gently fold into the rice mixture.

Spoon into the prepared ring mould. Bake in the preheated oven for 40 minutes, or until just set. Remove from the oven, allow to cool slightly, still in the tin, then sprinkle over the Kirsch and leave to cool completely.

When the cake is cool, melt the chocolate and the butter in a heatproof bowl set over a pan of gently simmering water, making sure the bottom of the bowl is not in contact with the water. Remove from the heat and mix until smooth.

Turn the cake out onto a wire rack and spoon the chocolate all over it. Allow the glaze to set completely before serving.

FRESH GINGER CAKE

What grows under the cacao trees at El Tesoro? The answer is ginger. It was brought over by colonists in the sixteenth century and has been quietly growing there, almost forgotten, ever since. Ginger has been given a new lease of life on the farm with this deliciously moist cake. It will crack slightly while cooking, so if you prefer a smoother top, place a tray of hot water in the bottom of the oven.

Serves 10

180g slightly salted butter

50g treacle

160g clear honey

150g dark muscovado sugar

120g Venezuelan Rio Caribe Superior 100% cacao, roughly chopped

120g fresh ginger, peeled and very finely chopped

100ml warm water

2 large eggs

180g plain flour

2 tsp baking powder

2 tsp ground cinnamon

2 tsp garam masala

50g ground almonds

2–3 pieces stem ginger, preserved in syrup

Equipment: 24 x 10-cm loaf tin, about 7cm deep

Preheat the oven to 160°C. Lightly grease the loaf tin with butter, then line with baking paper.

Melt the butter, molasses, honey and sugar together in a saucepan over a low heat, stirring until the sugar has dissolved and the ingredients are well combined. Stir in the cacao until melted and evenly mixed through. Remove from the heat and set aside to cool slightly.

Blend the chopped ginger and warm water to a paste, using either a mortar and pestle or an electric blender. Tip into a mixing bowl and stir in the slightly cooled cacao mixture. Beat in the eggs one at a time until well combined. Set aside.

Sift the flour with the baking powder, cinnamon and garam masala into a clean bowl. Stir in the ground almonds until evenly mixed through. Carefully fold the spiced flour mixture into the chocolate and ginger mixture until well combined. Pour into the prepared loaf tin and smooth the top.

Slice the pieces of preserved stem ginger thinly and sprinkle over the top of the cake. Bake in the centre of the preheated oven for 1 hour, or until a skewer inserted in the centre comes out clean. Remove from the oven and leave to cool completely in the tin before turning out. The cake will keep well for up to 5 days if stored in a cool place in an airtight container.

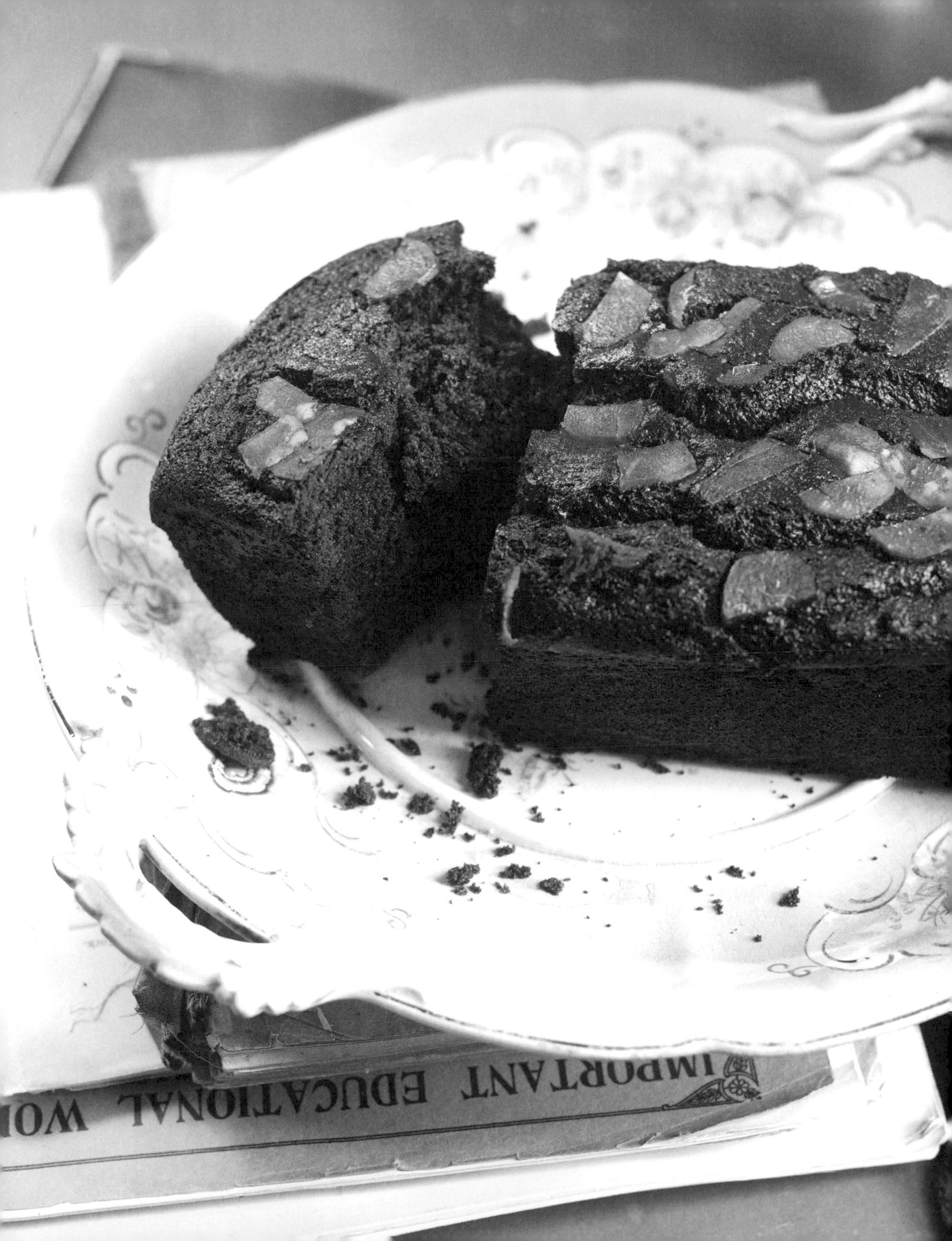
IMPORTANT EDUCATIONAL

CHOCOLATE GÉNOISE

A génoise is a basic sponge cake with the addition of a little butter, which helps it to remain moist for longer. This cake is lovely simply halved and sandwiched together with whipped cream, or it can be used as the base for Chocolate Truffle Cake (see page 253) or Black Forest Gateau (see page 258).

Serves 6–8

60g plain flour

35g cocoa powder

4 large eggs

120g caster sugar

1 tsp vanilla essence

50g unsalted butter, melted and slightly cooled

Equipment: 24-cm springform cake tin

Preheat the oven to 170°C. Lightly grease the cake tin with a little butter, then line with baking paper.

Sift the flour and cocoa powder together twice into a large bowl and set aside.

Warm a mixing bowl in freshly boiled water and dry thoroughly. Place the eggs, sugar and vanilla essence in the mixing bowl and whisk until the mixture is very light and fluffy and has almost tripled in volume.

Using a large metal spoon, carefully fold in half of the sifted flour and cocoa mixture, taking care not to overmix and deflate the egg mixture. Repeat with the remaining flour and cocoa, then very carefully fold in the still-warm butter until the mixture is just evenly combined.

Tip the mixture into the prepared tin and bake in the preheated oven for 20–25 minutes, or until the edges have shrunk away slightly and the top springs back when touched. Remove from the oven and allow to cool for 10 minutes in the tin. Turn out onto a wire rack and leave to cool completely. This cake will keep well in an airtight container in a cool place for 2–3 days, or can be frozen and kept for 2–3 months.

THE ULTIMATE FLOURLESS, SUGARLESS CHOCOLATE CAKE

I was at an event and a gentleman came up to me, gave me his card, and said he was a date farmer from Syria. Later, he kindly sent me some of the finest date syrup I've ever tasted. It was so sweet and nutty. Date syrup is a natural fruit sweetener and a great alternative to sugar, as in this lovely light, moist cake. It is available in most healthfood stores.

Serves 10

180g Venezuelan Rio Caribe Superior 100% cacao, roughly chopped

200g unsalted butter

6 eggs

180ml date syrup

Equipment: 28-cm springform cake tin

Preheat the oven to 150°C. Lightly grease the cake tin with a little butter, then line with baking paper.

Melt the cacao and butter in a heatproof bowl set over a pan of gently simmering water, making sure the bottom of the bowl is not in contact with the water. Remove from the heat, stir to mix well, then set aside to cool slightly.

Place the eggs in a mixing bowl and whisk until very light and fluffy and almost tripled in volume. Using a large metal spoon, carefully fold the date syrup into the beaten eggs until just combined, then fold about a third of the egg mixture into the melted cacao and butter until just combined. Add another third of the egg mixture and again mix until just combined. Repeat with the remaining egg mixture.

Pour the mixture into the prepared tin and place in a baking dish or roasting tin. Pour in enough freshly boiled water to come about halfway up the sides of the cake tin. Bake in the preheated oven for about 25 minutes, or until just set and springy to the touch. Remove from the oven and leave to cool completely in the tin.

This cake is delicious served on its own, or with whipped cream and a little raspberry and Kirsch sauce. It will keep well in an airtight container in a cool place for 2–3 days.

LEMON, ALMOND AND POLENTA CAKE WITH A CHOCOLATE GLAZE

This recipe makes a large cake and is lovely for a birthday or other celebration. It can be made several days in advance and stored in a cool place in an airtight container until ready to serve.

Serves 16

200g slightly salted butter, softened

200g caster sugar

250g ground almonds

1 tsp vanilla essence

3 eggs

Finely grated zest of 3 lemons

Juice of ½ lemon

75g fine or medium-ground polenta

½ tsp baking powder

½ tsp cream of tartar

FOR THE GLAZE:

180g Madagascan Sambirano Superior 71% chocolate, roughly chopped

90g unsalted butter

Equipment: 28-cm cake tin with sloping sides, about 6cm deep

Preheat the oven to 160°C. Lightly grease the cake tin with butter, then line with baking paper.

Beat the butter and sugar together in a large bowl until light and fluffy. Mix in the ground almonds and vanilla essence. Beat in the eggs one at a time, then beat in the lemon zest and juice.

Mix together the polenta, baking powder and cream of tartar in a clean bowl. Fold the polenta mixture into the butter, egg and almond mixture until evenly blended. Tip into the prepared cake tin. Smooth over the top, making a slight indent in the centre. Bake in the preheated oven for about 50 minutes, or until a skewer inserted in the centre comes out clean. Remove from the oven and allow to cool completely in the tin before turning onto a serving plate or cake board.

To prepare the glaze, melt the chocolate in a heatproof bowl set over a pan of gently simmering water, making sure that the bottom of the bowl is not in contact with the water. Stir in the butter until melted and the mixture is smooth and glossy. Using a flat spatula, spread the glaze evenly over the top and sides of the cake. Leave in a cool place for the glaze to set completely before serving.

CHOCOLATE CUPCAKES

Also known as fairy cakes, these are great for tea or birthday parties and are always fun to make with the kids. They will keep well for several days – just not in my house!

Makes 12

75g Venezuelan Rio Caribe Superior 100% cacao, roughly chopped

125g slightly salted butter

175g dark muscovado sugar

1 large egg

80g self-raising flour, sifted

100ml hot water

FOR THE ICING:

175ml double cream

150g Madagascan Sambirano Superior 71% chocolate, roughly chopped

50g milk chocolate, roughly chopped

15g icing sugar

1 tsp vanilla essence

Equipment: 12-hole muffin tin (optional); 12 paper cake cases

Preheat the oven to 180°C. Arrange the cake cases in the muffin tin or on a baking tray.

Melt the cacao in a heatproof bowl set over a pan of gently simmering water, making sure the bottom of the bowl is not in contact with the water. Remove from the heat and set aside to cool slightly.

Beat the butter and sugar in a large bowl until light and creamy. Beat in the egg, then the slightly cooled cacao until evenly combined. Fold in half the flour, then stir in half the hot water. Fold in the remaining flour, then stir in enough of the remaining hot water to form a sloppy but not runny mixture.

Divide the mixture between the paper cases and bake in the preheated oven for 15–20 minutes, until risen and springy. Remove from the oven and leave to cool in the tin.

While the cakes are cooling, prepare the icing. Heat the cream in a saucepan over a low heat until almost boiling. Remove from the heat and stir in both types of chocolate until melted. Stir in the icing sugar, followed by the vanilla essence. Set aside to cool slightly.

Spread about a tablespoon of icing on top of each cooled cake. Decorate as you wish.

BAKED CHOCOLATE CHEESECAKE

When summer is on its way, I start thinking of cheesecake, perhaps topped with a little fresh seasonal fruit and maybe some cream. This one, which has fresh cherries baked into it, is best prepared the day before you intend to serve it.

Serves 10

240g Madagascan Sambirano Superior 71% chocolate, roughly chopped

250g mascarpone cheese

400g full-fat cream cheese

4 large egg yolks

100g caster sugar

1 tsp vanilla essence

Pinch of salt

1 tbsp cornflour

20 fresh black cherries, halved and stoned

FOR THE CRUST:

70g Madagascan Sambirano Superior 71% chocolate, roughly chopped

40g coarse oatmeal biscuits

80g ground almonds

30g caster sugar

40g melted butter

Equipment: Deep 18-cm springform cake tin

Preheat the oven to 150°C. Lightly grease the cake tin and line with baking paper.

First make the crust. Melt the chocolate in a heatproof bowl set over a pan of gently simmering water, making sure the bottom of the bowl is not in contact with the water. Set aside.

Place the oatmeal biscuits in a clean plastic bag or wrap in cling film and crush with a rolling pin to form crumbs. Mix the biscuit crumbs with the melted chocolate, ground almonds, caster sugar and melted butter in a large bowl. Tip the mixture into the prepared cake tin and press down evenly with the back of a flexible spatula. Leave to chill in the fridge for 15 minutes, then bake in the preheated oven for 20 minutes. Remove from the oven and leave in the tin on a wire rack to cool. Leave the oven set to 150°C.

While the crust is cooling, prepare the filling. Melt the chocolate in a heatproof bowl set over a pan of gently simmering water, making sure the bottom of the bowl is not in contact with the water. Set aside to cool slightly.

Place the mascarpone and cream cheese in a large bowl and beat until well blended. Beat in the eggs one at a time, followed by the caster sugar, vanilla essence, salt and cornflour until well combined and smooth. Add the slightly cooled chocolate and beat again until evenly mixed through. Pour the mixture over the crust in the tin. Arrange the cherry halves evenly over the top and gently push them just beneath the surface. Place in the hot oven and cook for about 50 minutes, until the filling has set, but is still slightly wobbly in the middle.

Remove the cheesecake from the oven and leave to cool completely in the tin at room temperature. When cold, place in the fridge and leave to chill for at least 5 hours, preferably overnight. To serve, turn out of the tin, cut into slices and serve with cream, crème fraîche or Greek yoghurt.

CACAO NIB PRALINE, RUM AND CUSTARD CAKE

This lavish cake is perfect for a special occasion. Made up of layers of moist sponge soaked in rum syrup and sandwiched together with vanilla custard, it is covered with whipped cream, sprinkled with cacao nib praline and garnished with chocolate leaves. You can prepare most of it several days in advance, adding the final touches about an hour or so before serving.

Serves 10–12

6 eggs, separated

125ml full-fat milk

250g caster sugar

1 tsp vanilla essence

180g plain flour, sifted

FOR THE CUSTARD:

350ml full-fat milk

30g granulated sugar

½ vanilla pod, split

2 tbsp cornflour

5 egg yolks

FOR THE RUM SYRUP:

140g granulated sugar

140ml water

5 tbsp dark rum

FOR THE COATING:

300ml double cream

125g Cacao Nib Praline (see page 192), crushed

1 recipe quantity Chocolate Leaves (see page 219), to decorate

Equipment: 2 x 22-cm shallow cake tins

Preheat the oven to 170°C. Lightly grease the base of the cake tins with a little butter, then line with baking paper.

Make the sponge cake by whisking together the egg yolks and milk in a large bowl until combined. Add the sugar and vanilla essence and whisk the mixture until very light, thick and fluffy.

Carefully fold the sifted flour into the egg mixture until just amalgamated.

In a clean bowl, whisk the egg whites until they form soft peaks, then carefully fold into the egg and flour mixture until just combined. Spoon the mixture into the prepared cake tins, spread out evenly and bake in the preheated oven for 18–20 minutes, or until the cakes spring back when pressed in the middle. Remove from the oven and allow to cool for 5–10 minutes in the tins, before turning out onto a wire rack and leaving to cool completely.

While the cakes are baking, prepare the custard. Place 300ml of the milk and the sugar in a saucepan. Scrape the seeds out of the vanilla pod and add to the pan. Place over a medium heat and bring almost to the boil. Remove from the heat and set aside.

Blend the cornflour with the remaining milk in a small bowl. Place the egg yolks in a large heatproof bowl and beat in the cornflour and milk mixture until well blended. Pour on the hot milk, beating slowly as you add it to mix in evenly. Return the mixture to the pan and cook over a gentle heat, stirring constantly, until it thickens, taking care not to let it boil. Remove from the heat, pour into a bowl and set aside to cool completely. Chill in the fridge for at least an hour before using.

To prepare the rum syrup, place the sugar and water in a saucepan over a moderate heat, stirring until the sugar dissolves. Bring to the boil, then remove from the heat and stir in the rum. Set aside.

To assemble, slice each cake in half horizontally to give four layers of sponge. Place one layer on a cake board or serving plate. Sprinkle over about a quarter of the rum syrup, then spread about a third of the custard over the top. Place a layer of sponge on top and sprinkle another quarter of the rum syrup over that, followed by another third of the custard. Repeat with the remaining sponge layers, sprinkling only rum syrup over the top layer. Cover the cake and leave in the fridge to chill for at least 6 hours.

About 2 hours before serving, whip the cream for coating until just stiff. Using a flat spatula, spread it evenly and smoothly all over the cake. Sprinkle the crushed praline over the top and sides, then decorate with the chocolate leaves. Chill in the fridge until ready to serve. The cake will keep well for up to 5 days in the fridge, but the praline will start to soften.

MARJOLAINE

This cake was invented by the great French chef Fernand Point (1897–1955), who was influential in the development of *nouvelle cuisine* and trained many noted French chefs. I have adapted the cake to suit today's taste by substituting crème fraîche and cacao nib praline for the original buttercream and praline filling.

Serves 10–12

130g whole hazelnuts

130g whole blanched almonds

220g caster sugar

20g plain flour

6 large egg whites

Pinch of cream of tartar

50ml double cream

420ml crème fraîche

2 tbsp Chocolate Nocino (see page 34) or good-quality brandy

150g Cacao Nib Praline (see page 192), coarsely ground

220g Venezuelan Rio Caribe Superior 72% chocolate, roughly chopped

Preheat the oven to 180°C. Line a large baking tray with baking paper, then brush the paper lightly with a little melted butter and dust with a sprinkling of flour.

Spread the hazelnuts and almonds over another baking tray and toast in the hot oven for 10–15 minutes, until lightly golden. Set aside to cool. Lower the oven to 160°C.

Mix the toasted nuts with 100g of the sugar and all the flour, then crush coarsely, using either a pestle and mortar, a blender or food processor. Set aside.

Whisk the egg whites with the cream of tartar until they form stiff peaks. Whisk in the remaining sugar until stiff peaks form again, then carefully fold in the nut mixture. Spread the meringue evenly over the lined baking sheet, almost to the edge, and bake in the preheated oven for about 30 minutes, or until lightly browned. Remove and leave to cool on the baking sheet.

Whisk the cream, 220ml of the crème fraîche and the Nocino together until just stiff. Fold in the ground cacao nib praline and set aside.

Turn the meringue onto a large chopping board and peel off the baking paper. Using a large serrated knife, carefully slice the meringue into 4 lengthways pieces (note that it is easier to slice if you make it a day in advance and leave it to stand). Arrange the meringue pieces on top of each other, then again use a serrated knife to trim them to the same size.

Place one rectangle of meringue on a cake board or serving plate. Spread a third of the praline cream over the top of it, then place a second rectangle of meringue on top of that. Continue sandwiching the meringue layers together with the praline cream, finishing with a layer of meringue. Cover the cake loosely with greaseproof paper or cling film and leave in a cool place for at least an hour to settle.

Melt the chocolate in a heatproof bowl set over a pan of gently simmering water, making sure the bottom of the bowl is not in contact with the water. Remove from the heat and stir in the remaining crème fraîche. Set aside to cool until slightly thickened.

Uncover the cake carefully and spread the chocolate mixture evenly all over it. Leave in a cool place for the chocolate to set, then serve. It looks good decorated with gilded almonds and hazelnuts or a chocolate leaf (see page 219). To store, keep covered in the fridge for up to 3 days.

PUDDINGS AND MERINGUES

BONET

Originally from northern Italy, this pudding is an Italian version of crème caramel flavoured with chocolate, coffee and rum. While it is cooking, the amaretti biscuits rise to the top to form a separate layer, which becomes the base when the pudding is turned out. You'll love it.

Serves 4–6

100g granulated sugar

1 tbsp water

4 large eggs

500ml full-fat milk

40g Venezuelan Hacienda Las Trincheras 100% cacao, finely grated

100g amaretti biscuits, finely crumbled

2 tbsp dark rum or Amaretto liqueur

125ml freshly brewed strong coffee

Equipment: 22 x 11-cm loaf tin

Preheat the oven to 150°C.

Place 70g of the granulated sugar in a heavy-based pan and set over a medium heat. Stir until the sugar has melted, then continue cooking until a dark caramel starts to form. Take off the heat and stir in the water to 'loosen' the caramel. Pour into the loaf tin, tilting and turning it so that the caramel coats the base and goes about halfway up the sides.

Beat the remaining sugar with the eggs until well blended, then set aside. Heat the milk in a saucepan over a moderate heat until just beginning to boil. Take off the heat and stir in the grated cacao. Pour over the egg and sugar mixture and stir until well blended. Add the amaretti biscuits, the rum and coffee, then stir the mixture and pour into the caramel-coated loaf tin.

Stand the filled tin in a baking dish or roasting tin. Pour in enough freshly boiled water to come about a third of the way up the sides of the loaf tin. Bake in the preheated oven for 1 hour, or until set.

Remove from the oven and set aside to cool. Chill for 2–3 hours or overnight in the fridge before serving. To serve, slip a knife very gently around the top edge of the pudding, then turn out onto a deep-sided serving plate.

CHOCOLATE CRÈME BRÛLÉE

Breaking through the dark surface layer of this take on classic crème brûlée is exciting every time. Here, instead of caramel on the top, there is a thin coating of richly flavoured chocolate. In fact, by using Indonesian 69 with its distinctive caramel notes, you can enjoy the best of both worlds.

Serves 4–8

4 egg yolks

30g granulated sugar

500ml double cream

1 vanilla pod, split lengthways

100g Indonesian Javan Light Breaking 69% chocolate, roughly chopped

10g cacao butter (optional; you will achieve a thinner coating of chocolate if used)

Equipment: 4 x 125-ml or 8 x 75-ml ramekins

Mix the egg yolks with the sugar in a large heatproof bowl until well blended, then set aside. Place the cream and vanilla pod in a saucepan over a moderate heat and bring to just below boiling point. Remove from the heat and pour over the egg mixture, whisking continuously. Strain the mixture back into the saucepan, adding the vanilla pod from the sieve. Stir constantly with a wooden spoon over a gentle heat until the mixture thickens enough to coat the back of the spoon.

Remove from the heat and discard the vanilla pod. Divide the mixture between the ramekins. Leave to cool, not in the fridge, until a skin forms on each pot of custard. You can speed up this process by putting the filled ramekins in a 130°C oven for about 5 minutes.

When the custards are ready, melt the chocolate in a heatproof bowl set over a pan of gently simmering water, making sure the bottom of the bowl is not in contact with the water. Stir in the cacao butter, if using, until evenly mixed through.

Pour about a tablespoon of melted chocolate over the top of each 75-ml ramekin, or about 2 tablespoons over each 125-ml ramekin. Tilt the dishes so that chocolate completely covers the custard in them. This gives a smoother finish than spreading the chocolate with a spoon. Leave in a cool place for the chocolate to set before serving.

Don't chill the custards before pouring the chocolate on top or the chocolate will set too quickly and you'll end up with too thick a layer. The chocolate should be as thin as possible or it will be too difficult to break through when eating.

WHITE CHOCOLATE CRÈME BRÛLÉE

If you like white chocolate, you'll fall in love with this. There is only one word to describe it – heavenly! It's a classic crème brûlée with a caramelized topping, only the addition of white chocolate makes the custard even creamier.

Serves 4

3 egg yolks

30g granulated sugar, plus 2 tablespoons extra for sprinkling

125ml full-fat milk

125ml double cream

½ vanilla pod, split lengthways

100g white chocolate, roughly chopped

Equipment: 4 x 125-ml ramekins

Preheat the oven to 140°C.

Mix the egg yolks with the 30g sugar in a large heatproof bowl until well blended, then set aside. Place the milk, cream and vanilla pod in a saucepan over a moderate heat and bring to just below boiling point. Remove from the heat and pour over the egg mixture, whisking continuously. Strain the mixture back into the saucepan, adding the vanilla pod from the sieve. Stir constantly with a wooden spoon over a gentle heat until the mixture thickens enough to coat the back of the spoon.

Remove from the heat and stir in the white chocolate until melted. Remove the vanilla pod and divide the mixture between the ramekins. Bake in the preheated oven for 15 minutes, or until set.

Take out of the oven. Sprinkle a layer of sugar over the top of each baked custard and set aside to cool completely. When cool, place under a hot grill or use a small cook's blowtorch to caramelize the sugar. Chill in the fridge for at least an hour before serving.

CHOCOLATE PANNA COTTA WITH A RASPBERRY COULIS

This is one of the best recipes to reflect the flavour profile of my chocolate. I chose Las Trincheras because its classic chocolate taste goes well with the fruity note of the raspberries. These pussings can be made a day in advance of eating. Just remove from the fridge about 30 minutes before serving.

Serves 8

4 sheets leaf gelatine

500ml full-fat milk

200ml double cream

80g caster sugar

250g Venezuelan Hacienda Las Trincheras 72% chocolate, roughly chopped

FOR THE COULIS:

200g raspberries

Caster sugar, to taste

Kirsch, to taste (optional)

Equipment: 8 x 100-ml dariole moulds or ramekins

Place the gelatine in a shallow dish. Cover with cold water and leave to soak for 10 minutes.

Heat the milk, cream and sugar in a saucepan over a moderate heat, stirring until the sugar dissolves. Bring just to boiling point, then remove from the heat. Stir in the chocolate until melted.

Drain the gelatine and squeeze out any excess water. Stir into the warm chocolate mixture until it has completely dissolved. Divide the mixture between the dariole moulds or ramekins and leave to set in the fridge for at least 2 hours.

Meanwhile, prepare the coulis by pressing the raspberries through a sieve set over a clean bowl. Taste the thin purée in the bowl and add sugar to taste and Kirsch, if using.

To serve, dip each dish of panna cotta briefly into some hot water, then turn out onto a serving plate. Top with a teaspoon or two of the raspberry coulis.

LITTLE CUPS OF CHOCOLATE

These sensual petite desserts are full of delicate flavours (*opposite*). The geranium leaves and orange-blossom water give a fine fragrance to the chocolate. Try them with a garnish of Chocolate Candied Orange Peel (see page 234).

Makes 8

100ml full-fat milk

3 rose geranium leaves

300ml double cream

150g Venezuelan Rio Caribe Superior 72% chocolate, chopped into small pieces

1 tsp orange-blossom water

Equipment: 8 espresso cups or liqueur glasses

Place the milk and geranium leaves in a saucepan over a medium heat. Bring just to boiling point, then remove from the heat. Leave to stand for 10 minute to allow the geranium leaves to infuse.

Discard the geranium leaves, then stir in the cream. Return to the heat and again bring just to boiling point. Turn the heat down low and stir in the chocolate until melted. Remove from the heat and add the orange-blossom water. Leave to cool slightly.

Divide the mixture between the espresso cups or liqueur glasses. Leave in the fridge to set for at least 2 hours.

LITTLE POTS OF WHITE CHOCOLATE, BLUEBERRIES AND CRÈME FRAÎCHE

If you like blueberries with crème fraîche or with white chocolate, eating this dessert will bring you double the pleasure.

Makes 4

125g fresh blueberries

120g white chocolate

340g crème fraîche

Equipment: 4 x 125-ml ramekins

Preheat the oven to 140°C. Place the ramekins on a baking tray and put a quarter of the blueberries into each dish.

Melt the white chocolate in a heatproof bowl set over a pan of gently simmering water, making sure the bottom of the bowl is not in contact with the water. Remove from the heat and stir in the crème fraîche until well combined.

Divide the chocolate and crème fraîche mixture between the ramekins of blueberries. Bake in the preheated oven for 15 minutes. Remove from the oven and set aside to cool. Chill in the fridge for at least 2 hours.

To serve, slip a flat knife around the inside of each ramekin to loosen the chocolate cream and invert onto a serving plate.

CACAO PRALINE PANNA COTTA

Although lovely as it stands, this pudding is extra delicious if served with my Pumpkin, Quince and White Chocolate Sorbet (see page 92) and a dash of my Bitter Chocolate and Coffee Sauce (see page 124).

Serves 4–6

500ml double cream

100ml full-fat milk

60g caster sugar

80g cacao nibs, finely crushed with a rolling pin

4 sheets leaf gelatine

4–6 tsp Cacao Nib Praline (see page 192), finely crushed

Equipment: 4 x 150-ml or 6 x 100-ml dariole moulds or ramekins

Heat the cream, milk, sugar and cacao nibs in a saucepan over a medium heat, stirring until the sugar dissolves. Bring just to boiling point, then remove from heat and leave to stand for about 15 minutes, to allow the nibs to infuse.

Meanwhile, place the gelatine in a shallow dish. Cover with cold water and leave to soak for 10 minutes.

Bring the cream mixture back to the boil, then strain through a sieve, pressing the debris left in the sieve to squeeze out all the flavour (don't worry if a little comes through).

Drain the gelatine and squeeze out any excess water. Add to the hot cream mixture, stirring well until it has completely dissolved. Set the mixture aside to cool slightly.

Divide the warm mixture between the dariole moulds or ramekins and sprinkle a little cacao nib praline over each. Leave to set in the fridge for at least 2 hours.

To serve, briefly dip each dish of panna cotta into some hot water, then turn out onto a serving plate. Sprinkle over some extra crushed cacao nib praline and garnish with a few fresh raspberries if you wish. Alternatively, serve as suggested in the introduction above.

CHOCOLATE CHARLOTTE

This can be made a day or so in advance and kept in the fridge until needed. It is often made in two tiers, but can be made in three if you adjust the ingredients accordingly.

Serves 10–12

300g Madagascan Sambirano Superior 71% chocolate, roughly chopped

120g unsalted butter, softened

4 large eggs, separated

1 tsp vanilla essence

50g caster sugar

FOR THE BOUDOIR BISCUITS:

50g plain flour

50g cocoa powder

3 eggs

100g caster sugar

1 tsp vanilla essence

25g salted butter, melted

FOR THE SYRUP:

50g granulated sugar

50ml water

50ml dark rum

Equipment: 16-cm charlotte mould or deep springform cake tin; piping bag with 1-cm nozzle

Preheat the oven to 170°C. Line a large baking tray with baking paper. Line the charlotte mould or cake tin with baking paper.

First make the biscuits. Sift the flour and cocoa together into a bowl and set aside. In another bowl, whisk the eggs with the sugar and vanilla essence until thick and pale. Fold in the melted butter, followed by the flour and cocoa mixture until evenly combined. Spoon into the piping bag and pipe 8-cm-long fingers onto the prepared baking tray. Bake in the preheated oven for 8–10 minutes, until just firm. Transfer the biscuits to a wire rack and leave to cool completely.

While the biscuits are baking, make the syrup. Place the sugar and water in a saucepan over a low heat and stir until the sugar dissolves. Bring to just below boiling point, then remove from the heat and allow to cool slightly. Stir in the rum. One by one, dip cooled boudoir biscuits into the syrup and arrange them upright around the inside of the charlotte mould or cake tin. Set on one side, along with the remaining biscuits.

Melt the chocolate in a heatproof bowl set over a pan of gently simmering water, making sure the bottom of the bowl is not in contact with the water. Remove from the heat and spread about 4 tablespoons of the chocolate over some baking paper or a flexible plastic plate. Set aside to use later as decoration.

Stir the softened butter into the remaining melted chocolate, then carefully mix in the egg yolks and vanilla essence. Set aside. Whisk the egg whites with the sugar in a clean bowl until they form stiff peaks. Stir a large spoonful of egg white into the chocolate mixture to loosen it, then gently fold in the remainder until evenly combined. Spoon the mixture into the biscuit-lined mould, then cover the top with the reserved biscuits. Cover loosely with greaseproof paper or cling film and leave in the fridge to set for at least 2 hours.

To serve, turn the charlotte onto a plate and peel off any baking paper sticking to the outside. Take the hardened chocolate reserved earlier and break into large shards. Use to decorate the top, along with some flowers or a dusting of cocoa powder.

CHOCOLATE AND WILD STRAWBERRY TRIFLE

Trifle is always best made with a homemade sponge. If you cannot get any wild strawberries, this is still delicious made with other ripe fresh strawberries or with fresh raspberries.

Serves 8–10

4 eggs

100g caster sugar

1 tsp vanilla essence

40g slightly salted butter, melted

100g plain flour, sifted

200g wild strawberries

1 recipe quantity Chocolate Custard (see page 130)

400ml double cream

FOR THE RUM SYRUP:

30g caster sugar

50ml water

50ml dark rum

Equipment: 25-cm springform cake tin

Preheat the oven to 190°C. Lightly grease the cake tin with a little butter, then line with baking paper.

Place the eggs, sugar and vanilla essence together in a mixing bowl and whisk until the mixture is very light and fluffy and has almost tripled in volume.

Using a large metal spoon, carefully fold in the melted butter, followed by the sifted flour, until just evenly combined. Take care not to overmix and deflate the egg mixture.

Spoon the mixture into the prepared cake tin and bake in the preheated oven for 20–25 minutes, or until the edges have shrunk away slightly and the top springs back when touched. Remove from the oven and allow to cool for 10 minutes in the tin. Turn out onto a wire rack and leave to cool completely.

While the cake is baking, make the rum syrup. Place the sugar and water in a saucepan over a low heat, stirring until the sugar dissolves. Bring almost to the boil, then remove from the heat. Allow to cool slightly, then stir in the rum.

To assemble the trifle, slice up the sponge and arrange the pieces on the bottom of a large serving dish. Sprinkle over the rum syrup and allow it to soak into the cake. Top with the strawberries, setting a few aside for decoration. Pour in the custard to cover the fruit. Whip the cream until it is just stiff, then spoon over the custard.

Place the assembled trifle in the fridge to chill for at least 3 hours, preferably overnight. Just before serving, decorate the top with the reserved strawberries.

TARTUFFO

Taught to me by my great friend Marco Pierre White, this is a magnificent dessert that would grace any dinner party, and it's a wonderful way to sample the different flavour notes of the wide variety of dark chocolate now becoming more available. It's also very easy to make and can be prepared the day before serving.

Serves 12

180g Venezuelan Rio Caribe Superior 100% cacao, roughly grated

150g caster sugar

4 tbsp water

300ml double cream

Equipment: 15-cm springform cake tin or small loaf tin

Line the cake or loaf tin with greaseproof paper or cling film.

Melt the cacao by placing it in a heatproof bowl set over a pan of gently simmering water, making sure the bottom of the bowl is not in contact with the water. Set aside to cool slightly.

Meanwhile, place the caster sugar and water in a saucepan over a low heat, stirring until the sugar dissolves. Remove from the heat and set aside to cool slightly.

Beat the cream until it forms soft peaks, then gradually beat into the sugar syrup. Add a tablespoon of the cream mixture to the melted cacao and stir until just combined. Gently fold in the reminder of the cream mixture.

Pour the mixture into the prepared tin. Smooth the top and leave in the fridge until firm. To serve, turn out of the tin onto a serving plate, peel off the greaseproof paper or cling film and slice. Accompany each helping with some seasonal berries.

GOOEY CHOCOLATE PUDDINGS

Here's an all-time classic: a dynamite of a warm, gooey pudding in portions that you don't have to share. It's also easy to make.

Makes 6–8

180g 100% cacao, finely grated

200g unsalted butter

175g caster sugar

6 eggs

2 tsp vanilla essence

40g ground almonds

Equipment: 6 x 125-ml or 8 x 100-ml ramekins

Preheat the oven to 160°C. Grease the inside of the ramekins with a little butter.

Melt the cacao and butter by placing them, along with 60g of the caster sugar, in a large heatproof bowl set over a pan of gently simmering water, making sure the bottom of the bowl is not in contact with the water. Set aside to cool slightly.

Meanwhile, beat the eggs with the remaining caster sugar and the vanilla essence in a large bowl until pale and creamy.

Stir the ground almonds into the melted cacao and butter until evenly combined, then gradually fold this mixture into the eggs.

Divide the mixture between the prepared ramekins and bake in the preheated oven for 12–15 minutes, or until well risen and starting to split on top. Remove from the oven and serve immediately. For an adults-only twist, top each serving with some dried fruit that has been soaked in alcohol, such as apricots in brandy or raisins in rum.

SELF-SAUCING CHOCOLATE PUDDING

I've always loved pouring chocolate sauce on my desserts, so I thought why not try cooking a sauce into the dessert itself? The result is a total indulgence. This is so simple to prepare. The magic happens as you make it. You'll see!

Serves 6

125g plain flour

2 tsp baking powder

115g light muscovado sugar

150g Venezuelan Rio Caribe Superior 72% chocolate, roughly chopped

85g slightly salted butter

280ml full-fat milk, warmed

2 eggs, beaten

1 tsp vanilla essence

FOR THE SAUCE:

250ml water

55g Venezuelan Carenero Superior 100% cacao, roughly chopped

150g light muscovado sugar

Equipment: 1-litre baking dish, or 6 x 180-ml baking dishes

Preheat the oven to 180°C. Lightly grease the inside of the baking dish(es) with a little butter.

Sift the flour with the baking powder together into large mixing bowl. Stir in the sugar until evenly combined and set aside.

Melt the chocolate and butter in a heatproof bowl set over a pan of gently simmering water, making sure the bottom of the bowl is not in contact with the water. Remove from the heat and stir in the milk, beaten eggs and vanilla essence. Gradually beat the mixture into the bowl of flour until well blended. Pour into the prepared baking dish(es).

Make the sauce by bringing the water to the boil in a saucepan. Remove from the heat and stir in the chopped cacao until melted. Stir in the muscovado sugar, then pour carefully over the pudding mixture. Don't worry if it appears to curdle. It will separate out from the sauce when cooked to give a perfect sponge with a layer of syrupy sauce underneath.

Bake in the preheated oven: 20–25 minutes for the large pudding, or for 12–15 minutes for the individual puddings, or until just risen in the centre and still runny underneath. Serve hot with cream, crème fraîche or custard.

CHOCOLATE CRÊPES

If you ask children what they would like for breakfast, you are likely to hear a chorus of 'Crêpes!' Saturday was crêpe day because there was always a little more time to prepare them than on a school day.

Makes 16

80g Madagascan Sambirano Superior 71% chocolate, roughly chopped

350ml full-fat milk

6 tbsp caster sugar

200g plain flour

100ml water

3 eggs

½ tsp vanilla essence

butter, for frying

Place the chocolate and about 125ml of the milk in a saucepan over a low heat until the chocolate has melted. Remove from the heat and stir in the sugar and remaining milk. Set aside.

Sift the flour into a large bowl and make a well in the centre. Put the water, eggs and vanilla essence into the well. Using a wooden spoon or whisk, mix the liquid ingredients together, gradually drawing in the flour from the sides to form a thick batter about the consistency of double cream. Beat in the cooled chocolate mixture until well combined, then pour into a jug. Cover and place in the fridge or a cool place for at least an hour before using. The batter will keep in the fridge for up to 4 days.

To cook the crêpes, heat a heavy-based shallow frying pan or crêpe pan until it is very hot. Add a knob of butter and swirl it around the pan to coat it. Pour in a small ladleful of the batter and swirl it around, again to coat the surface of the pan.

Turn the heat down slightly and cook for about 1 minute (having sugar and chocolate in the mixture means that the crêpes will burn more easily than plain ones). Slip a spatula under the crêpe to loosen it and turn it over. Cook for a further 30 seconds, then transfer to a plate in a very low oven. Repeat this process with the remaining batter, interleaving the cooked crêpes with greaseproof paper to stop them from sticking together.

Serve topped with a fresh fruit sauce and whipped cream.

WHITE CHOCOLATE BREAD AND BUTTER PUDDING

Based on a great British favourite, this is rich and indulgent, creamy and seductive. Everyone will want a second helping.

Serves 6–8

400ml full-fat milk

400ml double cream

200g white chocolate, roughly chopped

4 large eggs

30g caster sugar

2 tsp vanilla essence

2 tbsp sultanas, soaked in dark rum or brandy for 1–2 days

30g unsalted butter

½ small baguette loaf, cut into about 24 slices 1cm thick

Equipment: 2-litre baking dish

Preheat the oven to 160°C. Lightly grease the inside of the baking dish with a little butter.

Place the milk and cream in a saucepan over a medium heat and bring just to the boil. Remove from the heat and stir in the white chocolate until melted. Set aside to cool slightly.

In a large bowl, whisk the eggs with the sugar and vanilla essence until pale and creamy, then stir into the cream and chocolate mixture.

Pour the mixture into the prepared baking dish and sprinkle over the sultanas. Butter the slices of bread and arrange them over the top of the custard. Place the baking dish in a roasting tin and pour in enough freshly boiled water to come about halfway up the sides. Bake in the preheated oven for about 40 minutes, or until just set. The pudding should still be slightly wobbly in the middle.

Serve hot or warm. It is fabulous with a little apricot jam, or a scattering of fresh raspberries and a dusting of icing sugar over the top, plus – for total indulgence – a little whipped cream!

CHOCOLATE ROULADE

Here's another classic, not to be forgotten in a hurry. You could even describe it as pure choc and roll!

Serves 8–10

250g Venezuelan Hacienda Las Trincheras 72% chocolate, roughly chopped

6 eggs, separated

130g caster sugar

300ml double cream

Icing sugar, to dust

Equipment: 33 x 23-cm Swiss roll tin

Preheat the oven to 170°C. Lightly grease the Swiss roll tin and line it with baking paper, pushing the paper firmly into the corners.

Melt the chocolate in a heatproof bowl set over a pan of gently simmering water, making sure the bottom of the bowl is not in contact with the water. Remove from the heat and set aside to cool slightly.

Beat the egg yolks with the sugar until very pale, thick and creamy. Stir in the slightly cooled chocolate until well blended.

Whisk the egg whites in a large bowl until just starting to form stiff peaks. Stir a large spoonful of egg white into the chocolate mixture to loosen it, then fold in the remaining egg white until evenly blended.

Pour the mixture into the prepared Swiss roll tin and gently level the surface. Bake in the preheated oven for 15–18 minutes, until the top is firm to the touch.

Remove from the oven. Gently slide the cake with the baking paper onto a wire rack and immediately cover with damp tea towel. Leave to cool completely. If the tea towel dries out, re-dampen it.

When the cake is cool, remove the baking paper. Dust a new sheet of baking paper with icing sugar and invert the cake onto it. Whip the cream until it forms soft peaks and spread it evenly over the top of the cake, leaving about a 2-cm border along one of the long edges. Roll up the sponge, starting with the long cream-free border edge furthest away from you, carefully lifting and peeling off the baking paper as you go. The roulade should have a slightly cracked appearance.

Chill in the fridge for at least an hour before serving to allow it to settle. This will also make the roulade easier to slice. Dust well with icing sugar before serving.

HOW TO MAKE A CHOCOLATE ROULADE

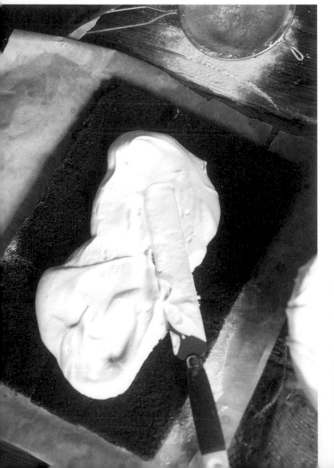

STUFFED PEACHES

When I was growing up in Ireland, we had two peach trees growing in a small wooden greenhouse. The fruit they produced was wonderfully succulent and juicy, so this dessert brings back lots of memories for me. Made in minutes, the cacao and amaretti biscuits are a perfect match for the luscious peaches.

Serves 4

4 large ripe
fresh peaches

4 tsp Kirsch or
Amaretto liqueur

4 tsp caster sugar

8 large amaretti biscuits

25g Madagascan
Sambirano Superior
100% cacao, grated

20g unsalted butter

Preheat the oven to 180°C.

Bring a large pan of water to a gentle boil. Drop in the peaches and leave for about 10 seconds, then drain. Peel, then halve the peaches and discard the stones. Using a teaspoon, carefully scrape away any fibres from the cavity where the stones were.

Pour the Kirsch or Amaretto into a shallow dish and stir in the caster sugar. Add the peach halves and turn gently to coat well with the liqueur and sugar mixture.

Lightly butter the inside of a baking dish large enough to hold the peach halves in a single layer. Arrange the peaches in the baking dish, cut side facing upward.

Crush the amaretti biscuits coarsely in a bowl, then mix in the grated cacao. Spoon this mixture equally into the hollow of each peach half and top with a shaving of the butter. Bake in the preheated oven for 25 minutes. Serve hot or warm, with a helping of crème fraîche or vanilla ice cream.

OEUFS À LA NEIGE AU CHOCOLAT

My variation of this French classic has islands of soft meringue spiked with ginger floating on a lake of rich chocolate custard. You can make this dessert several hours in advance, or even the day before it's needed.

Serves 6

6 egg whites

120g caster sugar

75g crystallized ginger, chopped into small pieces

750ml full-fat milk

80g Peruvian San Martin 70% chocolate, roughly chopped

1 recipe quantity Chocolate Custard (see page 130)

Make a meringue mixture by whisking the egg whites until they form stiff peaks. Beat in half the sugar until they become stiff again, then beat in the remaining sugar, again until stiff. Gently fold in the chopped ginger.

Place the milk in a large sauté pan or deep-sided frying pan over a low heat until gently simmering. Take about 2 tablespoons of the meringue mixture and shape into an oval mound about the size of a lemon. Drop a batch of these into the simmering milk and poach for 1 minute. Turn over and cook for 1 minute on the other side. Lift out with a slotted spoon and drain on kitchen paper. Repeat with the remaining egg white mixture. Set the cooked meringues on one side.

Melt the chocolate in a heatproof bowl set over a pan of gently simmering water, making sure the bottom of the bowl is not in contact with the water. Remove from the heat.

Using a fork, dribble melted chocolate, backwards and forwards over each meringue until they are generously coated. Allow the chocolate to set.

Pour the custard into one large serving dish or divide between individual serving bowls. Place the chocolate-drizzled meringues on top. Serve chilled.

POACHED PEAR PAVLOVA WITH A BITTER CHOCOLATE SAUCE

Named after the great Russian ballerina Anna Pavlova, this elegant creation has a meringue base that is crisp on the outside, but soft and yielding inside, with delectable pears sitting on top. Double the quantities for a really impressive dessert for 10–12.

Serves 6

120g granulated sugar

1 litre water

1 vanilla pod, split lengthways

6 ripe but firm pears (Comice are good)

200g Peruvian San Martin 70% chocolate, roughly chopped

5 large egg whites

300g caster sugar

1 tsp cornflour

1 tsp vanilla essence

1 tsp lemon juice

300ml double cream

Equipment: Baking tray about 36cm square

Heat the granulated sugar with the water in a large saucepan over a moderate heat, stirring until the sugar dissolves. Bring just to the boil, lower the heat and add the vanilla pod. Leave to simmer gently while you prepare the fruit.

Peel the pears, leaving the stalks on. Stand them in the syrup, then cover and poach very gently for about 1 hour, until soft but still holding their shape. Using a slotted spoon, carefully lift out the pears and set aside to cool. Turn up the heat under the syrup in the pan and reduce to about 150ml. Remove from the heat and stir in the chocolate until melted, then beat until smooth and well blended. Set aside to cool.

Preheat the oven to 140°C. Line the baking tray with baking paper.

Make a meringue mixture by whisking the egg whites until they form stiff peaks. Add a quarter of the caster sugar and again beat until stiff. Continue adding the sugar in this way until it is all used and the mixture is stiff. Carefully fold in the cornflour, vanilla essence and lemon juice until well combined.

Pile the meringue mixture onto the prepared baking tray, shaping it into a circular mound about 5cm from the edge of the tray: this gives it space to expand while cooking. Bake in the preheated oven for about 1¼ hours, or until the meringue is a very pale biscuit colour. Remove from the oven and set aside on the baking tray to cool completely.

When cold, very carefully turn the meringue over and peel off the baking paper. Turn it back over and place on a serving plate.

Lightly whip the cream until just stiff and spread it over the meringue, leaving about a 3-cm margin around the edge. Place the poached pears on top of the cream. Transfer to the fridge to chill for at least an hour, preferably longer. Just before serving, pour over about half of the cooled chocolate sauce, offering the remainder in a jug on the side.

CHOCOLATE BUGS

When you want to have some fun with the kids, make these edible insects. Part of the pleasure lies in getting creative with how you decorate them. Let your imagination run riot.

Makes about 18

2 egg whites

150g caster sugar

200g Venezuelan Hacienda Las Trincheras 72% chocolate

30g white chocolate

White and milk chocolate buttons (optional)

Equipment: Piping bag with a 2-cm nozzle; small freezer bag

Preheat the oven to 120°C. Line a large baking tray with baking paper.

Make a meringue mixture by whisking the egg whites in a large bowl until they form stiff peaks. Gradually add the sugar, whisking well between each addition, until the mixture is stiff again.

Fill the piping bag with the meringue mixture and pipe 'bug' bodies and heads onto the prepared baking tray: each body shape should be about 5cm long and 3cm wide, and each head about 1.5cm long and 1cm wide. Bake in the preheated oven for about 1½ hours, until the meringue is set and lifts easily off the baking paper. Remove from the oven and set aside to cool.

When the meringue pieces are cool, temper the Las Trincheras chocolate (see page 10). Dip each meringue piece into the tempered chocolate until well coated. Shake off any excess and return to the lined baking tray. Leave to set.

When the bug parts have set, melt the white chocolate in a heatproof bowl set over a pan of gently simmering water, making sure the bottom of the bowl does not touch the water. Remove from the heat and leave to cool a little.

Spoon the melted white chocolate into the freezer bag and snip off a very small tip from one corner of the bag. Pipe a little white chocolate onto one end of each body length and use this to 'glue' a head to each body. Pipe white chocolate eyes onto each head. If you are making ladybirds, pipe white chocolate spots onto each body, or attach chocolate buttons with a dab of white chocolate. Allow the chocolate on the bugs to set completely, then lift off the baking paper. These treats will store well in an airtight container for 3–4 days.

REDCURRANT AND WHITE CHOCOLATE MERINGUE CAKE

Delicious as well as eye-catching, this cake combines tangy redcurrants and sweet meringue to make a feast of flavour and colour. It's the ideal finale to a late-summer dinner party.

Serves 8-10

6 egg whites

375g caster sugar

FOR THE MOUSSE:

300g white chocolate, finely chopped

450ml double cream

3 egg whites

400g fresh redcurrants

Preheat the oven to 120°C. Line four baking trays with baking paper. In pencil, draw a circle 24cm in diameter on each sheet. Turn the paper over so that the circles are still visible but cannot mark the meringue.

Make the meringue by whisking the egg whites until they form stiff peaks. Add half the sugar, then whisk until the mixture is stiff again. Whisk in the remaining sugar, again until the mixture is stiff.

Divide the mixture between the circles drawn on the paper lining the baking trays. Spread out so that it fills each circle evenly and is as level as possible. Bake in the preheated oven for 3-4 hours, or until the meringue discs are set and lift off the baking paper easily. (You can make these 1-2 days in advance and store them in an airtight container.)

To make the mousse, place the chocolate in a heatproof bowl. Place 225ml of the cream in a saucepan over a moderate heat and bring just to the boil. Pour over the chocolate and stir until the chocolate has melted. Set aside to cool.

Meanwhile, whisk the egg whites in clean bowl until they form stiff peaks. Set aside. In another bowl, whip the remaining cream until thick. Quickly fold the egg whites into the cream, then fold this mixture into the cooled chocolate mixture. Set aside. Remove the redcurrants from their stalks.

Place one of the meringue discs on a serving plate and spread a quarter of the mousse over the top, followed by about a quarter of the redcurrants. Repeat with the remaining meringue discs, mousse and fruit, layering the cake up and finishing with a generous sprinkling of redcurrants. Leave in the fridge to chill for at least 2 hours before serving.

CHOCOLATE AND HAZELNUT MERINGUES WITH BLACKBERRIES IN KIRSCH

Madagascan Sambirano chocolate is the top choice here because its juicy summer-fruit notes blend so magnificently with the Kirsch-soaked blackberries.

Makes 8

200g blackberries

2 tbsp Kirsch

2 tbsp caster sugar

3 egg whites

Pinch of salt

150g caster sugar

Pinch of cream of tartar

100g hazelnuts, toasted, skinned and coarsely chopped

100g Madagascan Sambirano 71% chocolate, chopped into nut-size pieces

300ml double cream

1 recipe quantity Bitter Chocolate and Coffee Sauce (see page 124)

Place the blackberries in a bowl. Pour over the Kirsch and sprinkle with the granulated sugar. Stir so that the blackberries are well coated with both Kirsch and sugar. Cover and leave to stand in a cool place overnight.

Preheat the oven to 130°C. Line a large baking tray with baking paper.

Make a meringue mixture by whisking the egg whites in a large bowl with the pinch of salt until they form stiff peaks. Add 2–3 tablespoons of the sugar and whisk until stiff again. Continue adding the sugar in this way until it is all used, whisking each time until the mixture is stiff. Add the cream of tartar, whisk again until stiff, then fold in the hazelnuts and chocolate.

Spoon the meringue mixture onto the prepared baking tray in 8 heaped rounds. Bake in the preheated oven for about 1¼ hours, or until the meringues are set and lift easily and cleanly off the baking paper. (You can make these a couple of days in advance and store them in an airtight container if you wish.)

To assemble, whip the cream until stiff. Place a meringue on each serving plate and place a large spoonful of cream on top. Arrange some Kirsch-soaked blackberries on the cream and spoon a little juice around each meringue, along with a spoonful or two of the chocolate and coffee sauce. Serve immediately.

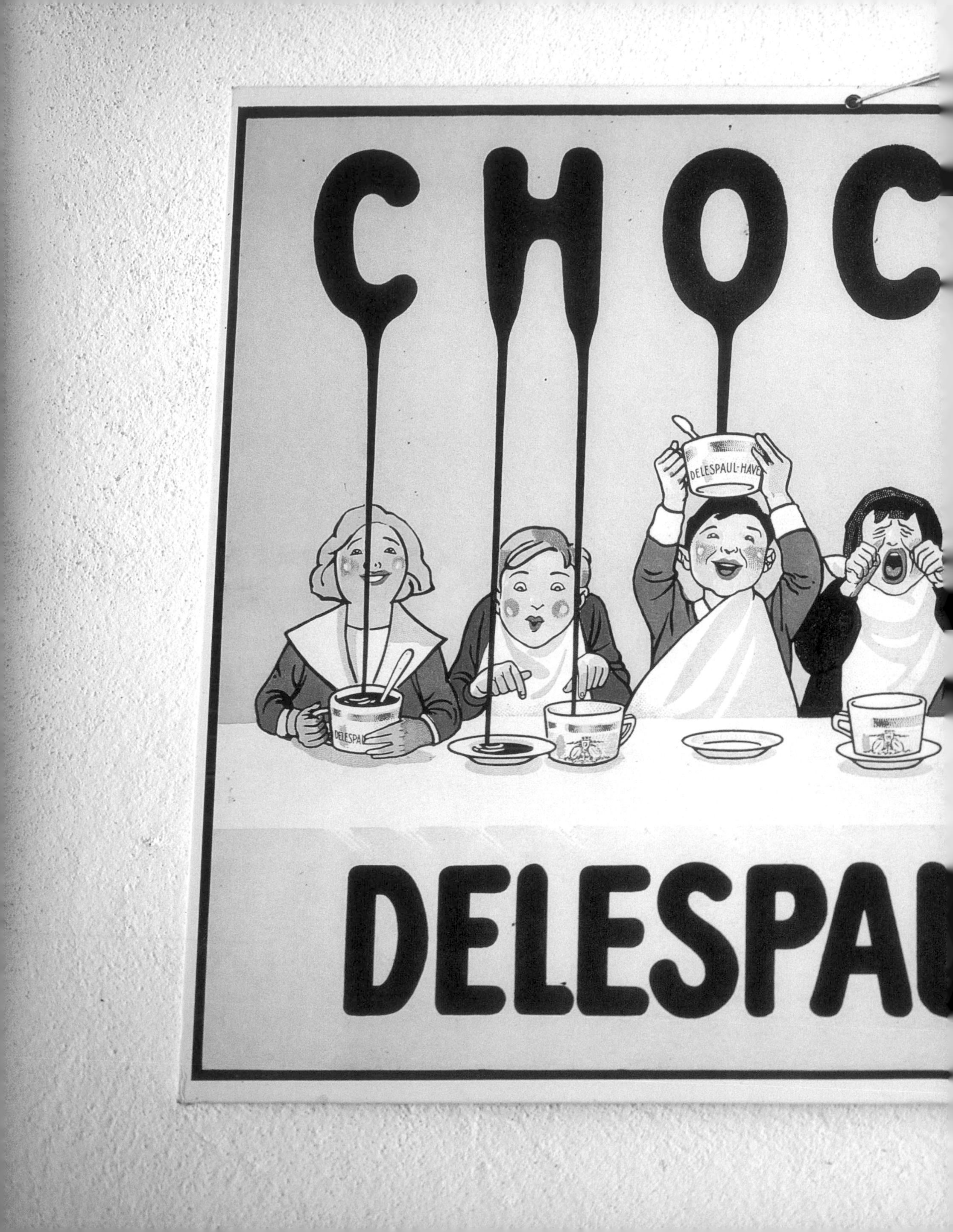
CHOC
DELESPAUL-HAVE
DELESPA
DELESPA

INDEX

ACKNOWLEDGMENTS

Thanks to all the chocolate romantics of the world who have supported me in my quest for the finest beans and chocolate making.

Thanks to my publishers, Hodder & Stoughton for their continuing belief in the Chocolate Man, especially Nicky Ross. Thanks to Sarah Hammond, Alice Wright, Kate Brunt, Camilla Dowse, Bill Jones, Cécile Landau, Trish Burgess, Lawrence Morton, Emma Lee, Jan Havemann-Bowser, Marina Filippelli, Laura Fyfe and Emma Thomas.

I am so lucky to have such fantastic sisters and a brother, who have helped tirelessly throughout the journey of this book. Sophie, Jessie, Harry: what would I have done without you?

I'm extremely grateful to my agents LAW, particularly to Araminta Whitley, who can only be described as fantastic, Alice Saunders, who is brilliant, and Harry The Man is simply The Man.

To Rebecca Cripps and Cristian Barnett, my chocolate musketeers: I look forward to many more adventures with you.

In Venezuela: my old faithful Arturo Sarmiento; Alfredo Astaburuaga and Alexandra de Yavorsky, for always being there; Tintin Arnal who's travelled great distances with me on my quest for the finest beans; Ricardo and Annabel Soto, farm manager and friend; Bertillio Araujo, the man with the knowledge of the mountains; the boys on the farm; the Franco for being such an incredibly helpful friend.

Franceschi family and San Jose Cacao, for all the fascinating facts and tasting information that they have always given me and for supplying me with some of the best cacao in the world;

To Willem Bolk and Jan Kips at Daarnhouwer & Co, for being the best premium bean suppliers in the world.

To Marisol, for her determination and support in sourcing Colombian beans; Miguel Angel Vargas Caro and Marlene Acevedo Romero for their kind attention and help in Colombia.

Back in England, firstly I would like to thank my sister Sein for her tireless tasting, testing and inspired creativity in the kitchen. Without Sein's brilliant contributions many of these recipes would never have seen the light of day.

To Marco Pierre White, a great friend and advisor; Dean Freeman who's always got some threads for me; Spencer Buck, Alex Bane, Ryan Wills and the rest of the dream team at Taxi Studio; Jim Bell and Gary Bell at Hass-Tek Services who have always lent technical support at Willie's Chocolate Factory; Chris Moore at Waitrose for understanding cacao and Louise O'Brien at Waitrose for knowing her chocolate; Ewan Venters, Food and Catering Director at Selfridges; at the factory Marlena Marynczak and Miroslaw Szafranski and the ever-changing temporary team; Mark Darlington and Toby Anderson on tunes; Stephen Beckett, Peter Cooke and Mike Gray, the chocolate romantics; Arthur Westbrook; Daniel Dultzin my friend and Mexican advisor; Ragus for being so sweet; Linny Lane, another chocolate romantic; Michael Kamlish at the Home Chocolate Factory, for technical support; David Kirkness and the team at Kirkness & Co; Lillia Frayre Sierre for all her kind care and attention in Mexico; JP Rathbone, an early chocolate romantic; Marcus Link, Richard Wain and Andrea Link.

To Liberty Bell/Doris who started the journey by making the series, my thanks especially to Stuart Prebble, Sam Richards, David Buckley, Southan Morris, Emma Robertson, Eli Hardy, Steve Lidgerwood and Little Steve.

To my dad, who taught me so much and gave me the skills to put together the machinery and build the chocolate factory.

To my children, Sophie, William and Evie, who make it all worthwhile.

First published in Great Britain in 2010 by Hodder & Stoughton
An Hachette UK company

1

Copyright © Willie Harcourt-Cooze 2010

A CIP catalogue record for this title is available from the British Library

ISBN 978 0 340 99356 9

Photography © Emma Lee
Pages: 4, 6, 8, 9, 14, 18, 23, 24, 25, 26, 27, 41, 49, 57, 57, 67, 68, 69, 70, 72, 74, 75,
76, 78, 79, 81, 102, 104, 108, 112, 115, 116, 118, 121, 174, 178, 180, 183, 184, 185,
186, 190, 198, 208, 210–211, 239, 240, 246, 249, 264, 293, 310 © Cristian Barnett.
Pages: 110, 242, and 244 from private collections.

Design by Lawrence Morton

Typeset in Clifford and Akzidenz Grotesk

Printed and bound by Graphicom, Italy

Hodder & Stoughton policy is to use papers that are natural, renewable and recyclable
products and made from wood grown in sustainable forests. The logging and
manufacturing processes are expected to conform to the environmental regulations of
the country of origin.

Hodder & Stoughton Ltd
338 Euston Road
London NW1 3BH

www.hodder.co.uk